Antelope Hill Writing Competition 2025
If Not Us, Who?

If Not Us, Who?

FIFTH ANNUAL

Antelope Hill Writing Competition

—2025—

ANTELOPE HILL PUBLISHING

Antelope Hill Publishing | antelopehillpublishing.com

Paperback ISBN: 979-8-89252-055-3
EPUB ISBN: 979-8-89252-056-0

CONTENTS

POETRY

Selected Poems by Author

Poetry Winners

SHORT STORIES
Selected Short Stories by Author

Short Story Winners

PUBLISHER'S FOREWORD

Antelope Hill Publishing is proud to present our Fifth Annual Writing Competition. For the fifth year, we were amazed by the creative responses to our theme "If not Us, Who?" This year, we intended the theme—a call to collective responsibility and action—to prompt participants to reflect on the imperatives of stepping forward in defense of one's heritage, values, and future, especially when others falter.

We want to thank all those who supported and promoted our competition, and especially all those who participated by submitting their writing, regardless of whether we accepted their submission or not. Our team loved reading and reviewing the submissions, and many were cut only after fierce debate. All participants who made it into the final print should hold their heads high as exemplifying some of the best among the pro-White cultural scene.

By hosting these competitions annually, we try to do our small part to inspire more writers in our sphere. One cannot overestimate the importance of literature and creative writing to the survival and self-knowledge of a people. It is all the more important for our people to create our own culture—to write our own stories, for our own consumption, and for our own benefit—because no one else will do it for us.

We hope that you enjoy the works in this collection as much as we have, and we look forward to having you, dear reader, share your talent with us in the future.

POETRY

Winding

A.D. Gudwynd

The God wind blows
A call that carves hard stone,
Cutting corridors to places unknown.

At His word we bow,
To the wind breaking the trees,
Splitting the seas, ravaging the cities.

Who are you, oh man?
In your cowardice, in your shame,
Show your face, you are His to claim.

Wulfila laid it down,
So that you could pick it up,
A bed of dust for an evergreen cup.

At His whim we rise,
The children of the heather,
By blood and soil bound together.

The Pond's Plea

Æ Firestone

In a pond where reeds hum soft and low,
Frogs croak their dreams to a sky aglow.
No king they have, yet chaos stings—
If not us, who mends broken things?

Their voices climb through mist's thin veil,
A chorus bold, yet doomed to fail.
God hears their cry, his laughter cold,
Sends a log to drift, no crown to hold.

It lies in silt, a splintered jest,
No pulse, no power, a throne unblessed.
They curse its weight, their hopes undone—
If not us, who sparks the sun?

Again they wail, their hunger raw,
Demand a lord to right their flaw.
God's shadow shifts, his patience thin,
A stork descends with beak of sin.

Its feathers gleam like fallen light,
Each step a theft through trembling night.
The pond grows still, their voices cease—
If not us, who brings us peace?

Now reeds stand lone where dreams once
stirred,
No croak, no cry, no desperate word.
The water holds their bones below—
If not us, who dares to grow?

Next Saint

Æwine

They did not come from your blood
But they learnt from you to hate,
from the lovely lips of liars
And what upon this earth befell
All cruel time shall tell
And old atomic fires--
Is this the coming kingdom they called hell?

The saints of the old blood
were bright and thin as glass;
Our next saint
shall be rough and grey as steel.
No dragon shall be spitted on his lance,
Only crawling serpents.
He hath no shield-brother,
No progenitors,
No heirs and no equal;
You will not see him coming
When he comes.

He will have no heralds, no harbingers, no
annunciation.
No trumpets shall blow,
The skies will not darken,
Though the streets will,
With your blood.

You may shriek and scold
To your maggot-sodden hearts' content.
You will not stop him;

You cannot:
You gave birth to him,
He is your own.
He is Ananke coming home.
He is the universe arighting itself.
He is the cosmos snapping back to order:
You dealt yourself your doom.

Your words avail naught to daunt him,
Your excommunication shall not damn him--
He was already damned;
You damned us all,
You damned yourselves.

What shall one say of this poor mis-made man
Whose part was not intended for this play.
The world wanted heroes
And we got him.
There was no one else--
He looked; he saw himself.

Much there was was wrong in him,
Much the mind recoils to retell,
Much we would have wished went otherwise;
We mourned to see the soft and seeming innocence
Of the mawless worms on which his sickle fell.

He was not of the brightest
Or the fairest
Or the wisest
Or the pure;
We have not the luxury of heroes
In an age when gods and kings are dead.
There are no more crusaders,

No clean and comely wars,
Only the knife, black and bloody, in the dark
And the pale clenching fist that vows revenge.
We fight not for a garland but for the garden,
The only Eden that our fathers ever knew.
The earth the Lamb trod down is now an island:
No other country calls us home;
We have nowhere else to go.

He was not chaste,
Yet he was a virgin.
He was brave,
Yet among his foes were women and the aged.
The only holiness he had was hate
For the hateful,
Most dearly that which he owned within himself
And the sewer-wastes of sin
he found himself surrounded in.
He knew only what all men know:
That home is in the heart
And the mind is in the eye;
That the stranger is not kin;
That a man must be a man;
That only fire may redeem flesh;
That this is our land
And they do not belong.
That none of this can last for very long.

And because he knew no more, he acted.
He was too young for caution
Or to care.

And so
From out all the holes of history,

From every oubliette of ideology
Behold them come,
A legion in motley,
A grinning regiment of clowns,
A sickled cell of cenobites,
Rank and monstrous as the grave;
Mishewn, malformed, fainting in their faith,
Fumbling even their curses,
Tongues ill-twisted round the truth.
Not white, not straight, not clean, not perfect,
A sacrifice the gods of old would not accept;
A stumbling three-legged lamb,
Black-spotted, perhaps black-hearted--
But the only one who kneels for the knife.

It is of no account:
Time will render their ignominy as fat is rendered by a
fire.
Necessity will purify their arms.
Posterity will white their tombs.

And now before us the long dark age stretches,
Soaring down from glory to the grave.
Yet even in the farthest depths of gloom
I see white lights flicker,
I see bright lines drawn,
I hear the clash of steel against the grain,
The cannonade of thunder--
I know whatever falls,
falls not alone.

I see a burning league of pale faces
Springing from the dragon's teeth you sowed
—You will never know who dies until it happens

In all our stolen streets,
Our haunted homes.

If we cannot be restored
At least we shall be revenged.
The land we could not rescue with our arms
We shall hallow with our blood
And yours.
A million innocents will die,
Not by your hand, yet their blood is upon you,
Who scorned
when warned that blood must flow.
There is at every hand
A generation rising,
Raised by you on treachery and hate,
Without faith, without remorse, without honor, without
mercy,
Perverse beyond repair,
Unmoored by fate.
Some of them will follow your commandment
And wallow like the worm in its own filth.
Some of them will turn aside in anguish
And grasp whatever weapon meets their hand.

And so, confronting you at every crossroads,
Tormenting us in every turn we take,
The eternal, aching question,
The question that you never dare forget:
Of all who writhe beneath your hand,
Who rise up from our soil,
The vision that I
Even in thy dark eye, descry:
grey-steeled to their duty,
iron-bent upon their task

And which of these young men
shall be our next sain

The Time Is Now

Æwine

Look not for a distant sign;
Not to the heavens for your hope,
Nor to a future age for your deliverance.
My message is this:
Thou art the man
And the time is now.

Get Up

Alexander Ross

There was an era, archer, when you never missed
your mark. When you were lean of speech, steady
of stride, and sure. No more. For the scribe has seen
you stumble, fumbling in the epochal dawn, riddled
blind by those merchants of milk and lead.

Yes, you, pilgrim, prostrate, swaddled in dogma,
who wear your blessings like a ball and chain
and hoist your fear like a flag. Whose incantations
tie your tongue? Whose black boots trod your
thoughts? Beggars in the guise of gods.

Let none but a brother be your keeper. In arms,
or blood, or both. May all your ties be the kind
that bind. The mightiest state, your state of mind.
Now name me the man who whimpered his way
to paradise. You have all the time in the world.

The Last Romanov

Alexander Ross

I could not have saved all of you,
the Urals being so unforgiving,
even in July. At best, one or two,
regrettably not the Tsar, that living

symbol of decency. Nor Tsarevich,
bless him, far too frail for such a drama.
But with one duchess, no Bolshevik
swine could find us. Tatianna,

Anastasia, Maria, or Olga.
I'd deliver you like a porcelain bird
beyond the wide waters of the Volga,
sustained by our cunning, my gentle words.

And you could grow old on the Thames or Seine,
wondering, with us, how things could have been.

The Prophecy of Merlin

Anonymous

There stood the Saxon freebooter
Who sought the British throne.
His arms were slick with British gore
Mingled with his own.

"Merlin!" growled the Saxon,
His baleful sword in hand,
"If knowest thou the future, tell:
Who shall rule this land?"

The wizard frowned and pondered.
At length he raised his head.
His gaze was cold, his voice was bold,
And this is what he said:

"Soon the House of Brutus
Shall furnish kings no more
And sink beneath the fiery tide
Of unforgiving war.
The Britons then shall flee their homes
As once they fled from Troy,
Before thy new Achaeans
Who plunder and destroy."

"But ere that fated hour comes
When Camelot crashes down
Shall reign a glorious British king
Of unsurpassed renown.
Thy folk shall feel his anger
And die upon his blade,

And e'er so long as Arthur lives
Is thine to be afraid."
"But in the after centuries
When long has ruled thy line,
Thou shalt look back on Arthur
And count him one of thine.
For the Saxons and the Britons
Shall blend their streams of blood,
And join the Gael and Norman too
In one great British flood.
And this new happy nation
Shall take thy tongue and name,
And peace and law and progress
Shall be its pride and fame."

The Saxon stood and pondered.
At length he asked "What then?"
And Merlin smiled knowingly
As he began again:

"Go forth! Saxon, plant thy flag
In every clime and place,
But more important than thy flag—
Saxon, plant thy race!"

"Leave to the French their artful dress,
Their canvases, and wine.
For music and philosophy,
Seek those beyond the Rhine.
Admit that Russia's daughters
Are loveliest in dance,
And Italy is first in verse
And songs of sweet romance."

"Thine, Saxon, is the longbow.
The bayonet is thine;
The cannon and the cutlass and
The warships of the line;
And thine the iron scepter,
Which makes the proud obey,
To guard a peerless empire
Of everlasting day."

"To the west of the Emerald Isle,
To the west of Avalon,
Thy people-laden vessels
Shall voyage on and on.
A lush and vasty continent
Lies waiting o'er the sea.
The red man dwells upon it now,
But it is meant for thee."

"The red man cannot stop thee,
Though brave and swift and cruel;
Thine endless waves of wagon folk
Shall vindicate thy rule.
The Spaniard's mongrel bastards
Shall stand athwart thy way.
Thou shalt kill them as an eagle kills
Its furtive, creeping prey."

"This conquered land shall make each man
Prosperous and free.
And pliant slaves shall plow thy fields
And pluck the fruits for thee."
"Around the cape of Africa
Thine other ships shall wend,
And on the slack, unready East

Thine armies shall descend.
The Hindoos and Mohammedans
Who dare to try the sword
Shall rue their swift correction
And learn to call thee lord.
Across the wild Orient
Thy vanguard shall advance
To subjugate the peoples of
A wondrous expanse!
To greet thy common soldiers
Brown emperors shall rise,
And the miscreants of India
Shall dread to tell thee lies!"

"Then sailing ever onwards,
Thy restless folk shall range
To lands beyond the ken of men
Where e'en the stars are strange.
The creatures on this continent
Are few and dark and crude.
Thou shalt plant there to replace them
Thine own superior brood."

"Then, proud of thy dominion,
And witting of thy worth,
Thou shalt resolve to conquer the
Remainder of the earth."

"The warriors of Africa
Shall learn to reckon then:
A single British soldier's equals
Twenty negro men."

"The Middle Kingdom's millions

Shall know which men are best.
Thou shalt rule the yellow races
As easily as the rest."

"The greatest weapons in the world
Shall guarantee thy rights
And stock the nightmares of mankind:
Blue eyes and iron sights."

"In time thy kindred nations
Shall follow in thy train,
And steadily across the earth
Increase the white domain.
Together ye shall drive the Turk
From European soil,
And make the rebel Chinaman
Resume his proper toil.
So long as Europeans keep
Their bonds as brothers true,
The sundry folk of all the world
Shall swear their oaths to you."

"And wisely thou shalt govern—
Never cruel nor rash.
With justice thou shalt give decrees,
With justice wield the lash.
By white commands and colored hands
New cities shall be built,
And thou shalt banish sickness, light the dark,
And punish guilt.
No other race with power
Has ever been so fair;
The load of mankind's leadership
Must be Whites' to bear."

"True, some malcontents will grumble,
But in every darky's mind,
He'll know he's better ruled by thee
Than ruled by his own kind.
For someday thou shalt leave them,
And swarms of swarthy men
Shall brave the desert, woods, and sea
To be with thee again."

"Yes, someday thou shalt leave them.
Thine empire shall end
When thou forgetest color marks
A rival from a friend."

"Thy jealousy of Germany
Shall be the cause of doom—
To stop the peeking German dawn
Thou'lt plunge the world in gloom.
Thou shalt march against the fatherland
That nurtured thee of yore,
And wash away the white man's sway
In fratricidal gore."

"Thou shalt emerge the victor;
Aye, but not the same.
Triumphant pride shall swiftly turn
To all-consuming shame—
Not just shame for slaughtering
And shackling thy kin,
But shame for all that thou hast done
And all that thou hast been."

"That driving force shall drain away
Which animates thee now,

And lesser breeds shall take from thee
Who used to scrape and bow.
The refuse of the tropics
Shall ring thy lands about
With greedy hand, with grasping hand,
With pressing maw and snout."

"These foreigners without a fight
Shall flood through gaping walls,
And all thy children yet unborn
Shall haunt thee with their calls:
"Where now are the pitiless archers
Who slew the Frankish knights?
Where are the grenadiers who won
A hundred close-run fights?
Where now are the fearsome pirates
That Spain's armada faced?
Where are the bomber pilots who
Laid Germany to waste?"

"Are there no more Saxon men
As resolute and brave,
When rather than to slay their kin,
Their children they must save?"

"In every Western country
The scene is now the same:
Niggers loot and swagger;
White men nurse their shame.
The alien hordes upon our lands
Grow and grow and grow.
Wilt thou not resist them?
Hast thou fall'n so low?
Is this the end for our fair race

That Providence had planned?
To meekly shuffle off the earth?
We who were so grand?"

"Father, Father, do not fail—
I wish so much to be!
Don't let strangers fill the homes
Thy forbears built for me!"

"At last thou shalt awaken.
Their calls shall stir thy blood.
And thou shalt rise with all thy kin
In one great Aryan flood!"
"Then all the other races—red,
Yellow, brown, and black—
Shall breath a frightened whisper:
The master has come back!
Thou shalt chastise these usurpers,
Whether short or long the fight,
Till as of yore they'll bow before
The people of the light."

"Then forth again to plant thy flag
On every star in space,
But more important than thy flag—
White man, plant thy race!"

Mightiest Alone

Caleb Ó Muireadhaigh

A new century had just begun but the Earls had fallen
low
They shook the hands at Mellifont and soon they fled
their home
Our people gazed at empty thrones: "Are the nobles
gone now and for all time?"
No! Aristocracy is inborn in our race, whether in home
or foreign clime

With a belief in noble Gaelic blood, Féilim raised the
sword
To smite invading planters and expel the foreign horde
For God, King and Country the Gael did wage his war
And for longer than a decade his blood pervade and
spilled galore

At the behest of foreign Parliamentarians, the Gael had
fall upon his back
But with belief in Christ, he rose again, and readied for
attack
Then came the foreign Dutchman, paid by those who
spit upon the cross
Enemies not just of dear Ireland, but of Europe, and of
God

Near three years the war did rage, till the Wild Geese
spread their wings and flew
The Gael did look around, consolidate, and begin the
struggle all anew

Famine struck our brothers yonder sea, and sailed they
to our shores
Our men flocked all over Europe and we fought in
Stuart wars

And when the Jacobites did rise in the year one seven
forty-five
Gideon cursed their faith and honor, and he funded
their demise
Then came our valiant heroes, pikemen ready for to die
And die they did unceasing, as the bodies piled on high

As Tone took his blade and slit his throat, Dwyer
manned the mountains
Emmet was soon beheaded and blood did flow down as
a fountain
No one will ever save us, only we can end our peoples'
pouring tears
The Young Movement rose and failed, then reinforced,
and tried again in nineteen years

"If not us, then who?" one asked, and Griffith
answered: "Ourselves Alone!"
Through the will of our own people we will resurrect
the Gaelic throne
It is deep within our memory, unconscious within our
souls
The true nobility of Éire know that we are Mightiest
Alone

And with that all in mind, the Seven signed the
Proclamation
At Easter time to tame the tide of foreign domination

Sixteen heroes executed, in the future thousands more
will die
Brother will kill brother and father kill his own dear
child

And in '69 our heroes raised the rifle, and fought for
30 years
But subversion was put in place by men of foreign
mindset, who did tout to British ears
And now my dear young Gaelic brethren, fight tooth,
nail, and bone
Flock to your family through Clann Éireann, for we are
Mightiest Alone

The Ballad of a Pilgrim of Earth

Cornelius Taylor

Hebrews 11:13~16

Section I: The Journey Through

Along the road where all have gone
Passed by, or soon forgot,
On the Trav'ler's Quest I was drawn,
A far off land I sought.

I sought a land—I knew not where—
Like Abraham of old,
Wishing for hopes and joys to share
With all those brave and bold.

I knew not the way, but I thought:
"Someone I'll surely find,
I'll ask them of the land I sought,
They'll answer and be kind."

The Cynic
I asked a wise man as I walked,
But me he answered not;
I asked again, he only mocked.
"He's not so wise," I thought.

The Fool
I saw a fool—he only glared
And brushed his hand at me.
He raised his voice and rudely blared;
I left and let him be.

The Timid
I saw a timid, lonesome man,
Hiding behind a stone,
I went to ask him but he ran—
I sighed, and left alone.

The Procrastinator
I saw a man in a tree top,
I asked "What are you doing?"
"I must escape—I will not stop,
My pathway I am viewing."
"Come down," I said, "and we will go
And find our way together."
"No—I'm afraid I can't do so,
I'll wait for better weather!"

The Politician
I saw a man above a crowd,
Who spoke high and lofty words;
"Thou know'st the way?" I asked aloud,
But my voice he never heard.

The Pessimist
I saw a man wandering west,
Towards the low, setting sun.
I asked him which way was the best,
But he grimly answered "None."

The "Educated Person"
I saw a man of learnéd look
Laying upon the ground,
I went to ask—but saw his book:
He held it upside down.
The Fearful

I saw a young man standing by
An old lamppost in the night,
I asked him to accompany,
But he feared to leave the light.

The Dead
I saw a man in dreadful state—
All in the gutter he lay;
I knelt to help but 'twas too late,
And I turned my face away.

The Crisis & The Resolve
In my dismay I looked around—
The night was falling soon,
I threw my staff unto the ground,
And called out to the moon:

"There is no way that I can find,
There is no time to borrow,
There is no stranger that is kind—
I fear to see tomorrow."

Then clouds rolled back, and moonful light
Shone down upon my face,
A shooting star burst forth in flight,
And hope I did embrace.

I looked and saw a sign o'er-grown,
And hidden with Ivy leaves:
"Farthest Gate to the Land Unknown:
Pass free if you believe."

Section II: The Journey Out

The Gatekeeper
I reached the man guarding the gate,
I asked him but he said "No,
I only guard—I stand and wait,
Your land I do not know."

Puzzled, I said "But how can you
Guard a path you do not know?"
"I cannot say—my words are few:
They tell me I cannot go."

"Then tell me—only if you can—
What lies beyond this gate?"
"You see that tree? There sits a man
They say can tell your fate.

"Beyond him are mountains and hills
Which no man ever crossed
Or if they had the strength and will,
They've gone—and now are lost.
"Sir, do not pass! For if you do,
You may ne'er enter this gate."
"I shall not fear if words be true,
I must, it is all too late."

Upon a grassy sunlit hill,
Where flowers bowed in the breeze
I saw a poplar, tall and still,
With whispering yellow leaves.

The Encourager
Under the waving poplar tree,
A man in a cloak of blue,
Sat and slowly peered up at me,

"I've been waiting here for you.

"Of all the men that walked this way—
Through dark tempests, mists, or fair—
Out of the many that did stray,
You followed and did not err.
"The Poplar's heart-leaf I bestow,
Upon your chest make fast,
To guide, protect, and courage grow,
So you shall safely pass."

I sojourned on, until the road
Became so hard and steep,
I could not climb; my pace it slowed,
Stones cut my hands and feet.

The True Wise Man
Then on a ledge so high and thin,
Sat a man, all old and grey—
A long white beard upon his chin,
His eyes closed as if to pray.

He smiled and said "For you, my friend,
Your journey's nearly done.
The road is almost at an end—
Keep on, follow the sun."

"Who are you and how do you know,
The things of which you speak?"
He blinked, then whispered, soft and low:
"I know the land you seek.

"I've been there long years and lingered,
But now I have journeyed back,

To beckon the lost and the hindered
So that they may not turn back.

"If thou art pure of heart and mind,
And truthful in word and tongue,
Nor fond of what you leave behind,
Nor fearful to be unsung:

"Upon this mountain when you reach,
The wind-swept summit so bare,
Do not turn back, I do beseech—
But behold a view most fair."

"But who are you? What is your name?"
"I embody men of old—
Their wisdom, words, virtue and fame—
Ensure their memory's told.

"They walked down this path before us,
Past jeering crowds of fools,
They persevered and labored—thus,
Their words are more than jewels."

I nodded—he nodded again;
I looked up into the clouds,
And with my dimming eyes did strain,
To see their beckoning crowds.

And then he went—I saw no more,
His lantern, staff, and beard;
I looked ahead, and courage bore—
The path no more I feared.

The Summit

I held my staff, my pack threadbare,

My poplar brooch and cloak.
I closed my eyes and breathed the air—
I knew my soul awoke.

I climbed and strove—my hands they bled;
Ice winds my face did sting.
I thought on all the words they said—
Turned mind to higher things.

I spied the summit, gleaming white,
Through blinding snow I fought.
Now stood upon the looming height
I found the land I sought.

Lest We Forget/Je me souviens

Daniel Creighton

The land God gave Cain
The craggy battered costa
Awash with sea salt spray
Wind swept desolate plains
La forêt silencieuse verte et brune
L'hurlement de loups à la lune
The white snow with red blood stains

Les natifs du paysage
À la point de disparaître sans traces
Vous pouvez voir d'inquiétude sur leurs faces
Tout ce qu'ils entendent est "Quel dommage!"
Alors ils souffrent silencieusement
Pendant que le temps passe doucement
Jusqu'à la fin d'âge

The nightingale who sings on MacLeods Hill
The ancient tune our fathers brought West
Frae auld Scotland's Isles o' the Blest
Les français fiers comme Swill
The Irish fishermen whose work ne'er ceases
T'was in England they sewed the pieces
Thistle, lily, shamrock, and rose entwine still

The cherished memories still haunt me
'May these ties of love be fore'er ours'
Those desires shining bright like the stars
In the darkest night you are all I see
That starlight which sparkles in your eyes
Dream awa' wi' me the time that flies

One day we will wake together, bound by love,
and free

Run the Colors!

Danny Död

Hoist high the Jolly Roger!
Too long you've dwelt on land.
Your strength is haste'ly wasting
So come lend us hand.
Your gaze, it looks so sullen,
Legs bandy and arms weak.
Rise like the bloody sea-foam
That crowns the briny deep!

Let others toil in sorrow
Or sit on paper thrones
And covet beans and pennies
As time does rend them old.
For Fate abhors the coward
and Fate adores the bold:
You shall surf the ocean's waves
And fly the Skull and Bones.

There's halyards that need hauling.
Rusty swords that need thrust,
Each canon must be roaring
To cast away the dust.
Hark the tide's ebb a-calling
The pirate's siren song,
While young men are a-purring
To enter Neptune's throng.
Far away on distant shores
Await us fame and gold
For those brave and daring youths
Beneath the Skull and Bones.

A Lament to a Son

Edward Delacroix

A foreign plain, filled with fire and smoke
Lying here, fatal bullet in my side
I unhappily lay down my life's yoke
And think to you, my boy, my greatest pride

How I wish I had stayed to watch you grow
And spend days together in merry bliss
Imparting all the things you need to know
Instead of "Farewell" and a parting kiss

But in such evil times a man must fight
With hope forever blooming in his heart
That your life may be long and filled with light
And from your home, you never need to part

One day, when you have a son of your own
You'll und'rstand my charge into the unknown

Academics

F.A.

A white paper sat, with pity evokes
The passion of eunuchs,
of scholars. And strokes
of dead ink
lay dormant and seething
like yesterday's blood
like dust in a corner.
Sterile and aging
like salt on the tarmac
like brittle dry leaves.

Heroism

F.A.

The slow stale eternity
Of mass unmarked graves
A trial by fire
Is what the world needs

No more patience and waiting
Like a pious old wife
The life of a sailor
Will set a man free

A and B

Fury

I ask, You think we can catch that rabbit?
He says, It's fast but together we can.

The first time I met him all the chairs were taken.
Save the one beside him, so I sat down.
We used to play a lot in the sandbox.
We were playing and he caught me off guard,
and he put a twig in my mouth.
I didn't ask him why he did that
I didn't cry, there was just grit in my mouth
bit crunchy, but not filthy in hindsight.
We had arguments but we never fought.
We mimed fits but we were just bored young kids.

There never really was a falling out, we just woke
up one day, quarter century later, he moved north
and I moved away south and we drifted apart.
Chasing rabbits up the hill, to nowhere in particular
chasing shadows in the night, the rain, the dark.

He had the patter, the jokes, the energy, the dreams
the first girlfriend who I later found out was actually
into me. His dreams got shattered first, his light
went out first.

And there was no passing of the mantle, no
unsheathing
swords from rocks, no rituals, no rites, no whispers
over candles in the dark. Just the ticking of the clock,
the sands of time and dust in the wind and the wind

through blades of grass and the grass over empty hills
and the hills with no rabbits and the dying of friendship
who I was, who he was.

I could have said something and so could he.
We knew we would just be wasting our breath.

The sun goes down and the light dissipates
The shadows lengthen and the birds migrate
and hunters in vain chase after rabbits.

The cold blue embers of our children hearts burn
like sticking two fingers inside a monster's heart
there is no scream, there's just the twinge
and the eyes twitch but do not flinch
and then the evening redness comes and we shatter
apart. No breath wasted. Like arrows that blot out
the sun, while warriors dash to their fateful doom.

As teenagers we had birthday parties and he gave me
an amulet representing friendship and brotherhood
I still have it, but it's just a bauble, not a token of
anything.
Its bronze rots and its green patina shines like the
rolling
evergreen damp hills where the rabbits slip away from
us.

Right before the first time I broke my heart I told him
it was going to be the last time. It was at the
playground
close to midnight and it was dark but safe back then.
I told him my dreams then and he listened but now he's
gone

or rather, I am gone, we are both gone, he north and I
south
and he has a girlfriend and they live together and I
became
a ronin and moved about and have the written word
but I'd rather had gone to war with my brother
beside me, swords on our hips and dreams behind me
and enemies and goals before us, mountains to conquer
now there are just black holes and amnesia and
insomnia
and the abyss and the regrets of broken friendships.

My hair has grown longer and my eyes have grown
colder.
His hair has grown more gray and whiter and shorter.
And the flames of despair and of counter pasts and
alternative histories and stories untold and things
unsaid
encircle me and the flames rise higher and it burns,
burns,
burns and in my infernal nightmares we stare at each
other
but neither of us turns to stone because we never did
face
the gorgons together so we don't know what it means
to
face ourselves in the mirror and be warriors of destiny.

the kids we killed off they do not scream in anguish
and horror and sadness there is really nothing
but the blue emptiness and the passing hellos
of our mothers on the streets, the sins of our fathers
and things they wished they would have told us
or done for us. But there are no breaths wasted.

You are north, I am south. I am A. You are B.

*   *   *

I look up at blue stars in the blue night.
I imagine holy and blue arrows and crosses and faith.
I desire children, family, a clan.
But you do not desire such things, and your line will
end with you.
When I see you play with your nephew you try, you
stumble and fall.
You know it, and you're fine with it, that's why you
ain't having kids.
I nod because our friend already told me and I pretend
I'm fine with it, I mean, we stopped sharing our
dreams long ago.
Why waste breath, why waste time and energy
and sweat and blood and tears chasing rabbits.

you think we can catch 'em

Our arctic fortress of solitude bolsters and the castles
of both our pasts and futures tumble down.
I build new bridges of steel and concrete
and between other people and so do you. The dust
settles.

The riders in the night come and get us
the officers in white and with their caps
their spears and lances and swords on their hips
and I look at that one sword which has a token clipped
to it,
something that looks like the letter B, something that
dreams and has

40

meaning and grows and laughs just like you did when
you were a kid
and your hair was jet black and you put a dark twig in
my mouth
the times I asked how fast we had to run to catch the
rabbits
and you said to me, "Don't worry they'll be there when
we get there."

*   *   *

Your knee got shot. So did your top athlete career.
I fucked up my knees and I got jacked up running
marathons.
You're still working on your first degree. I got mine.
I worked some dead-end jobs, the ball and chain
and all my dreams got crushed and I picked up chain-
smoking, drinking,
cigars, travel and loose women and writing and I'll see
you
at our friend's wedding in Portugal that summer and I
talk
to women and you stop me and don't like it. But you
have a girl
and live north without me, what's it to you, get out of
my way
you stopped talking to me. What happened to not
wasting our breath
we both went our separate paths. Even though our eyes
reflect
the same pain we both bear in the blue dark and the
inky nights.

41

I was training in the snow and in the mountains in
Norway
and there was an avalanche and I almost died
and you were not there to watch me chase.
I met the world's most famous people, you were
not there. You moved in with your girl up north
and you didn't tell me and the invite must've gotten
lost.

The shooting stars at night like blue arrows,
those ones that blot out all suns, and tracing the dark
like comets
demons and shadows that creep up and broken dreams
that grovel and howl in despairing dark and petrifying
past
of regret, dead friendships and bleeding brotherhoods.
all the scars we got and shared, all the scars
when we were not there and all that was left
was the inky black heart
looking for the temple of our fathers
the swords of lost heroes
the shields of first maidens
and last dragons we did not dare to face
because we couldn't stare at our own fate
in the reflection of dirty mirrors.

*   *   *

I no longer want to catch the rabbit
I want to take all the pain I have
all the things we left unsaid and did not waste
our breath on, and I want to turn it into
an arrow of light
and shoot it straight out.

I want to watch the blood smear on the white
of the snow and trail all the way into the forest
over the damp hills that are no longer green
but white and wet and blue and cold.

You can shoot your arrows too, B
Shoot your arrows at me
I don't mind, you cannot kill me
nothing can, you can no longer kill me
for if you could, you could once
but that time is gone and that kid is dead
my heart is already broken, my dreams are dead
and I've broken my fist on the cold damp earth.
and on a steel pole and now it tells me of storms
and blue lightning like celestial arrows of god
but you no longer care you don't have faith
you no longer think of such things
go ahead, pound the ground, scream at the night
like you used to, tear your gray hairs out
go ahead bleed it all out
I am not there.

I sheathe my sword, without an amulet
this sword is not for rabbits, it's not for you
it's for my own destiny, my own path, my own clan
my own castles in the sand.

*   *   *

Give it a rest, B
The two of us never had to fight
no breaths wasted
and it didn't benefit us one bit.
Look at me, I know there's a bleeding

43

hole in your chest, where your burning
soul and heart still bleed for the dreams
you used to tell me in the sandbox
tell me, how do we catch the rabbits
tell *me*, will we do it.

the violin plays and the fingers burn
the violin plays long and through the night
the strings burn and screech and scream
of all the pain and all the things left unsaid
the things we never did
all the dreams we did not face together
all the broken swords left in the tombs
of the fathers before us
the violin howls into the long night
and the fingers burn

it's fast but we can do it together

blood drips out of your mouth
blood drips out of your soul and heart
it leaves a trail in the snow

you used to love war and had aspirations
of going over the top and into no man's land
we were in the trenches together
and would crawl through the mud
and carry the pounds of our same blood
it wouldn't have matter if your arm got chopped
all the blood would have been for your battles
and your war and your dreams and your soul
your faith and it would have been for our chase.

go ahead, burn, B, blaze into the dying of the night

toss up smoke and let me vanish like a white mage in
flight
come on B, cough it all out, give it to me, I want to
hear you say it. Say it. Say you hate me. Say you loved
me.
Say something B, you coward. I've said enough.
I'll draw my sword rather than paint you words
Or you're a pacifist now and want me to sheathe again
Give me your full self, that's all I ever wanted
and all you wanted of me, all we wanted. To be full.

You've stuck all your fingers in my heart.
I bleed too. I crawl just like you.
That's why I scrawl these black blots like little lost
buzzards in the dark. Like little white rabbits
searching for their holes of escape in the hills
their white furs quaking with fear for the big bad wolf
that would chomp of their arms and neck
and let it crawl and bleed out.

Come on B put your burning hand on my heart.
Let's dream together one last time.
Put your fuming fingers on my scarred chest
look me into my scarred eyes
say something just like when we were kids.
This is not some basketball game we used to play
There are no winners or losers, this is life.
What are you expecting, what are we staking.

And the pillars of the world's night stand tall
and broad and thick and devastatingly immortal.

I must leave you now. I ascend the concrete white
steps and I walk tall and sheathe my sword

and think of the bronze amulet, my friend.
Step by step, I will walk the path, climb the stairs
to our destiny and the dreams you entrusted to me
leave it to me, things better left unsaid right
no breath wasted
there is no pain
as long as my eyes are set
on the balance of our fate.
I will go on our wild childish hunt
one last time into the long blue night
over the long evergreen hills
watch me B
we'll do it together, my friend.

The Statue That Could Have Been

H. Martins

*Dedicated to the pioneer Joseph Bishop, who
helped to settle Middle Tennessee and whose
name is largely unknown.*

Nearby there is a statue
of a man that settled the land.
No great Achilles was the man,
nor are his feats in common view.
It matters not that passers-by
walk down his namesake avenue.
His statue is there, that is true,
but too few look up even one moment
to see his triumph that has been rent
from the likewise ignorant hands of his
inheritors.

This man came over mountains steep
and fought off wolves
for the raising of sheep
and cleared off the land
for the building of stations
to fight of the many Indian nations
who slaughtered women and children alike
and whose knives cut a mite deeper than
Delilah's blade.

Betwixt his station and those of others
a village began to grow
and the village into a city
and the rolling stone of time rolled on

and ground his shaping into dust, and his body
too.
The place of his station still bears his name,
though his statue, still there against the odds,
is eyed maliciously by modern artists who
might stoop to spit on his statue.

This man might be forgotten now,
his pursuits wiped away.
Yet one thing is for certain still:
if good men do nothing,
as they say,
then the trees will grow untamed again
and the wolves would hunt the lambs
and the Indians would ride armed again
and no men would man the stations.

Catasterism

H.D. Withrow

In the auric morn, as I rise along with the sun, I'm betaken
To the skies with wings waxed of dreams.
Ah, feathers of phantoms, how can I fly with these?
Faith in a dream!
A height hitherto unseen!
A youthful dream of glory caught in glory's gleam . . .

I am Icarus; I tarry the path of clouds, of heights unbeknown,
Carrying a hope unhoped for and a half-dream unsewn.
I, lover of loftiness, was unaware my wings were vain,
As a mortal aim—would this phantasmal
plumage turn to stone,
Should I plummet to where I began—
a slumber of hope and dreams

In the silence of my fall, my wings beat
Against the weight of gravity
But it is not gravity—
it is my *sins* that tether me to soil.

The Weight of Regret

Hamfari

Upon his bed, so frail and worn,
An old man lay, his spirit torn.
The air was thick with sorrow deep,
As shadows gathered, soft and steep.

His eyes beheld the ghosts of time,
The love he'd lost, the wasted prime.
A world once bright, now cold and bare,
A graveyard built from his despair.

He saw their faces, one by one,
His wife, his child, all come undone.
By fear, by silence, by delay,
They slipped like embers burned away.

He'd watched as tyrants rose in might,
Yet never dared to stand and fight.
He'd let the fire scorch the land,
And now he lay with empty hands.

A whisper curled within his chest,
A dying breath, a last request—
"If only I had fought," he wept,
And into endless dark he stepped . . .

But sudden light! A gasp! A cry!
His weary bones unbent, stood high.
His hands were strong, his chest drew deep,
The weight of age no more to keep.

A dream, a warning, not his fate!
His chance remained—it's not too late.
He rose, his heart both fierce and true,
"If not I . . . If not us . . . Who?"

The Turncoat Prince

Jeremy Davies

Ambivalence! Too oft the state of man
Who nobly strives, ne'er entirely he can
Encapsulate the spirit of his time
In dusty pamphlets, deeds of sale or rhyme.
What follows then? A moral tale of old
Which came to me within a dream so bold
It did so seem that I was there, I say,
Just as, just here, I clearly seem this day.
The Good Book's land it seem'd to be, and though
So much was gain'd, so little's to bestow.

In righteous vengeance regicide was done:
A bloody giant on a mountain won
The day, but in descent from there he glimps'd
Ascending thus, in haste, a turncoat prince.
They lov'd each other once, but then betrayed:
The giant had his heart through hate re-made.
His sword, still wet with blood, still keen to kill
Sang lusty songs of veng'ance and its thrill
And yet, despite the hate that burned so bright
Inside his faithful breast, he ran from sight

In faith the giant hid, but faith misplaced:
So giant he, far less the land embraced!
More body was unhid than hid; of course.
The turncoat Prince prepared himself for force.
Approaching though, his thoughts did twirl anew:
With thoughts came words, with words a plot soon grew:

"Alive, a giant as an ally is
far more politic to my cause, and his."
So, thus, as he approached with guile, he hailed:
"O giant knight of old, my friend, please tell
me why, in open ambush, bold you wait;
Your lust for royal blood is yet to sate?
Come now, remember? We were once in love!
Let other men have hawks. For us? A dove."

The giant stayed in place, concealed he thought,
Still bent on murder, though on less resort.
But then, the Prince drew forth a weapon sharp:
For what will soothe the savage beast? A harp.
For soothing is a death of sorts, you see;
Sans rage, the turncoat's victim turns to me
And whispers: "Yea, though Beauty be no beast
And Splendor be no fool, O God, at least
This sound loves me! And ev'ry beast's a fool
Who cannot hear their doom in Beauty's rule!"

The turncoat Prince, a David of the Jews,
In the giant the love of Spring imbues:
The daffodils, the violets and the rose,
The dancing lamb, the babbling brook: all foes!
So easy do the lovely turn their coats
When Princes use their cunning: sheep to goats.
Emerges he, our hero giant's frame,
And dances, smiles, and sings: so quick, so tame.
But now, with me, he shakes with rage a'new
To see himself, en'storied, falsely true.

"Lie down," the Prince he croons, "beside this brook

The water's clear, the stones so smooth, and look!
Just there! A doe doth drink her fill, so sweet!
Such beauty, yea, so tender, and such meat!"
So swift the Prince picked up a stone and cast:
Fair beauty into beautiful repast.
The giant Knight saw not a thing struck down
His bread and circus head upon the ground
His bag of bloody royal heads forgot
Empty of who or where or why or what.

For princes or for philistines, what next?
This giant fallen in this field of text?
Which coat to wear, when ev'ry coat is worn
concurrently by ev'ry man who's born?
The turncoat Prince observes the offer'd head
Decapitation? Worse: a kiss instead.
The giant's weapon stolen thus and used
Against the vase where flower'd thought abus'd.
Less bloody, true, less bones left in the grass
The coat sown up with threaded pain, aghast.

But still, the giant hears the Prince descend
So left with bitter idyll to contend
The bag of royal heads across his back
The psalmic Prince sings to the bloody sack:
"False fields! False fields! How can you be so true?
Weapons of war so fallen with the dew!
If I can stop the dew and rain with words
The mighty thus are fallen for the birds.
O Jonathan, the Prince of just one coat:
Your head is so much heavier to tote!
And as for old King Saul I must agree

That such a merrie old soul was he.”

And see, the giant’s tale to me runs short:
The swiftness of our loss brooks no retort.
The Prince, a giant-killer did become,
From strength to strength and coat to coat he spun
The giant grew e’er larger as he shrank
The more he striv’d, more perfectly he sank
Until he all but disappeared from view,
Save troubl’d voices, hereby troubling you.

Thy Brow, Thy Quick Bright Eyes

Lue-Yee Tsang

A MUWASHSHAH OF LUE-YEE TSANG,
AS BOMBS RAINED DOWN ON HOMES IN YEMEN BY
NIGHT.

Refrain:
Thy brow, thy quick bright eyes, passed by my door,
And in the golden sun resistance slew.

O glory and confusion, save me! Now
I know the meaning of a willing death,
As lips sublime bewitch me and I bow
Me prostrate, captive to thy merest breath;
Speak no longer, peace or else I die –
Enough I burn up by thy wine-dark eye.
Thou dwell'st within me, love, so make no war
Against me; every whispered word is true.

A hush falls over Bethlem's Christian homes
As bombs fall on their brethren on the plain
Of Gaza: Herod is afoot, the domes
Of churches ringing with the sound of gain
For Pharisees who seize the weeping land
From Mary's people, damn the Lord's command.
Thy forehead, like a mountain, I adore;
Yet in an evil time thy words are few.
Whatever did a man of Palæstine
To you, that ye should slay him? Will ye sell
Your bombs to butchers, slaughter as the swine
Those men who'd stop them? Traffic, hear this knell!
My lord will not, to keep thee going, slay

The innocent and call it duty's way.
My love, thine eye that sees the desert shore—
Which they call peace—can make it bloom anew.
How long, O Lord? Must nine, ten thousand more
Children be slain, called Amalek by those
Who call Christ's body Ishmaël? Abhor
What deeds are evil; see Christ's bitter foes,
And love your enemies indeed, but see!
They are your enemies, acknowledge ye.
Vīvāmus! Curse my mouth, thee I forswore
But perjured me. O mercy, see me through!

Arise, καιρὸς δ' ἐστίν! Now if thou take
Thy mantle, oh! how burns my heart to see
That noble splendor; lo! my innards ache
For trunk and branches of a lordly tree.
How quick my days, how trembling are my years,
Swift, lusty soul! Then spoke for me my tears:
Say to the Pharisee, "No more, no more"—
Or for these words wilt thou deport me, too?

UPON A FLUTE AND PLUCKED STRINGS.

First Achilles

Lusty Foe

Twice had he seen
When Wihrós brought him
Knotted heads nodding
Among the boulders
Shouts thrown like spears
Through the long grass.

His arm hair stands tall
Hands clap breasts as lightning
cracks
Feet tread with thunder
Spears swing, clubs swipe
But none dare get close.

To club a fox is not war.

Thunder rumbles longest yet
Men tread in place
And shout without meaning—
Do wolves howl after the hunt
with no hare in the den?

He did not come to dance.

Clouds scour the sky.
Clouds scour his mind.
Ragged his breath.
Clenched his club and spear.

The dance has a step-beat:
Foe steps forward
Friend steps back.
He breaks it.

Lightning he feels
In his thighs
As he leaps left
As he bounds right
As the wolf closes for the kill.

Two eyes cross
As he flies
Weapons aloft

FLASH

Light rends the sky
Club cracks the skull
Gurgling sounds life's wane.

He spears the heart
Before him and growls
As the glutting bear
When vermin press in.

Hooting like apes
His foes stop Their treading
to stare
Before they fly.

His brothers watch
Him give chase
And feel new powers

In their limbs.

One
Then another
Then all
Spring forth
To give chase.
A thrusting spear, a cry
A swinging club, a thud.

None could stop
His rampage
None tried.

Is this how gods feel
To walk among men?

Bodies round the hill
Bottom lay strewn
As the wolf pack howls
In a round.

Who can stop
The first men
Who take life
In their hands?

Smearing red up his arms
And across his brow
A flint sparks
Behind his eyes—

What can't I do now?

The Return of Odysseus

Michael Classen

Our hero rows, upon the throes, of Neptune near to land
With burdened limb and features grim, he banks upon the sands.
Tis not the shore he left for war, nor faces of his past
A tragic twist has caused this miss, of oar and wind and mast.

His wearied feet pace cobbled streets, observes a horrid scene
The noble stock that set this rock, are few and far between
A land bereft of all he left, a scourge of blight and sin
He stares aghast as faces pass, through noise and foreign din.

Amongst the crowds that seem so loud, he sights one here and there
Men who could, and likely would, in his great honor share.
Men who stand upon these lands, and witness as he does
A noble hearth which lost all worth, no longer *is* but *was*.

He views a sight near to his right, where men lay block and stone
They toil well upon the cell, together and alone.
He calls to one, *"what have they done, betrayed your ancient home?"*
The man says, *"Well, we have far fell in London, Paris, Rome."*

Our hero hears of hopes and fears, of battles won and lost
Of men who swore to fight these wars, not knowing yet the cost.
They tell him still how lands have filled, with vulgar foreign hordes
How men of power came and devoured, left neither land nor lords.

One man says, *"Wait! You know our fate, you come of our own hearts?"*
Our hero stoops, removes his boots, the man steps back and starts.
A jagged slash down near the calf, a wound of ancient age
He stands up high and sees their eyes, perceives no scorn nor rage.

"How can this be, you come to me? Surely I know your name . . ."
Our hero nods, the men applaud, *"I am one and the same."*
"We've read that you had battled through, and won your Queen and
State?"
"Sadly not, my path is wrought, with sudden twists of fate."

The men discuss and argue thus, *"This sign can't be in vain!"*
"Will our king stay here in our day, our people rife with pain?"
"The sign is here! Our people fear, but now they'll stand and fight!"
"Who are we to speak for thee? Our king is not our right."

Our hero tells of caverned wells, he quells their haste, their angst
He tells of days long past away, when ancient portals sank.
"Show me now and show me how, to reach the place I seek . . .
If I reach home upon my throne, these lands are yours this week."

An inner voice informs their choice, the men lead off at once
Something calls down by the falls, more than mere wish or hunch.
Cascading wash upon the rocks, obscures what lies within
Our hero tells, *"You've led me well, our battle now begins."*

Now crossing streams, 'neath rainbow beams, a flash of light in dark
They're taken forth far from the North, Athena's flagrant ark.
Our hero leads his men by threes, disguised now with a crutch
"Too right you all, those ancient falls, led back to Ithaca."

They then arrive with splendid skies, and clouds of flowing silk
Exclaim, *"Of course! This radiant source, of our ancient ilk!"*
Emotions bleed for when they'd read, of all that came before
They never knew they'd pass on through, this long-lost hidden door

As they walk they dare not talk, for bloodshed comes at noon
They pass through trees and auburn leaves, and pray for victory soon
When they draw near to drunken sneers, and sight the king's great walls

Indeed they must, feel rank disgust, as suitors scheme and crawl.

Ahead with hate on through the gate, the king he leads his men
Throws off disguise and sees their eyes, these cowards in their den.
With one great roar he's seized his sword, the next he's strung his bow
His men all rear now armed with spears, the suitors down below.

He takes first shot and misses not, the first of many die
They twist and scream and wish to dream, as spears and arrows fly
His men explode on this abode, they fight with anger plain
They will endow their king's old crown, upon his royal name

An hours past and long sweet last, the suitors all are dead
Some impaled as they flailed, and some are missing heads.
The blood attests to all the rest, his reign has now been gleaned
They soon arrive from far and wide, to hail their king and queen.

For when the death had come to rest, appeared then on the stairs
His darling wife who'd spent her life, in wait and soft despair
She'd always known he'd seize their throne, restore the order due
She strikes a pace, sweet love's embrace, a kingdom now anew.

The king adores his honored lords, bestows them gifts and praise
They take a knee down by the sea, amidst light rain and haze
They risked so much and left as such, to seek this honor dear
And now await that glory great, so vaulted and so near.

Our king he speaks, *"Brave men I seek, and brave is what has come . . .*
Now on your way my knights of day, God bless you all and one."
His men say, *"How? You leave us now? You swore we'd have our*
lands!
How can we hope to climb that slope with our mere working hands?"

"You fought with pride yet now decide, this time will be your last?

You look to me as if you need this remnant of your past.
My spirit will be with you still, though not my flesh and bones,
You've learned the might of men that fight, now go reclaim your
homes . . ."

Voices of the Dead

Nick Griffin

I wandered through my native land
And stood aghast at what I saw
As she wept under foreign hands:
No justice, truth or rule of law.
So laid me down in troubles deep

And fell into a fitful sleep.
I dreamt the dead came back and spoke
Of deeds long done, of blood and sword.
They died to fend off alien yoke,
To save our land from foreign hordes.
And, win or lose, each one had tried
To throw back the invading tide.

First came a warrior, noble queen,
Who led her men 'gainst Casesar's might;
"Gray beards, strong chiefs and striplings
green,
We showed proud Rome how men can fight
And o'er three cities smoke rose high
To prove that we'd live free or die.

Next spoke a Saxon, gold-haired
Who swung his axe on Senlac field.
"A fight too fair, and ill it faired,
But as night fell we would not yield,
And through long centuries of night
Our children knew that we scorned flight."

"I fought with Drake, as up the coast,

We chased the mighty Spanish ships.
Our guns and fireships broke the host
Of those who came with racks and whips
And would-be tyrants, rich and grand
Found only graves in our England."

"In Flanders fields, me and my mates
From cities, towns and leafy lanes
Died in the war that fools called 'Great'.
'To end all wars', we fell in vain.
In truth we fought the Kaiser's crew
To hand our country on to you."

Last came a lad in pilot's blue
With sadness in his eyes of grey.
I knew him straight—one of the Few
Who stood when others ran away.
"I shot down boys of our own kind
To save your right to speak your mind."

Then all of them looked round our land,
For which they went to early graves.
I saw they couldn't understand
The evils wrought by fools and knaves.
But them on me they all did turn
And 'neath their gaze my soul did burn.

"Win or lose, and came what might,
On land, in air or on the waves
At least we all put up a fight
And now rest easy in our graves.
But what of you, faced by the same
And finding just excuses lame?"

Defiance kindles in my heart and I hear
It drives away unhopeful fear.
Win or lose, and come what might
Once more we'll stand. We'll stand and fight.

Aeneas' Duty

Orbis Tertius

What greater tale of sacrifice exists;
        What more heroic story have we known—
Than that of brave Aeneas, prince of Troy,
        Who watched as Grecian flame consumed his
        home?

Cast out to sea, engulfed by Juno's storm,
        A foreign coast gave refuge to his men.
More welcome still were palace halls, the likes
        Of which they never thought they'd see again.

Queen Dido took them in and fed them well,
        She listened to their tales and their laments;
Upon her though was set a lover's curse:
        And to her longing she could but relent.

Regardless of poor Dido's love for him,
        The pious Trojan was by duty bound—
A noble race of men to raise anew;
        A legendary empire yet to found.

And so the Trojan thence put back to sea
        In search of lands to make this fated home;
Behind he left the smoke of Dido's pyre,
        And too the love that nigh prevented Rome.

Albion

Orbis Tertius

It gives me great pains to see
    This great country I was raised to adore—
With her culture, her achievements, her fine history—
    Slowly fade into the mists of yore
In the name of tolerance and diversity;
    The Britain of old exists no more.

Destiny

Reb Kittredge

My time was now, it seems.
When I caught up to my past.
All those mistakes—

girls not chosen for a mate,
sweet children not to be,
cast down into the dungeon

of mere possibility—
were steppingstones on the twisting
path that led to me.

Battles I was born to fight,
dreams bring down to earth:
All in the fabric of the suit

I was designed to wear today.
Some flowers blossom early, shed
their buds by dusk;

I blossomed late.
Our destiny's not written
in the stars. It's in those

double-helix constellations
spiraling within.
So take heart, give credit

where it's due. Withhold the blame.
We become more who we are

with age. Like a tree

filling out its nascent shape—
fully sprung, we see, at last,
our fate.

Grandfather

Roman Emerald

The scent of a workshop
The hardware and grime
Tinkering away to pass the time
Ham radio equipment in musty cellar
Coded language adds to the mystery
So many artifacts that fascinated me

The mystique, of not remembering much
But just enough of a masculine touch
Forward thinking, computer games
Apple trees on the land
Small, tart, and green
picking them by hand
A science set for Christmas,
A fun toy racing track
A world in monochrome, a simpler time
Before smart phones, and terror attacks

I saw a bit of you in my old man
He was never the same after you were gone
He felt Guilt and shame for not taking the time
For not visiting more before you died
An Ability to fix things and organize
A love for angling and fish fries

But he turned to the bottle, and gave up on life
Neglecting his son and abusing his wife
A cautionary tale, a sad cliché
Many have gone the self-same way
I survived all of that, and it makes me think

Only God knows, but I choose not to drink

I'd often wish you were still around
When false idols had let me down
An adolescent, learning to live
I wondered what advice you'd give

Now my own son, I wonder how he'll be
Did a generational curse merely skip me?
We'll raise him well, but at times he'll stray
I hope he grows up to be like you one day

Old South Charm, New South Progress?

Roman Emerald

Gravel driveway winding
Flanked by plank fence guiding

White columns behind oaken bowers hiding
Secluded from highway traffic sighing

Seemingly removed from harm
Dust settles on Antebellum charm

Closer still with window down
Cattle grazing, hear the sound
Of Barking Lab aging grey from brown

Welcomed by brick stair and screen
And by kin not often seen
Trivial matters, wasting time
No utility, still sublime
Memory, Light, Matter, and Time
Gliding in through the blinds

Wisdom Unheard

Roman Emerald

Timeless and evergreen
Seasons in flow
Always relevant
With wisdom in tow
Sound advice
And the written word
Seem to many
To be absurd

Taken for granted
As millennia pass
Warnings unheard
As Questions amass

Reinhilde's Speech from Act 1 Scene 2 of Arminius

Seamus Tout-Cœur

*[Arminius attends a play within the play, written in
honor of Drusus the Elder's campaigns against the
Germanic tribes. In it, a Germanic seeress speaks the
following last words, as she dies to the Roman invasion
force]*

RUFUS QUINTILLIUS
And now thee wench—
Thou beast of a sow god
Mired in muck and filth,
Scry thee thy own end!

REINHILDE Scry I?
If so:
By Wind, by Water.
And by Earth and Fire—
Those forces that shaped me
Since birth,
Through Odin-scar to eye.
Witness now my fall,
So that I may see true.

**Above, within, amongst, and below—
Listen now and well:**

A hand, held fast or let to slip
Bids time to attend or fate to grip!
Or bids to loose what none have claimed—
For who but us, might grasp at flame?

Aye, ye who wane! Ye who wilt!
O, who shall stand as thou dost tilt?
If not we, who wends this weight?
If not we, who tempers fate?
—Halt—
Hear hush—
For silence builds as winter's hoarfrost:
Thin and light first,
Yet soon hardened to cold and loss.

A breath unspent, is deed not did—
Thou think the tides turn by such naught?
Dost believe Sun is wont to rise unbid?

Wait long, and all may be lost.

Shall lips press firm, or wilt they stay
Locked as a tomb beneath the clay?
I pray thee, love, steady thy gaze,
For folly feasts on faltering ways.

Gods hear not the hush of cowards,
Nor can any wall defend the still.

In deed, in lack, each choice shall chime,
A knell, a song, in marked-out rhyme.
A step, a slip, a vow to bide—
Thou tarry long? Dost step aside?

Time's tread feels light upon air,
But heavy where it settles.

Or shalt thou stand, as by law with lance?
Shalt thou move? Shalt thou advance?

—Lo!—
The hush is rent, the call is made;
If not us, then none shall wade
Through waters cold, through dust and deep,
Through bridges burned, through oaths to
keep.

So yield thee not—nor bow thy nape,
For time takes all, as all its claim.
Yet here remains fleeting spark,
This breath, this pulse—our herald's mark.
Who, if not we, shall stir the dawn?
Take up hymn to Sun— Sing even, Sing on!

Or let it fall. And know thy part.

ARMINIUS (in whisper)
Rome asked for mockery,
Yet Germania sings
Through her
To me—
And her son may yet shine.
Yet what she resounded,
I dare now only whisper.
How could it ever be else?

The Avenging Son (for Octavian)

T. Petera

My eyes beheld my father's sword
Sheathed and dull and never drawn
The statesmen mocked
The scholars schemed
The merchant's gold
Burst at the seams

The jackal cried
The carrion fed
A beggar's feast
My father bled

Breaking ancient law I grasped
My father's sword, which now was sharp
And then I struck
And then I slew
Those traitors all
Whose blood I drew

The people safe
The land restored
Because I drew
My father's sword.

An Ode to a Lazy Murderer

TOM

A shadow on a shadow
A line of light outline
Constant motion halted
A killer laid supine

Lightened eyes reflect
A fire trapped inside
Fragments of our star now fled
'Cross day and night's divide

A silent rush
Disturbs the hush
Of crickets, frogs and hare

The pounce, the shriek
The final squeak
And back he pads to lair

The killer with a thousand kills
Has claimed yet one kill more
The drops of blood that softly thud
On master's old plank floor

Soon enough the mouthful's down
And sated purrs commence
He'll leave some bones, and gullet stones
As shelter's recompense

And Glorious Dead of the Past

TOM

When the moon is bright
And the air is just right
And autumn has laid low the bugs

The pack dogs all howl
For a wolf on the prowl
Seeking livestock that's grown too snug

On nights like these
With no whisper of breeze
And silence like primeval stone

A man should sit long
Whether he's weak or he's strong
In the deep dark, all on his own

The wolf will be wary
For the shape still is scary;
That shadow of men now long past

It may deign to be daring
And stalk close after staring
To leap and bite down and hold fast

And that weak or strong man
All alone, and in hand
The weapon he chooses to trust

Will be given his chance
To hold fast to his lance

And slake the nearly lost lust
He will rise up but fail
Or stumble yet prevail
As he takes on the beast in the night

Death will be dealt
Both steel and tooth felt
By the creatures that meet in this fight

The victor will stagger
And the vanquished will swagger
As they move off on opposite paths

One to the living
And the other, to the grinning
And glorious dead of the Past

Fibrous Fascism

TOM

The stolid march of sun and clouds is nearing
culmination
The birds retreat to canopy, hierarchy marking their
station
The gloaming marks midday for the dawn and dusk
survivors
The rising moon a lodestone for many leg-ed strivers
The orchestra of crickets tune their scratchy mandolins
A threat'ning hooting chorus signals hunts will soon
begin
Both predators and prey dance in natural confusion
The swoop, the stoop, the dodging loop beget a shared
delusion

The greatest lie we sold ourselves to shield us from the
dark
Was Nature's God has different rules for each and
every part
From levels cellular up to the stellar plane
The rules are writ' in blood an' flame
And every line's the same
You'll hunt
You'll flee
You'll captive be

To urge
To need
To mate and eat

A life is born, it lives then dies

And spirit, like flame, forever survives
So long as its offspring swims, runs, or flies

Freedom is death, submission is rest, nothing is
measured until death
You live just as long as you do, not one day more or
less

If Not You, Then Whom?

Toxic Brodude

I. The Call

Lo, inaction is death.
A truth lies deep, unyielding within,
A lineage traced through a thousand years,
Of suffering, of battle, of blood unbowed.
The truth of who you are,
And whence you came,
Burns bright beneath your ribs.

When the mewling comes,
From self-victimizing heifers,
Their dross thoughts
Spoken near your noble ears,
Rise, speak.
Some beast they are,
That your ancestors
Would spear through the heart
Without a moment's pause.

II. The Silence of Good Men

The mutants of the left
Have crept like rot,
Infecting the minds of the young,
Pure, natural, and decent.
How?
Through silence,
Through good men
Who did not speak.

Yet the cure lies sharp,
A tongue honed keen
Can tear through the veil,
Their neuroses unraveled
In one fell stroke.
Rest not on laurels
When your people,
Your homeland,
Are cursed by savage tongues
Of un-noble blood.

III. The Fallen West

Weak men
Let the truth-deniers rise.
They watched the West, once green,
Turned grey, sullied, spoiled.
Yet the future,
A prize still to seize,
May be wrenched
From the hands of the brow-beaten,
Spiritually dead.

What is gold will endure.
What is debased
Will fade,
Will crumble,
Will vanish into ash.

IV. Blood and Faith

Let conviction dwell
Within your heart.
Let the blood in your veins

Guide you.
Hold faith
In what is right,
And honest,
And natural,
And good.

Let doubt fester
Only upon the false,
The crimes against God.
And if not God,
Then crimes against the world,
Against the land,
Against the sanctity of nature.

V. The Eternal Loss

For what stands to be lost
Is just that,
And what is lost
Is lost forever.
No more shall the land
Be unsullied.
No more shall what is pure
Shine golden in the sun.

VI. The Solitary Flame

If you feel yourself
One man, alone,
Crushed by the vastness of the world,
Know this.
No man is exempt
From his place in the tale.

The story of Man
Is billions of stories,
Each one a soul like yours.
This lonesome ache
Serves only misery,
Feeds defeat,
Steals hope,
Joy,
Light.

Stand,
As proud men stood before you.
For your role
Is yours alone.
Not one living soul
Could play it in your stead.

The Newland Saga

By Tanner MacPhee

Lo! The lay of the Newlanders
Long ere dispatched from Vinland's hearth
To find new earth; and sailing south
The ship's prow, donned with dragon's mouth
Crashed on this foreign, rocky land
With tragic woe and consequence
For six upon the ship had died
And three more taken by the tide . . .
They set up camp; and as years passed
Newland fair was built at last;
They cleared the land, harvested trees
And took themselves to shipbuilding

Newland's king was chieftain Björn
The Bear, to whom a son was born:
Fair Arvid, son of Björn, the tall
And Johan was Björn's wretched thrall
Who envied Arvid Björnsson fair
The brown eyed boy with golden hair;
He met the Skræling witch, Felgoth
And many curses did she wrought
Against his master's good bloodline
But in Arvid, she saw a sign:
For Arvid's beloved was Lina pure
Daughter of Hafþor, carpenter
And sister to good Wulf, the strong -
The fisherboy, and archer long
The witch bade Johan: "seize the girl
And I will many curses hurl
Against Arvid your enemy
Against whom you in vengeance seek
To ruin forever Björn the Bear
Your master and your slave-driver;
You must pay the highest price

But I cannot ensure your life"

Johan spoke: "Indeed, good witch
I will kidnap that sordid bitch
So that Arvid will come searching
And I will trap him in a string
And kill that son of Hafþor, Wulf
With your curséd and evil knife
And slay Arvid once and for all
And send him down to Hell's long halls"
Many years after that night
Newland fell into a fright
For Lina, Hafþor's daughter fair
Went missing; and Arvid was scared;
"Where is my beloved?" said he
While Wulf did many answers seek:
"My sister would not leave us thus
This is much more than mere bad luck
A curse has fallen on this realm -
A Skræling curse, at whose fell helm
A traitor stands; a mystery
Has now been laid down at our feet"

Hafþor spoke: "Now hear me folk
Lina's disappearance won't
Slow down our busy industry;
We must send forth a search party
Have we any volunteers?"
Wulf then raised his hand, "hear, hear"
Arvid too, and Erik bold
And Harold Ragnsarsson the old
"So be it" said Hafþor, waving his hand
"Set forth into the Skræling lands
And find Lina, my good daughter

And thence, Arvid shall marry her"

The four brave men set out that night
With swords of steel ready to fight
The Skrælings and their other foes
To save their Newland from its woes
And to their aid was swiftly found
Wulf's good strong and trusty hound;
The hound set forth, set on her trail
And in their quest, they would not fail
For Lina was beloved so
To Arvid, as in tales of old

They set up camp in the woods that night
And sang some songs to Thor's delight
But 'midst their singing swiftly came
A pack of wolves with eyes of flame;
They rose, and Wulf did fetch is bow
And, with his sword, Arvid fell blows
But Erik, succumbing to fear
Was torn apart by canine spear;
Harold Ragnarsson did bleed
But kept his wits and fought indeed
Until those three did wolfpack slay
Until the misty dawn of day

"Gird your loins, my men," said Wulf
"Erik is gone by teeth of wolf
This venture shall be fell indeed
So pack your things and follow me"
And so the party set forth thence;
To Erik, they vowed recompense
"Not in vain did our friend die
To Valhalla shall Erik fly"

The sky was red at dawn that day
As Wulf's hound led them to a glade
Where they found rest and healed their wounds
So Lina would be at last found
"Where, O hound, have you led us to?"
Spoke Arvid, peering keenly through
The trees and bushes of that dark wood
As Wulf let down his darkling hood
And spoke thus: "We shall see quite soon
Indeed, it shall not be till noon
That we shall navigate these lands
In which no man has worked his hands
But Skrælings—savages, the lot
Have many evil curses wrought
Against our proud and noble kin . . ."
And Lo! There swiftly flew by him
A poison arrow, straight and sound
Which cut the hound down to the ground;
"What is this!" did Wulf then scream
While fetching his quiver, speedily

Then there came the queerest sound
Yelping, barking, moaning, growls
"The Skrælings are at last at hand"
And surely, near them was a band
Of goblin men of swarthy skin
Short and lean and fierce and thin
Welding bows and spears to boot
And trinkets from their dead man's loot
"Wulf! Now! Let your arrow fly!"
Said Harold Ragnsarsson the wise
But wiser Wulf did then abstain
"Great magic have these men attained
Such that they can shape and shift;

My good arrows would pass adrift"

Before them then a Skræling came
An elder of the sons of Cain
Wielding him a mighty staff
On which there was a skull attached
And donned he raiment evil-like
That Arvid backed away in fright
But Wulf stood firm and stared at him:
"Who are you? Are you a foe or friend?"
The Skræling smirked and slithered; "Say!
Who are you and your company?"
Said Harold, but to no avail
To speak in Skræling-tongue, he failed
But then the elder raised his staff
And from his mouth there came a bat
Then two, then three, then thousands more
Wulf then cried: "To war! To war!"
Many bats surrounded them
So that the wizard fled from thence
While they in agony did fight
Those rodents of the airy night
Then arrows poured in from the wood
And struck down old Harold, the good:
"Why, O Tyr, have you let me die
With such fallen indignity
Fighting bats from Skræling-mouth?
Why not in my goodly house?"
Then, old Harold passed away
Carried thence by Valkyrie
To Odin's halls for meat and mead
Gladly did he Arvid leave

Soon the bats did disappear

And Wulf and Arvid stood tiredly there
In that fell glade, where Skræling men
Came forth, and pointed spears at them
"We cannot fight these many foes
O Wulf, would you now drop your bow?"
Wulf did ponder, wearily
And lowered his bow quite steadily
But in this act, he heard a noise
A scream: and those two kept their poise
The Skrælings turned, to the northward wind
Where they beheld one slay their kin
"Who is that?" said Arvid tall
"It's Johan!" answered Wulf the bold
And raised did he his bow again
And felled the goblin in front of him
And great mayhem did thence unfold
Till all the Skrælings lay down cold
"Good Johan, it is my delight!"
Said Arvid, bowing at his sight
"My friends, my friends, I've seen your maid
I believe she simply lost her way
In these fell woods; I've looked for you
Since you set out a night ago"

"What great news!" said Arvid, blind
But Wulf did peer with his keen eyes
Into the depths of Johan's soul;
Thought he; "This man is long-gone foul"
"Take us, then!" said the chieftain's son
Wulf spoke up: "I'll follow along"
And turning, Johan gave a glare
And Wulf was sure what he saw there

Through trees and bushes and swamps they
rode
Down to the Skræling witch's abode
But unbeknownst to them, they walked
Amidst the traitor of their flock
For this was all Johan's design
The false Christian of poisoned wine
The Judas of the Newlanders
'Long ere dispatched from Vinland's hearth'
From whence they left their Norsemen-kin
To find these Skræling woods and glens

They walked for two days, while at night
They camped and ate with the evil wight -
Fell Johan, of the curséd name;
They ate and slept till morning came
When Arvid, peering through the wood
Saw Lina, beautiful and good
Standing nude by maple tree
"My Lina, come over here to me!"
Wulf woke up, and Johan too
The latter grinning tooth by tooth
For this was a deception pure
On Arvid's heart, Johan was sure

Arvid leapt up, running forth
Leaving there his mighty sword
Wulf spoke: "Arvid! Don't! Come back!"
You know not now what might attack!"
But it was too late, for Arvid then
Lost Lina midst a boggy fen
Nor was it even truly her
But a vision cast on Arvid's heart
"We must go find her now!" said he

But Wulf bade Arvid save his speech:
"The Devil lives in this dark wood
A trickster, who appears all good"
Johan brought Arvid his sword
And spoke thus: "We must go forward
And find your young princess-to-be
And put to rest this fell journey"

They walked from thence till highest noon
Johan leading those twain through
Until they came upon a hut -
A yurt of which the door was shut
Arvid spoke: "Shall we go in?"
Johan said: "Come on, my friends
A shamaness does live in here
With tales of old and trinkets weird
She has great wisdom of these lands
She'll read the fate written on our hands"

They entered thence and met the witch -
A blind old woman who had a stitch
Over her eye, whence she drew blood
To cast a spell on Johan's luck;
Arvid sat, and Johan too
But Wulf stood back with notched arrow
"Three Norsemen do an oracle seek
Now, what have you to do with me?"
Johan spoke, while pretending
Not to know the Skræling fiend:
We've come to find a younger girl
With fairest hair of finest curls
She lost herself in this forest
And Newland sent four of its best;
Two of us have already died

The other two have thus survived"
The witch then laughed: "The Norns of late
Have woven you a deadly fate
Stick out your hands, so I can read
What other fates I might now see"
Arvid then put out his palm
"Oh, young one, you have waited long
To wed your maiden, I can see
What fate now shows itself to me:
A naive lover have I found here
And in Johan, a Christian queer;
But what of Wulf, the archer brave;
Are you not but a youngling knave?
A worshipper of Thor I find
Searching for his sister-kind"
Wulf then drew on his bowstring
"Silence, witch, you nasty thing!
You know not of whom you now speak
Great havoc do you long to wreak
On our fair realm—the Newlanders
Have lost too much to your fell work!"

Arvid spoke: "Wulf! Lower your bow
For I do seek to learn and know
Where our fair Lina surely lay
Here and now on just this day!"
The witch spoke thus: "I am Felgoth
And many magics have I wrought
But in finding Lina I shall aid
If you prove to be truly brave;
Slice your hand with my good knife
And give to me your blood of life
In exchange for Lina fair -
The pretty girl with golden hair

"I shall" said Arvid, dauntlessly
"Arvid, you know not what you speak
This witch will keep you from Odin's throne
We shall find Lina on our own"
But Wulf's fine words did not avail
And Arvid bled till he was pale
Over the witch's cauldron fell
And she cursed Arvid down to Hell

"Go and find your damsel-girl"
Said the witch, with finger curled
"Your beloved lay in the southwest wind
Surely there you will her find"
And thus did they then leave the yurt
And plunge forth in a world of hurt
With Arvid's sword steady in hand
And Wulf, with bow, following behind

They stumbled, hacked, plunged, and struck
To find Lina with newfound luck
And bring her back to Newland fair;
Deep into the woods, they dared
Until they lastly came upon
A river long with current strong
On whose long banks a Skræling camp
Did sit, with many Skræling tents
And midst them all, a pole was hung
And strapped to this was a maiden young;
Lina had they found at last!
As moonlight had near come to pass

"Lina!" yelled young Arvid fair
Wulf whispered: "No! Stand back from there!
Go not beyond this dark tree line

Or else you will forfeit our lives
Our Lina is to burn at stake
And then be thrown into the lake
We must go fetch her at nightfall
Or else we'll become Skræling-thralls"
Johan spoke: "It is a plan
We shall venture the Skræling-land
Quite soon, under the guise of night
And fetch Lina to her delight"
Arvid was ready, sword in hand
Which he did cut for his woman
Eager then to save his love
And honor Thor, his god above

Later, as the sun did set
The Skræling men went in their tents
So they set out, the Norsemen three;
Arvid's eyes were wide and keen
They crept up to where Lina stood;
She seemed asleep; Arvid lowered his hood
And grabbed her hand: "Lina, wake up"
But she did not, with any luck;
He drew his knife to cut her loose
And then did Johan cut Wulf's throat!
In stealth did Johan do this deed
That Wulf began to gag and bleed

Unbeknownst, Arvid cut her down
And Johan took up Wulf's fine bow
And notched an arrow from his quiver
And shot it into Lina's liver
"No!" screamed Arvid, shocked and dazed;
He grabbed his sword and went to fray
Against Johan, his mighty foe

As Lina screamed: "Oh, awful woe!"

There the two men fought and dueled
In that fell Skræling camp of old
Till all the goblin-men awoke
As Wulf did bleed out from his throat
"A curse is laid on your bloodline!"
Said Johan, "Arvid, your soul is mine!"
Arvid fought with him, enraged
Clashing swords; and out there came
The Skrælings, wielding many spears
The sound of battle in their ears
They watched as those Norsemen did fight
That woeful, cursed, evil night

"What have you to earn this day?
O Arvid, your kinsmen are slain!
Kill me, prove your Thor your worth
And Christ will take me from this earth
And send you down to Hell's tortures
Where belong all idolaters!"
Arvid then let out a cry
And swung his blade, strong and high
And took off Johan's wretched head
Till that false Christian lay down dead

"Arvid, kiss me one last time"
Said Lina, "I'm about to die"
And as the Skrælings pointed spears
Arvid dropped and knelt by her
And spoke: "No, Lina, not down here
In Valhalla, I'll meet you there
And Wulf, your finest brother fair
I'll see you all in Odin's lair"

And with that, Lina slowly passed
And Arvid wept and screamed aghast
And took again his bloody sword
And fought the Skrælings till no more;
Ten he slew till they cut him down
And he lay breathless on the ground
Till Valkyries did thus descend
To collect Lina, Wulf, and Arvid.

Many weeks did slowly pass
Till Björn the Bear stood up at last
And spoke thus: "People, we must find
My finest son—that son of mine
And Lina, and our other kin
Lost in the land of the Skrælings".
"But with what force?" said Hafþor wise
"We have nought but small bows and knives
We must go back to Vinland strong
Where Karlsefni and our kin do throng"
Björn smote the table of his mead hall
"I will not be a Vinland-thrall
We left that place to forge our own
Newland is my forever home!"
Hafþor spoke to Björn the Bear:
"No, my lord, we must haste there
To ask for aid; we cannot fight
The Skrælings in one single night!"
Stubborn Björn did ponder long
"To Vinland, then, where Thorfinn throngs
Whence we set out so long ago
And raise an army, like days of old"

They readied their wave-chariot
And set out thence from their Heorot

To find Thorfinn Karlsefni old
In his northern, Vinland abode
And after days of navigation
They came upon their destination
Where Thorfinn did welcome them home
In his mead hall and on his throne
Thorfinn spoke: "O Björn the Bear
The skalds do tell of your fair hair
And of your big and mighty hands
And of your colony, Newland!"

Björn then bowed: "Behold, fair chief
I come but as a soldier-thief
My prince is lost in Skræling-wood
I humbly request, O Thorfinn, could
You send some men to help us fight
The Skrælings of the wood tonight?"
Thorfinn laughed: "O humble Björn
To me of late as son is born
I have no time to thus partake
In warfare; but go to the lake
And see the seer, Flokisson
Who shall tell you the wisdom of Odin;
And if indeed your quest is true
And Odin does so favor you
I will send forth my finest men
And you will see your prince again"
Björn then bowed, but with a whisper:
"Shall I seek a witch's favor?"

Björn ventured into the night
Guided thence by pale moonlight
Until he came upon the lake
And spoke thus: "Seer, read my fate!"

Suddenly, then, out there came
A hunched old man wielding a cane
With a snowy beard and eyes so green -
The ugliest wretch he'd ever seen;
The elder spoke: "Old Björn the Bear
Has sought the seer for Newland's heir
And Odin's wealth of wisdom while
He searches for his Arvid child"

"You know his name" spoke Björn, weary
The seer replied: "Do not query
About the wisdom of Flokisson
As one is two and two are one"
"What say the gods of my Arvid?"
Asked Björn, with hand on his hilt
The seer laughed: "O Björn, my child
In Skræling woods has Arvid died;
In Felgoth's curse did he partake;
He cut himself for Lina's sake
With Johan, the Christian slave of yours
Who wrought and schemed an evil curse;
You have come here all in vain
And Thor shall pour his mighty rain
Upon your quest, upon your war;
The Newlanders will be no more
Tell your men to pack and leave
Go back to Greenland; there you'll see
What fate is true 'neath Yggdrasil
Before your men in graveyards dwell"

Björn let out a mighty scream
And took his sword out from its sheath
And slew the seer with his broadsword
The seer laughed and was no more

"Odin, favor me in quest
And I will prove that I'm the best
Of all the Vikings on these seas
For Arvid do I long to see"

Björn returned to Thorfinn king
Who gathered a most grand meeting
To judge the tidings of chieftain Björn
And the fate the Newlanders had borne
"What say the seer by the lake?"
Spoke Thorfinn as the others drank
"Flokisson has blessed our war;
Odin and Frigg and Tyr and Thor
Are on our side in this venture
Our victory is thus assured"
Thus did Björn let out this lie
That all his men would go to die
In vain, for Björn's fell stubbornness;
For never was his venture blessed

"If Flokisson did so prophecy
Then we are more than thus obliged
To aid the Newland king of yore
Till all the Skrælings are no more"
Björn then felt such guilt and pain
But pushed it down, and thus refrained
From telling Hafþor wise the truth
And thus rain fell on Thorfinn's roof
And thunderbolts sent down from Thor
In mighty wrath, and evermore
Did Björn the Bear this burden carry
And ever so was he thus weary

Two Viking ships were loaded thence

With swords and shields and bows and tents
And they set out from Vinland's hearth
To prove the gods, in vain, their worth
At last, they came to Newland's shores
Underneath the rain that poured
They left the ships, all eighty men
As Newland's women greeted them;
The men brought forth their shields and swords
Till eventide, when mead did pour
Then morning came, and Björn awoke
By his wife's side; the king then spoke:
"We must now fetch Arvid, my son
Underneath this morning sun
And Wulf and Lina, Hafþor's kin
And Erik and Harold Ragnarsson
And Johan, my damn Christian thrall
And bring them back to this mead hall"
Girded with their swords of steel
And bows and quivers and mighty shields
Guided by their many hounds
They marched to drums, and horns did sound
As Björn strode forth beside Hafþor—
The Newlanders had gone to war

Following the path that Wulf's hound took
The dogs did bark, the tall trees shook
Till they found Erik's rotten corpse
Hafþor sang: "O mighty Thor
Receive our Erik into Valhalla
And aid us forth in Ragnarok
The Skræling-fiends shall taste our steel"
Thus ended his lamenting reel

They strode forth under clouds so grey

And thunder clapped amidst the glade
Eighty mighty Vikings strong
Did walk along and beat their drums;
But the drums did stop, as they did see
A woman before their company;
Nude was she, with golden locks
She stood there smiling in the lot
Then ran away; the men pursued
Till lost was she, no longer found
But from the woods then came a growl;
A wight appeared, donning a cowl
It stood over six meters tall -
It stood there moaning with a drawl
Lina then appeared at last
Behind the beast; and ever fast
The beast leapt forth and drew its fangs
And all the horns of war then sang;
Björn set foot, leading the charge
Against the beast, ever large;
He swung his axe with his bear-hands
On that wight's head—the axe did land
It flinched, then cast Björn to the side
And crushed another until he died
And many more went into fray -
As many thence did lifeless lay -
Till Björn rose up and ran thence forth -
The strongest man of all the north -
And leaped onto the wight's shoulders
And choked it, brought it to the earth
Then let out one great battle-cry
Took up his axe and swung it high
And smashed the skull of the evil wight
Again and again until out of sight
That fell beast was; it lay bleeding

Lifeless, it laid there wretchedly
Björn then turned to Lina fair
Who morphed into a snowy hare
The hare turned thence, and forth it trot
And Hafþor was gravely distraught

"What is this that happened here?"
Björn spoke: "Things aren't as they appear"
The men took rest there in the glen
And swift did two ravens then descend
Crowing there that fateful morn
Hafþor spoke: "Lo! Hugin and Munin!"
And as they feasted on carcasses
Björn reckoned there his dark promise
To Odin, Hugin and Munin's lord
The ravens whispered thence to Björn:
"Nevermore will your plans avail;
Go back to Newland and set your sails
For Greenland, as the seer foretold;
For what shall avail a heart so bold?"
But Björn desired to weave his fate
And filled was he with such great hate
That Thor poured down his mighty rain
Upon the proud Viking again
That Björn might finally take heed;
But stubborn was Björn's heart indeed

They proceeded thence, from the glade
Beneath the falling, heavy rain
Till at last they came unto the lake
Where Lina did once hang at stake;
The Skræling camp was nowhere found
For they, as nomads, were so bound
To scavenge land and hunt and fish;

They left nought but a petty ditch
Wherein a bonfire once did lay;
For after Johan and Arvid's fray
They cooked and ate their lifeless flesh
A savagery—a curse of death
And Hafþor's kin did they eat too
Till all of them were thus consumed;
But four fell stakes did there remain
The heads of four Norsepeople slain:
Arvid, Wulf, Lina, and Johan -
Heads impaled on stakes so long
That when Björn went to take them down
Their blood did drip upon his crown
"O what evil! Arvid, my son!"
Yelled Björn, wheezing from his lungs
For he was gravely misshapen
Never to see his son again
"By Mjolnir's wrath, I swear vengeance
Forever and until death against
The Skrælings who did this to me
For I am Björn of the western seas!"
Hafþor spoke: "Fear not, O Björn
I will not turn away in scorn
But aid you in your quest of glory
And avenge your son of this crime so gory
And of all you who will, say 'Aye'"
Eleven others did then say aye;
The rest did turn to Newland fair
To embark again to Vinland's hearth:
"Of this quest we are not obliged
We shall go back to Newland this night
And leave you in your misery
We are no longer your company"
"Cowards!" yelled Björn, thus distraught

Hafþor spoke: "They've seen enough blood
Let them go into the night
Tomorrow we shall have our fight"

They set up camp by the river long
And there those twelve Norsemen and Björn
Did sing, lament, and play the lyre
Sitting and laying around a bonfire
"Tomorrow we shall die" said Björn,
"Tonight we shall sing our last song to Thor"

The sun did rise, as did the men
And those thirteen set out from thence
Upon their quest for glory and pain
And surely did Thor pour more rain
They came upon a cleared-through trail
Which the Skrælings were known to travail;
They followed it forward, with their hounds
Stomping over Skræling-ground
Bows and spears and swords in hand
They sought the Skrælings in the land
The ravens crowed, the wolves did howl
For surely they did know the hour
Was near that Björn and men would die;
The Vikings gave a battle-cry
They tread along until high noon
On that long trail, and they came soon
Upon a band of Skræling hunters;
Björn yelled out with mighty thunder
"Curse and kill these goblins all!"
Under Viking-blade did all of them fall
Save one, who ran back cowardly
To the rest of his Skræling company
Which those great Norsemen then pursued -

Surely they were a horrid brood

They came at last unto a clearing
Women and children deathly screaming
As the Norsemen set to their Viking ways
Entering all into the fray
Slashing, slaying, drawing blood;
The Skræling-women thus did run
As the men leapt forth, a hundred-fold
With spears so sharp and eyes so cold;
They battled there, and all did fall
Till at last there stood only Björn the tall
The king then knelt, bloodied and battered
hard
"Surely I have come long and far
To receive my pound of flesh; and whence
Has come my fallen recompense?
My son lay dead, and all my kin
All because of my fallen sin
My pride, my cursed stubbornness
I've fought my war; there's nothing left
'The gods help those who help themselves'
Or so I thought; I must bid farewell
To all my dreams for mighty glory
As I kneel in this field alone, so gory
Odin, will you forgive my ways?
Shall I die in honor here this day?"

A shuffle came then from the wood:
Felgoth appeared and lowered her hood
And wielding in her hand a sword
She spoke to Björn a final word:
"King Björn, I've come to meet you here
And at your prayer I am moved to tears

But you have slain many of my kin
And Thorfinn's seer back in Vinland
As I can tell by the breeze that blows
And tickles the hairlets of my nose
From the northward gulf, from whence you
came
Back to my realm beneath Thor's rain
And now I've come to put an end
To your forsaken settlement
And send the Norsemen overseas
And regain my sacred home and peace!"

Björn rose up with axe in hand:
"This is mine, I've cleared this land
If you shall take my son from me
Then I shall take your damn country!"
The witch leapt forth, with lightning-feet;
The Newland king did gladly greet
Her blows with blows, and stabs with slashes
And in each other they left great gashes;
For one half hour, those enemies dueled
To find which one would truly rule;
They swung and struck until, at last
That final moment came to pass
That Björn did split the witch's head
And Felgoth there did lay down dead
But not before she stabbed with sword
The heart of king and chieftain Björn

The Valkyrie came, collected him
And surely he saw his son again
In Odin's hall, where they did feast;
Wulf and Lina did he also greet
While down in Midgard, Newland fell

And Johan rotted down in Hell
Rejected even by the Christ;
Surely Johan paid the price

Thus ends Newland's tale, whose teller
Retires, until he finds a better
Song to sing, or poem to write
To all who read, I say: good bye.

O Colonel! My Colonel!

By Alexander Ross

For L. Degrelle

O colonel! my colonel! the long campaign is through.
The tank has taken every shell, every shell but two.
The first, a burst of liquid heat, of shrapnel and of flame.
The second wielding hist'rys pen, blackening your name.
          O fate! fate! fate!
              What a world its twists have sown,
                  where, banished, you must mine the past,
                      a thousand miles from home.

O colonel! my colonel! you watched us laid to rest,
between the rows of sunflower stalks, somewhere upon the steppe.
At final siege, you took your leave. You made that great escape,
with half your life ahead of you to pray, and write, and wait.
          Here colonel! dear poet!
              You are beckoned to the throne.
                  It is some dream your years have fled
                      a thousand miles from home.

My colonel, he does answer, but in a voice so far away.
No gathered crowd or banners proud await to hear him say
that in the end, the deeds of men are cast in gold and bronze,
but it takes a tongue, a land, a song, to let a Folk live on.
          The guns have fallen silent now.
              My colonel stands alone,
                  calling for Europa's sons
                      a thousand miles from home.

115

Music

By Edward Schofield

A certain music lingers in the air,
what muse and voice of man once dared to call
the timeless grace of God. A hymn of fair,
dark flowers, birds in chorus, pregnant all
with high symphonic light, with notes that speed
on ray and leaf -- a siren song indeed!

The sacred: aged, but strangely lively fresh.
So close it brushes with the body's hairs;
yet farther than the stars to human flesh,
it moves unnervingly; aloof, yet glares
on deep foundations of the inmost mind.
Enmeshed, estranged -- apart, but one in kind.

There is no glory like this summer sun,
when morning shudders, opening a trove
of wealth untouched; as if the world had run
it course, then planted paradise: all wove
in mystic, chanting, glistening tones. Our peace,
if men will grasp it, here has lasting lease.

No law, nor rule, or theory here contains
the craft of art, our faith in man's ascents,
the fecund harvest of the heart's rich pains.
Potential! Boundless as the elements
of endless land, quick winds, the foam-capped sea,
that power of voice and pen and ringing key!

But in the harmony of dance and tune,
a distant discord seems to echo down.
Afar, and barely heard; but as the moon
projects to silver clouds a drifting frown,
so threatens this grim dissonance to crowd
and suffocate . . . and thence, the burial shroud.

This wheel of black impersonality
grinds near: our songs to pulp, their notes to meal.
Beneath the treads, machine-men crawl unfree,
as worms are trod, revealed by rain's grey heel;
the new technology in lustre dead,
in eyes all blank, in stars descending red.

Now darkly luminous, the evening skies,
once beautiful in effervescent blades
of sapphire chorus, close. Emerging spies
of winter's death-dirge bid their cold brigades
to screech. The cheerless noises all resound
throughout the realms of day's last whispered sound.

O ghostly fading! Frost to glaze the dark,
deep shadow's killing stroke in twilight's end;
we, too afraid to sing, destroyed. The stark
penumbran orchestra makes cease
our golden eves, our canticles turn mute.
No elegy for sad inaction's fruit.

The seasons, haughty over time's great flood,
guard last domains of hearts that clung to myths,
as if old Father Time, with fervent blood,
had Europe's carven rocks and blade-bound smiths
raced past: the maker of the highest throne,
And drive of all that once we dared to own.

But does the final silence of our round
have fate's inevitable stamp and seal?
Can man the epitaph of tacit sound
still read, interpret, and revive with zeal?
Or will the false responds and columns now
upholding bleak cathedrals crush our vow?

Example still abounds from ancient days!
When, even in the age of dark (supposed),
a flickering ember lit the greying haze
with epic poems, tales, and lays. Composed
despite their artlessness and beauty's debts
to creditors come daily for their bets.

For even from a thousand years of wait,
when triumphs seemed forgotten things, too drained
of color to attempt display—too late,
it seemed, to many in excuses chained—
lyres that were broken, mended and restrung;
bronze that was tarnished, cleaned then proudly hung!

Yes, if that old arcadian breeze abides,
—and can it die, that lives in lineage,
that rises out of kinship's very sides?—
then man has but to listen, and the bridge
that fords the summer streams to that high place
will build on solid piers of stock and race.

The only lacking thing is one small chord,
to modulate, to alter night to day,
a simple triad every man has stored
within the musics of his mental fray:
a fundament of hope, defiant dreams,
and sweat-drenched work to spite foes' haughty
screams.

What fear can manhood shelter in its soul,
when through the world of memory alight
the spirits of its heroes past, whose whole
and mighty beauty gave us all our right?
Whose fertile kingship must we hold in awe:

their flights of destiny, of will made raw.

The clarion-call is echoing through the West;
its herald blasts from some eternal hill:
'Bring forth thine own, thy great, thy best;
with fire-borne strength, tremendous in their will!'
So I, if merit rests in me, should heed;
And you? Shall doubt deny the hour its plead?

SHORT STORIES

Outside Your Room

A.J. Bell

The young couple next door argued a lot, mostly yelling back and forth; and when they eventually made up, their lovemaking showed an equal lack of consideration for the units around them. The cycle went round and round, every few days it seemed. Kasie would listen to them; he'd tap the space bar on her laptop, freezing whatever she was doing, then cock her head to the side so that her left ear was tilted up like a rabbit on the prairie. She felt only mildly guilty for doing this.

As time went on, Kasie couldn't shake the feeling that she had somehow cynically manifested this duo, to punish and torment herself for her own recent breakup and subsequent loneliness. She'd never seen them, after all. She'd never spoken to either of them. They weren't fully real—phantoms trapped inside the walls in the throes of a passion just beyond her reach. She knew, once the weather warmed up, it would be better; people would be outside more. They'll have their windows open. The collective noise would drown them out. She wanted to believe that. The cold and the snow made everything still, made the apartment feel like a cave. At night when she couldn't sleep, and she could hear them in bed through the wall, she told herself she was happy for them. She wanted to believe that too.

*   *   *

It had been an especially long day at the hospital, and Kasie was in no mood to be bothered, or for anyone else's drama. But whoever was knocking on the door was not letting up. She had quickly closed her laptop, then fast-tiptoed to hit the light at the first sound. She sat in the dark, and waited. But the knocking continued. Finally, anger overwhelmed her patience, and she answered the door. There she found a young woman with dirty blonde hair standing in the hall, in her pajamas. Her eyes were red and puffy from crying. She was clutching her phone to her chest. Kasie just stared at her.

"I'm so sorry. I hate to bother you," the young woman said.

Kasie asked her if she was okay. She knew that was the right thing to say. The girl just scrunched up her face, and shook her head. Kasie quickly brought her inside, hoping whatever this was wouldn't take too long.

"Can I use your bathroom?" Kasie flicked the light back on, then gestured in the direction of it. All the apartments had the same basic layout; the bathrooms were all connected back-to-back, each unit directly mirrored the one next to it. "Thank you so much. I'm so sorry, I know you don't even know me. I'm a good person." Kasie gave her a stern but knowing look, like all these facts were well-established.

The girl was in there a long time. Her phone kept going off. Sometimes she silenced it right away; a couple times she answered, pleading with the person on the other end to stop calling. That she just needed time to think, to calm down, to be by herself for a while. Each time it rang, Kasie crept closer to the door.

"Hey," she said, tapping on it gently, "do you want me to call the cops for you? I don't mind." Truthfully, Kasie was counting on the girl saying no, and when that was the answer she got, she let out a huge sigh of relief. The girl said she'd be out in a minute.

Kasie retreated back out into the living room, with her arms crossed. She did a silent hallelujah when she heard the toilet flush. We were making progress.

The girl came out, plopping down on the couch beside her without being asked. Her face stayed locked on her phone. She seemed to have regained some of her composure.

"You have a nice bathroom."

"Thank you."

The girl took a deep breath, darkening her phone, then looking finally at her hostess. "I'm so sorry about all this. I'll get out of here soon."

"It's okay."

"My fiancé and I were fighting."

"I understand."

"My name's Luna."

Kasie waved hello at her, even though she was right next to her. "Hi, Luna. I'm Kasie."

"Nice to meet you."

Her and her fiancé had only known each other for five months, and had been living together only a few weeks. Luna seemed to have a very clear but ironic understanding that this didn't bode well. Most of the conversation consisted of Kasie nodding her head respectfully as Luna shared while she texted, in between awkward stretches of nothing being said by either of them. Simple but condescending advice rested on the tip of Kasie's tongue. But she grit her teeth, and was proud of herself for keeping it in. When Luna finally got up to leave, saying thank you, telling her she's the best, Kasie made her promise to come by anytime if she needed to decompress or needed someone to talk to. She knew that was the right thing to say. She even briefly rubbed the girl's shoulder at the door, like a big sister.

Naturally, Kasie assumed this was half of the couple next door. But after Luna left, there was no sound from that apartment; no raised voices, no slamming of doors. She knew it didn't matter really, but she felt she had to be certain. She couldn't say exactly why. She listened carefully, but the walls stayed quiet. Then, just as she was finally about to drift off underneath the covers, she sensed the creak of a mattress not so far away.

*　　*　　*

The housekeeping job at the hospital was only temporary, to pay the rent while she did college. But college was about to be over. Kasie knew the longer she stayed, the worse it looked. Yet she felt so drained lately, she didn't even want to think about all the things that would need to happen in order to reach escape velocity. She knew the breakup had bought her some time from inquiries about her future, and she was perversely thankful for that.

Anyway, it was an easy job. In fact, this was the most mellow job she'd ever had. Just cleaning. The closest thing to customer service she had to do was direct someone here to visit a loved one back to the lobby, or the parking garage. Being on night shift helped. Otherwise, she was left alone. She was assigned a room, through her housekeeping phone, then just followed the steps. Trash and linen. High dust. High-touch surfaces. Make the bed. Clean the restroom. Mop. Inspect. Go to the next room. It was mindless, but that was a relief after spending the morning reading and writing in class.

The phone went off. It was her supervisor. "What's up?" she asked.

"Are you almost done in that room?"

"No, it was really bad in here. Why?"

"I need a favor."

"What?"

"Would you go check Vascular real quick?"

"It's Saturday. There's no one over there."

"I know, but I have to be able to sign off on it being done. And the person I normally have do it is on vacation."

"Do I need to put on scrubs?"

"No. Don't worry about that. Forget about the procedure rooms. Just make a loop, make sure everything's good, trash and dash."

"Trash and dash? Okay, I can do that."

"You're the best, Kasie. Thank you."

"No problem. It'll get done." She hung up.

She was a good employee and, as a good employee, she was rewarded with more work.

This was nothing new.

Vascular was closed on the weekends, except when the hospital staff needed to use one of the procedure rooms, in an emergency. There were six of them, and then there was a suite of recovery bays. The waiting area made up the final third of this rectangle. This was where she went, after swiftly patrolling through the dark empty rooms and scanning anything metal for handprints or blood. Screen savers with inspirational photos and text sleepily blinked from every monitor.

Someone had left the lights on in the waiting area. She had already shut the door behind her with her cleaning cart, when she realized someone was in there.

*   *   *

Kasie had thought of this scenario many times before. What if one night she went in there to check and make sure everything was in order, and she found one of the doctors making out with one of the nurses? Or a homeless person, looking for a warm place to spend the night? Or a guy in a clown suit with a knife? So far, these situations had stayed firmly in the realm of her bored daydreams. And, luckily, this wasn't the case now.

It was just an old woman sitting in the far corner. She was praying softly over a tea light on a small side table next to her chair. Kasie sighed.

"Hello?" she said. "Ma'am?"

Instead of answering her, the old woman clapped her hands together, and blew out the candle.

"Hello?" Kasie said again. "I don't mean to be rude, but you can't be in here."

"Do you know my daughter?"

"No. Is she a patient here?"

The woman nodded. She said, "Yes, she is having her gallbladder taken out. I was told to wait in here."

"Well, you must have gotten turned around. There's no one over here now. Do you know what room your daughter is in?"

"No, the nurse said she'd come get me, once they were done. The door was unlocked."

Kasie sighed again. "I understand that. There's a nurses' station just up the hall from here. I can take you there. Someone will know where you need to be."

The woman spent a long time pondering over this. "Alright. But I want to give you something first."

"What?"

She started rummaging in the large bag she had with her. "It's a gift."

Kasie said, "I can't accept any gifts, it's hospital policy, thank you but I can get in trouble—"

"You can give it to your daughter."

"I don't have a daughter. I don't even have a boyfriend right now —"

"Here."

The woman held out something in her hand that Kasie couldn't see. She took a step back away from her. The woman asked, "What is your name?" Then she snatched up the spent tea light, and tossed it in a nearby trash.

"Kasie."

"Kasie, do you believe in magick?"

"Magick?"

"Yes, magick. That which we cannot see or easily explain."

"Sure, why not? But I still can't accept gifts from patients or visitors to the hospital."

"I'll take that as a no. I used to be just like you. I'll leave this here. I don't want to get

you in trouble." She placed a small white crystal on the table, in the spot where the tea light had been. It was roughly the size of a finger.

The woman continued, "Let me explain magick to you. And then we can be on our way. Magick is like saying 'I love you.' What if you went up to some random person, a total stranger, and told them you loved them?"

"They would probably think I was nuts," said Kasie, sending a death ray to the crystal with her eyes.

"Right. It would be a little awkward, to say the least. It would just be words. They wouldn't mean anything. You don't even know that person. Now, imagine you meet someone, you feel a connection with them, you get to know each other, you become very close—and then you tell them you love them. It's a world of difference, isn't it?"

"Yeah. Okay."

"Magick is the same way. It's a relationship, it's about what the individual brings to it.

Anyone can learn magick words, or play dress up. But a shallow understanding will bring about a shallow result. A selfish heart will draw, shall we say, unwanted attention."

"Why are you telling me this?"

"Because I believe fate has brought us together. I had intended to give this crystal to my daughter, to help give her a speedy recovery. But here you are. It's clearly for you."

"I'm here five nights a week. I don't know if fate comes into it."

The woman smiled at her. "But you said yourself: no one is supposed to be in here."

"Someone forgot to lock the door on their way out. Happens all the time. What about your daughter?"

"My daughter will be fine. She will understand."

Kasie started toward the door. "C'mon, let's go find your family member. That's very kind of you, but take the crystal, please."

"Alright," the woman said. Kasie watched her pick up her gift, and return it to her bag. They quickly found her daughter, who was sleeping peacefully in a room on the third floor. The woman gently squeezed Kasie's arm, and thanked her for her help. They said goodnight. When Kasie got back to her cart to resume her shift, she mysteriously found the crystal there, hiding in between her duster and her mop. She held it up to the light, and shook her head.

*   *   *

The next morning Kasie woke up to the sound of power tools, and hammering. She growled, and hid under her pillow. Eventually she got up to put on coffee. Then she stood by the front window with her mug. Maintenance men were dragging out some rolled up carpet, going in and out.

After she got ready for work, on her way to the parking lot to leave, she stopped one of the men. He smelled like paint.

"Did that young couple move out?" she asked.

The man looked confused. He said, "That unit is empty." Kasie didn't know his name, but they'd spoken before when her refrigerator had stopped working.

"But a guy and a girl lived there. Two noisy kids?"

He shook his head. "That apartment's been empty for months."

"I hear them all the time. The girl came over to my house the other night, she was having a bit of a meltdown. They were fighting."

The man just shrugged. "I don't know what to tell you. Probably a different unit. A lot of people have moved out recently. We've been so shorthanded, we're just now getting it ready for someone new."

Kasie gazed up at the side of the building as if they would suddenly appear in a window and prove her right. But the glass only reflected the tops of trees, and the sky. She said, "Yeah, I guess so," then went to her car. She sat there a long time before driving away. The crystal was in her pocket. It was a warm day.

The Cathedral

Aethelray

"People around here speak Russian, but the trees whisper in German."

Kurt was fumbling the fountain pen—his nerves carried his mind away from writing—then he jotted down a few more sentences:

"I'm worried. A police officer—or was he with the army? showed up this morning, asking if we heard anything from Papa. Of course, we didn't. We don't even know if they want to help him, or they think he's a deserter, or if he's even alive."

He wasn't certain where his train of thought would lead him, but he felt he had to continue for there was not much else to do to exercise focus, and relax at the same time. Kurt's fingers began to sweat; it was Charlotte he couldn't stop dwelling on. He had bought it. It had cost him a true fortune, but it was worth every single reichsmark.

He put down the pen. There was no use. Kurt slouched and pondered whether he should go out today at all. What a dumb question! Naturally he had to! 'Never forget to catch a break of fresh air.' he'd tell himself when feeling down and apathetic towards his surroundings. Daylight poured into his room through the roof windows, and behind one Kurt eyed the cropped-out castle top. The summer sky covered in peaceful blue—"peaceful" was such a rare word to utter now—it reassured Kurt he absolutely had to treat himself to a walk outside. Besides, it would be a perfect opportunity to steal a few moments from her. Accepting this moral obligation, he slipped on his school-old jacket, slightly worn-out trousers with the occasional, sticking-out thread, and hurried downstairs.

His little sister, Greta, was doing her homework in the kitchen whilst their mother was managing a few chores simultaneously.

"You going outside, Kurt? Make sure you pick these from the list, please," the mother handed a note.

"Do you think they actually have it in the shops?" Kurt glanced through some of the items. "I can't remember—"

"Well, just, get what you can find, alright?" she departed into the living room. "I still have some saved up," Kurt shouted from the kitchen.

"Oh, good, good, then all's good," Mother gave him a quick kiss on the cheek.

Kurt's mother was always very efficient in the household, never appearing one bit tired from all the hard work she'd had to endure as all major responsibilities piled up on top of her shoulders. Kurt volunteered to help when he could, but he was most useful now making whatever money they could earn. His mother had repeatedly told him though to apply for university in Berlin—something he'd genuinely planned— but when Papa had been sent off to the front, he put down the idea for good. Mother's blessings didn't encourage him, and there was also Greta, she was only twelve. And Charlotte . . . Leaving the town would also mean leaving Charlotte. Should he say the words tonight?

The moment Kurt made it out of the house, a muscular horse neighed into his face. A cart was driving by down the tight cobble street, the same direction Kurt intended to take. It smelled of cabbage and other vegetables, the cart must be laden with some. Little eddies of wind hit Kurt's face as he walked down the path, passing by a few closed shops with empty windows that resembled dull mirrors.

The road ahead opened view to a much livelier world of intersected tram lines, busy crowds, news boards with multiple posters tacked to it, Kurt would only read a few headlines from the local paper. Despite their generally optimistic tone, the climate here made a quiet, yet uneasy impression.

Kurt strolled down past a line of buildings nestled against the side of the river, towards the bridge to densely constructed Kneiphof island. Charlotte's family resided in one of the higher-end apartments, her room was upstairs. Once Kurt had 'conspired' with a neighbor, and sneaked his way into Charlotte's chamber right through the two windows in a single, audacious jump. Even though she'd been expecting him, it gave her quite a fright. But then, initial fear had quickly given way to passion Kurt had ever experienced only with her. Those were the nights, and to believe it was only but a bit more than half a year back!

A tram rolled by, squealing against the rails, clearing the path to cross the road. Kurt knew Charlotte's weekday routine so perfectly he could predict her day as accurately as public transport schedule. Kurt chuckled at the spontaneous comparison; he never fancied any kinds of transportation and avoided traveling when possible.

The rather narrow central street brimmed with local folk always on the move, hustling with their business—Kurt was so slow in his steps he mentally isolated himself from the rest. The buildings of old stood silent, they passed the test of time, and yet they failed to speak to Kurt: their poetic language lay in an inaccessible realm. Unlike trees. Trees spoke a quiet whisper, Kurt would have to silence his mind first, and the melodies he heard gifted him the opportunity to translate them to his dear Charlotte.

An imposing cathedral cut itself out into the air, its spire-topped windows always emanating some kind of inner light through the stained glass, and the spire gracefully looked down upon the helms and cross-shaped roofs. Kurt tarried in the courtyard for a short while, hoping he would find Charlotte nearby. He then headed towards the nearby park—it wasn't an actual park, but the few trees grouped together as if dwarfed by the wall-like buildings dotted the surroundings beautifully.

Kurt spotted Charlotte—he instantly recognized her blueish dress, the colors of today's sky. She turned around nonchalantly, her hat keeping her sharp face in its shadow.

"I was beginning to think you'd miss me today," she smiled at him.

"I didn't know we had an arrangement," Kurt joked back. His heart was beating frantically against his chest. He had to bring *it* up, but how?

"You're a man of arrangement, Kurt, you should know it yourself by now," Charlotte leaned closer. "Speaking of. I was hoping to see you today, I have some news."

Kurt looked at her quizzically. Her voice didn't sound happy.

"My father is sending me off to Copenhagen to his brother. I don't know when I'll be catching my train, might be as early as next week, Kurt."

"But—" Kurt was lost for words. This update was of little help.

"I know," Charlotte leaned even closer, her head under his chin. "But the recent bombing . . . He doesn't think it's safe for me anymore. And I don't think it's safe for you."

"This should be over soon."

"When?" she stepped away. "When is it going to be over? Everyone keeps saying that, but things have only been getting worse, Kurt."

"Things will get better," he rested his hands on her shoulders. "Tonight. Will you be able to see me closer to midnight?"

"What, you're planning to summon Stalin and Churchill and Führer and scold them into peace?" she laughed.

"Well," Kurt couldn't resist a grin. "I might not possess *that* kind of power. But I can promise you this, I'll never leave you," he said the last words with the most confident quality of his voice. They surprised Charlotte visibly, and she didn't respond instantly as she normally would.

"You have me convinced, Kurt, at least for now," she laughed again.

The couple continued on walking, hand in hand, as Kurt loved it. He had no idea what he was doing or even saying, doubt clouded him, but he would show none of it. When speaking with Charlotte, his intuition was his only ally, it had bonded him to her, and he cherished this bond.

Kurt kissed Charlotte goodbye on the bridge, and traveled all the way back to the market. A sudden sweat had broken out over his body. What was he actually planning? She was set on leaving, she had no choice, and even if she said 'yes', it wouldn't change anything!

The eastern part of Königsberg horrified with the bombed sites where the dust still swirled in the air, and the heaps of rubble were being shoveled away. The bombs had demolished a few buildings completely, leaving jagged holes in the belt of houses. Kurt preferred to avoid the crowd, and took a side-street. There were men with roughened faces—their spades resting on the rubble—reading newspapers. Kurt headed further off haunted by a certain dizziness.

He returned home before evening, carrying bags with food, mostly vegetables. His mother greeted him momentarily and took the bags into the kitchen. Kurt later found his little sister in the living room; she was writing a letter.

"Oh, whom are you writing to?" he asked with enthusiasm. He noted a bunch of lovely little pictures she'd drawn all around the paper.

"To Papa," Greta answered quietly. She didn't look up.

"Want to tell him about school?" Kurt played along. Mother must be picking up those letters in secret.

"Not only," Greta sipped off some of her tea. "Let him know I got a nice job!"

"Why don't you write him yourself?"

"I did," said Kurt after a short pause. "I just thought you'd want to –" he didn't finish. Greta didn't comment either. Perhaps she knew all along Papa was missing, and Kurt was lying, and Mother was lying. He couldn't tell.

In thought, Kurt made it upstairs to his room. He didn't change. Back at his table, journal open, he penned:

"Still the evening of August 29th. I'm feeling like I'm shaking from fever. I am about to propose to Charlotte, she's going to meet me tonight near the cathedral. I don't know. My thoughts are a mess. I know I have to do it, this might be my only chance. Even when she

departs, she will have the ring, and she will remember me. This way she will always have a piece of my love, whatever the grim future holds for us both. I have to do it!"

Kurt pushed the journal aside, and took out the ring. He'd secretly measured her other rings, so he'd made certain it was the right size. His fingers were trembling as he was holding it, its neat blue stone reflected the dazzling color of her eyes. Kurt smiled. He would finally do it.

Kurt whiled the rest of his time reading—or attempting to read. Pacing the floor, speaking to himself, rehearsing the lines, none of that helped him to calm down. A minute dragged into an hour, an hour dragged into a few hours, then he simply cast the book onto the bed, and rushed outside the house, without any goodbyes.

The night had conquered the sky, there wasn't a single star above, the clouds stretched far, covering the city. It was dark, not all street lamps were working properly. Kurt's mind was furiously busy with the train of thought he had begun in his room. The chill wind blew, and his pumped-up euphoria subsided somewhat. Kurt recollected himself, fingered the ring in his pocket, and continued with a firm walk towards the island.

Having acquired a feeling of assurance, the further direction of his life was once more in his own hands. It would be a new Kurt who would emerge out of this day, an engaged young man who would wait out any war to reunite with his beloved one at whatever cost.

There was no tram, very few cars driving by, the city was both asleep and awake. Kurt inspected Charlotte's house. The lights were out. She must have left already. He slowed down his pace, making a weak echo with each step. Charlotte was nowhere in the courtyard, nor was she around the trees. Kurt wandered all the way towards the bridge, and she was standing there, resting onto the railing, gazing into the water. Kurt stood in place for a brief moment, in complete amazement.

"Well, well, wizard. It's about time," Charlotte finally noticed him. "Time to demonstrate the magic you promised," she giggled.

Kurt didn't say a word at first. There was no need for a prelude, it'd lasted for way too many months . . . He took her hand tenderly, kissed it, then he went down on his knee.

"What are you doing?"

"Will you marry me?" as he produced the ring out of his pocket, her shocked and joyful face radiated such a magnitude of emotions Kurt wasn't able to move. There was his answer. Charlotte carefully accepted the ring, and it fit her finger perfectly, and it was also a fine addition to her bird-styled earrings. She was about to utter the fateful word –

The siren howled. It signaled another air raid. The sudden ringing caught both of them off-guard, and as the city's projectors shot up light into the night, Kurt grabbed Charlotte's hand to lead her away to the nearest shelter.

"Stay close to me, alright? We need to hurry," he said with all the seriousness of his voice. She held onto his arm tight, he could even feel her breathing. There was a sudden commotion: a few other residents followed them, the rest were probably hiding in their basements. Like a disorganized column of pilgrims, they ventured away under the menacing rhythm of the sirens.

Then a not-so-distant whistle came down, and a deafening explosion enveloped the roof of a house, cracked bricks littered the ground, fragments of glass scattered, dust clouding up the further path. The very foundation tremored, then there was a roar that seemingly made the ground heave. There was another not too far, and then another. Smoke reigned above, and the air was filled up with screams— and destruction raining down.

Another building smashed into rubble, nearly collapsing onto Kurt and Charlotte; it blocked the narrow strip off the island.

"Go back, we need to go back!" Kurt shouted, his face and clothes caked in grey. Charlotte only had time to gasp:

"But my parents!"

"We can't get there! They'll be fine! Come on, we can hide in the cathedral!"

Not a single bomb hit the ground as they raced towards the

miraculously undamaged temple. Yet the chilling whistles pierced Kurt's ears, he was no longer able to hear anything else, and his eyes targeted the doors to safety.

They rushed through into the cathedral along with a few others, nearly losing their balance and dropping onto the stone floor. The interior welcomed them into cold refuge, the unceasing thunder of the bombardment rattled noisily.

Kurt along with Charlotte shambled into the hall, shocked after the experience. He sat her onto the nearby bench, giving the obscure walls and windows a skeptical look.

"Sit down with me, please," she said.

"I don't understand," he kept looking nervously. "How they haven't hit us

yet?"

"Must be him," Charlotte pointed upwards. Kurt noted a giant cross with the

figure of Jesus crucified hanging above the altar. Unsure whether the cathedral had indeed been heavenly blessed and shielded from the catastrophe.

Kurt planted himself onto the bench, sighing from exhaustion, shaking whenever another bomb landed nearby. Each blast echoed: a woman with a kid retreated under a bench, the priest was comforting those surrounding him, reading prayers from his book, and Kurt could only hold Charlotte's hands, his ring resting on her finger. He stroked it with his thumb, as though trying to calm himself down the movement.

"And my answer is 'yes'," she whispered to him. Her words injected more feverish warmth than any other act of love they'd shared so far. For a few moments, Kurt quit listening for the bombs, and embraced his fiancée, shedding ash and dust off the shoulders.

A trail of black smoke descended slowly from the roof. Its bulbs twisted their way around, and the imminent danger became evident.

"Oh, God," let out Kurt. "We have to run, now!"

Not many followed him and Charlotte at once, and as soon as he opened the door outside, a bomb fell into the courtyard, and in a flash,

Kurt lost his footing, hitting his knees and elbows hard. Charlotte, being a short distance behind, stayed on her legs, helping Kurt up and fall back into cover.

"Jesus, Kurt! Please, stop running! Just stop!" her voice bordering hysteria implored him to stay with her. Kurt's face remained shocked from the blast, he wasn't sure he'd heard Charlotte well.

Now led by Charlotte, he was returned to the hall to a scene of panic. The smoke was crawling down the walls and windows, and the roof was being swallowed by the first visible tongues of flame! A few men attempted to flee, following Kurt's poor example, their fate was unknown. Charlotte kept encouraging Kurt to go after the priest— presumably to the lower levels—and the burning cross collapsed into the central aisle. The smoke had encroached upon them, leaving hardly any space to breathe. Both Kurt and Charlotte erupted into an uncontrollable cough, suffocating. They backed away, and the burning roof spilled fire into the interior, the glorious organ now too gave in, creating a whole cacophony of noises. The hall transformed into a fiery labyrinth which there was no clear escape from. Kurt barely had time to regain his faculties, to see the smoke-poisoned face of Charlotte, when the debris buried them both.

* * *

"Look, I think we can go in now, the concert will start in," Konstantin checked his watch, "twenty minutes. Yeah, we'd better catch good seats."

"Nobody's going to steal your seat," Lena reproached, clearly unenthusiastic about waiting for another twenty minutes just idling in the hall.

"Well, I'm excited! I've never been in there, and I love this Brick Gothic! I mean, just look at the size of this thing!" he took another dozen pictures.

Lena didn't comment. Not that Konstantin could hear her well anyway: the weird mini-skirt drum troupe wouldn't stop playing loud

138

music, what were the crowd even applauding to?

"Do you think I should get us some water?" Lena asked.

"Here? These are all souvenir booths, it's overpriced as hell. This bottle alone cost 125 rubles!"

"I'll be quick," she departed.

Konstantin didn't mind. He was psyched to check out the cathedral: he'd already explored the museum upstairs, and the absolutely stunning Teutonic armor sets, older maps of Königsberg, Prussian folk costumes —all of that spoke to him in an incompressible language, exciting him to bits!

He made it inside, showed his QR code of the e-ticket, and proceeded into the main hall. They only allowed indoors when playing a concert, so finally Konstantin had his opportunity to appreciate the restored beauty of German architecture. The white walls, two magnificent organs, little sculptures of angels delicately placed at the top of the balcony. He was breathless as he took a couple of more pictures, and then hid away his smart phone, feeling a strange urge to take it all in with his own eyes. There was a good seat pretty close to the balcony with the main organ, he quickly took it, waiting for Lena at leisure, enjoying the little details of the interior that sparkled with grandeur.

Most of the good seats were being taken within minutes, Konstantin commended himself for his biological sense of time. Shortly the organist stepped up to the balcony, making his introduction:

"Good evening, ladies and gentlemen!" there was a round of applause. What was taking Lena so long? "I would like to welcome you all in this cathedral of our beautiful city of Kaliningrad, and congratulate you on the Victory Day, in honor of which we are playing this concert today. I believe the occasion is suitable enough to share with you a little bit of history. What you can observe today, was only recently restored, as all that was left after the war, were the walls you could see on the outside. Major works took place between 1996 and 1998. You must have also explored the green park that surrounds this building. It used to be a very lively district, full of historical houses that—unfortunately

—did not survive the fatal Allied air raid in August, in 1944. The RAF pilots didn't target the cathedral specifically, most likely using its spire as a handy landmark to bomb all the rest that was around it. And yet, the dark hand of circumstance allowed the neighboring fire to spread onto the roof which collapsed completely, leaving nothing but ruins on the inside."

"Finally found you," Lena squeezed in onto the bench. "Hey, you okay?" she saw Konstantin completely paralyzed as he listened to the musician speaking. She gave him a gentle shake she'd normally do when she thought she wasn't heard. Konstantin then turned to her, slowly, breathing heavily.

"Are you alright? You don't look well, at all," she tried to speak quietly as a few elderly ladies gave her an evil eye.

Konstantin was breathing through his mouth now, hot sweat trickled down his temples. For no apparent reason, a feeling of deep sorrow and fear gripped his heart, and it submerged him into a pool of tragic memories—it was so painful Konstantin could hardly sit still. Memories that weren't his, and yet they were!

It seemed he was having a sort of panic attack. Lena was at a loss; her boyfriend had never had any such episodes!

Konstantin stood up with a jerk and quickly escaped into the lobby. Lena followed him.

"What the hell is wrong? Do you need a doctor?" she appeared both pissed and worried. Konstantin avoided eye contact.

"Mein armes Mädchen, oh, no!" Konstantin broke out into a cry. Tears streamed down his cheeks, his face reddened. He buried it in his hands, as if ashamed, sobbing and sniffling. He could see the faces, but couldn't tell the names. He had been here before, but he wasn't *him* now. He could feel what *he* felt—but there was no end.

Lena was standing there in astonishment. Her boyfriend never learned German. And now he was crying uncontrollably, shaking with his all body, without making any sense.

Clay Things

Bill Vitiello

PART I

Sitting under a snow-covered evergreen, Pete exhaled heavily, followed by another quick inhale. He was beginning to catch his breath. Looking at his watch [23:38], he snaked a hand through his gear into his smock and found the pack of Marlboros. He began pulling out cigarettes—broken in half, broken, broken, crushed—and tossing them. Finally, a smokable stick came out, and he lit it with a match stored in the Marlboro box. Taking a long drag, he exhaled with a cough. Chunky blood was typically suboptimal for a smoker's cough, but in this case, not all that surprising. Another drag, another cough, more pain, more blood. His breathing recovered, he worked up the nerve and fished his other hand under the bottom of his coat, feeling for the wound.

Searing pain at the slightest touch. Removing his hand, he could see his glove was covered in blood. "Damn," he paused, "he got me good." Another long drag, another cough, more chunky bloody crap. Thinking about the past few hours, he began to laugh, bringing on more coughing and a flash of pain. He doubled over, clutching his side. When the pain let up a bit, he sat back up, gathering snow in his hands. He lifted his smock as best he could, and began packing the wound with his mix of slurry and snow. It simultaneously relieved and increased the pain. After a few moments, it began to numb.

Trading one cigarette for another, he finally examined his rifle, noting there was no magazine inserted. More had transpired in those few seconds that felt like hours, than he could scarcely believe. He

141

retrieved another mag from his chest rig, and inserted it with a louder clunk than he would've liked, using the palm of his hand to seat the mag with a slap. A cold wind blew through the trees, chilling Pete to the bone. "Motherfucker," he thought, shivering, "I should probably get moving." Digging his rifle butt into the snow, he used it to push himself onto his knees, and then up onto his feet.

He was stiff from resting, and that stiffness was causing him for more pain in his side than he'd expected. He took a step and fell back against the tree. Searing pain shot through him again. He clutched his side, swearing, coughing, and wheezing all at once. "Maybe this is it," he said to himself, followed by another long drag, another cough, more blood. He shivered and knew he had to get moving. Bracing his abdomen with one hand, he attempted to stand again, this time rising fully to his feet. He stood still for a moment, one hand pressuring the wound, the other gripping his rifle with the stock tucked under his arm. "Okay. I can do this." He took a step, and another. Each step caused more pain, and what felt like tearing at the slash in his abdomen. He continued to put one foot in front of the other. Before long he could feel himself moving at pace, and he slipped into the brush of the forest on his way down the mountain.

PART II

Pete's career had taken him across the globe, sometimes for morally righteous causes, and other times for less-than-savory ones. Yet, without fail, he'd followed orders every time. He'd done as he was told, and he'd gotten the job done, and all it had cost him was everything else. His first wife had left while he was still with the Rhodesian SAS back in '79. She could apparently see the writing on the wall that Pete couldn't. Tired of being alone for months or even years at a time, she unceremoniously sold everything and moved to Australia. The big gut punch came in 1980 when Pete's unit was stood down in surrender to the communists, years of fighting, losing his family, it had all been for naught.

Pete arrived in DC in June of 1980, his contacts in the British SAS put him in touch with the right people at Langley, and in no time at all he was back in business. This time, however, he was a "contractor" for GRS, a "private" firm that was, in reality, a single-client organization (for the CIA) providing an opaque barrier for clandestine operatives and operations. This suited Pete fine, as anything that allowed him to fight the blight of communism, which had consumed his homeland, was a net positive in his book.

By 1984, Pete had been promoted to station chief in Nicaragua. He assisted with the buildup of Contra forces, funneled them weapons, trained their trainers, and directly oversaw multiple operations and raids carried out against the Sandinista commies. It's usually at the top, of course, where things start to go downhill.

During a raid against a communist training camp in the jungle, Pete's radio signal became jammed. "Eagle Eye, come in. Over. I'm not reading you," he called up, over and over, with no response on any channel. Without air observation, the raid would be perilous for himself and the Contra fighters, but they were already on the X. He made the call, hand signaling to the Contra commander "Go. Go. Go." In a flash of fury, Pete's team opened up machine gun fire on the camp, while the Contra's flanked right around the camp.

"Shift fire, shift fire!" Pete called to his men, instructing them to fire parallel to the camp, but not directly into it, allowing the fighters to begin clearing the camp. As the Contra fighters cleared out the communists, Pete's team stopped firing complete and began to clean up behind them, scanning for any potential intelligence assets (or liabilities).

As he was picking through the pockets of a dead communist officer, hoping for a map, communique, memorandum, or anything else actionable, a young contra fighter came running up.

"Gee arrr ehss! Gee arrr ehss!"

Pete looked up, and saw the young man sprinting toward him. "What?"

"Come! Come! Gee arr ehss! Come!" he spoke all the English he could and Pete followed him through the camp to where the Contra commander had established his command post. "What's your man on about?" he said, aggravated at being interrupted. "We thought you might like to see this?" the commander said through a thick accent, handing Pete the wallet of a man they'd captured.

Opening the wallet, Pete recognized immediately the GRS ID card in the window pocket, he had one just like it. He read the name, but didn't recognize it.

"Where is this man?" he asked the commander, more abusively than intended.

"Over there," he pointed in the direction of a dead communist insurgent. Pete felt like he'd been smacked in the head with a sledge hammer as he slowly made his way to the body. Rolling the man onto his back, he compared the photo laminated onto the GRS ID card to the face of this dead man, and it was no doubt the same person.

"What is going on here?" he thought to himself. "Why would a CIA contractor be fighting for the communists?" He quickly checked the body for any other identifying articles, or intel, and rolled him back onto his face.

Returning to the Contra commander, he gave strict orders: "Bury him with the rest. I'm keeping this," he motioned with the wallet, sliding it into his back pocket.

Arriving back at the station HQ (the US consulate in Managua), he ran through a rolodex of GRS employees currently in country. "I should know about this guy, but more importantly, what was he doing with the commies?" he thought, flipping one card after the next. No matches. "Is it a fake?" he slid the card out of the wallet, comparing it to his own. It was too good to be fake, GRS used a pressure stamp to affix your photo to the card, and that would be nearly impossible to fake. "Besides," he thought, "who the hell makes a fake contractor ID just to sign up with the commies?"

He phoned GRS HQ in DC and received the answering machine as was standard. "Papa Bravo Two Four Zero One-One Bravo," he read into the recorder, identifying himself and finishing the message with "requesting immediate callback."

After only a few minutes, his secure phone line rang and he picked up. "Lima Kilo One Nine Eleven Four Two Alpha." Pete heard the ID code of his recipient read into the line.

"Pete, what's so important? It's after 2300 here, ya know?" he skipped right past the time question and got to the point.

"Well Larry, I have one K.I.A. GRS here," he paused for reaction before continuing, but no reaction came "which isn't the weird part. The weird thing is that he was K.I.A. when I found him, sporting Sandinista fatigues." There was a long silence on the line

"You there, Lar?" Pete was impatient and he knew something wasn't right. "Pete, listen, this is a compartmentalized operation. You understand. Not everything is need-to-know, and this is above your pay grade. Fax any identifying documents to plus-one-five-five-five-one-eight-six-four and then destroy them. Thanks for the heads up." *Click.* As the line went dead, Pete knew he had a much larger problem on his hands than a contractor going native and getting wasted.

Exiting his consular office, he took the elevator up to the fifth floor, where personnel records were stored. Reaching a door with a keypad, he punched in his identification code and entered the room. He searched for the G filing cabinet and opened the first drawer, flicking quickly through the file tags before moving to the second drawer down. Finally, on the third drawer he found a file titled "GRS-A" and directly behind it "GRS-B"—he grabbed both files and headed for the door.

PART III

"It felt like days had passed, but it was likely only a few hours," Pete thought to himself, using tree trunks, boulders, and his rifle as a walking stick to keep him upright as he moved. He checked his watch "only twenty-five minutes??" he said to himself aloud. The walk was taxing, partially because going down a mountain can be just as difficult as climbing up, but his blood loss was also sub-optimal. Still, the movement had been slower and more painful than he'd expected.

Sitting on a boulder, he opened his canteen only to find it empty. He chuckled to himself again, coughing—no blood this time—unsure of whether that was good or bad, he closed his eyes and hung his head, with his hands planted on his rifle, its butt firmly planted in the snow.

Considering his situation, Pete decided now was probably a good time for a quick prayer: "Lord Jesus Christ, Son of God, have mercy upon me—a sinner." He spoke just low enough for himself to hear, repeating the prayer again "Lord Jesus Christ, Son of God, have mercy upon me—a sinner." Pausing to catch his breath, he began a third time: "Lord Jesus Christ. Son—"

He was cut off suddenly by the ground beneath him beginning to shake and rattle. The boulder under him split in two and he fell sideways onto the ground, the muzzle of his rifle smacking him in the lip on the way down. Clenching his jaw, he couldn't believe his eyes.

As the ground shook, the snow began to melt and mix with the dirt below it. A slush of muddy clay began to swirl and bubble. He watched with a mix of horror and amazement as the figure began to rise from the slurry concoction in the shape of a hulking man. "You gotta be fuckin' kidding me," he said, getting to his feet, wounds forgotten. As the figure came into full formation, it began to move toward him, more sloshing than walking, and the only sound was that of Pete's rifle, as he fired direct hit after direct hit into its chest, with no effect at all.

PART IV

Pete upended the instant ramen into a pot of boiling water and moved to his kitchen table, sitting down with the files. He unwound the cord of string keeping GRS-A closed, and revealed its contents: personnel files of GRS employees currently stationed in Nicaragua, including a half-dozen direct action contractors, a handful of intel and support guys, and the station chief. The only problem was that he had never seen any of the men in this file before, to include the chief. Well, he did recognize one of them.

"James Williams . . . doesn't ring a bell," he muttered to himself.

The K.I.A. from the camp was right there in the file. "Five years USMC, served in Nam, Laos, and Cambodia. Two years CIA before 'resigning' and joining GRS." Pete was well aware that no one left the Agency, and a file suggesting someone resigned simply meant reassigned to a division that doesn't exist on paper.

Flipping through the other personnel, he couldn't believe that there was an entire secondary station here that he had no idea about. He heard the pot boiling over as he began to unwrap GRS-B's cord. Noodles in hand, he opened the B file, finding the personnel records of himself and his team. "Why are we the B team?" he thought to himself, realizing he hadn't eaten today until now. Flipping through his team's files, he noted a red square stamped in the upper right-hand corner of each of their jackets, something that was absent from any of the GRS-A files—something that, as far as he knew, had no meaning in GRS, but was definitely a deliberate addition to their records.

After finishing his noodles, he decided to head back to the station. He wouldn't be able to sleep unless he got to the bottom of this. Checking his watch, he noted it was 12:43 a.m. and the night guard should be making their first rounds.

He arrived at the consulate and badged through the gate as normal, parked in his designated spot, marked out for the Head of Janitorial Services and wondered which other fake department spot was marked out for his rival chief. Making his way back up to the fifth floor, he walked past the personnel file office and made a left down a long corridor with a single door at the end of it. Arriving at the door, the sign above it read "SCIF—FOUO" and he reached for his badge. This door required a badge scan as well as a thumb scan to confirm your identity both to enter and to leave. Upon entering, a guard checked Pete for any type of recording or photography device, and upon clearing him, buzzed him through the next door and into the Sensitive Compartmented Information Facility. In this room, microfilms of classified top secret documents, videos, and intelligence reports were gathered, cataloged, and stored floor to ceiling, with a single microfilm viewer. He began hunting for anything "GRS."

He came across a small box labeled "GRS Activities Branch" and began to rifle through the films in the box. Most were debriefs of operations he and his predecessors had managed or prosecuted against the Sandinista regime to root out communism from Central & South America. Some were of their GRS counterparts in neighboring nations performing the same work, where intel overlapped. None appeared to contain anything revelatory, and he began to place the box back on the shelf when he discovered a spool with a small red square stamped on it, just above "TS/SCI" [Top Secret-Sensitive Compartmented Information]. He felt as if a weight pressed down on his chest.

Loading the spool into the microfilm viewer, he began to scroll through the documents contained within the films. Most were again standard post-activity debriefs and reports, until he saw a name: James Williams. His K.I.A. compatriot was very much alive, AK in hand, smiling for the camera flanked by Sandinista sicarios, standing atop a handful of dead Contra fighters. "Mission Status: Success" read the memorandum headline that the photo was attached to. It went on to describe a multi-month operation to embed GRS into the Sandinista forces, in an effort to force multiply their fighting capability, and decimate the Contras. Pete felt like the weight on his chest was an anvil.

Scrolling to the next page he saw more GRS-A members, all involved in countering every effort his team made, and in most cases using the intel his team passed up to preempt Contra movements, attacks, and raids. Yesterday's raid had been spontaneous, the result of actionable intel from inside sources revealing the location of the communist's training camp, which probably explained why they'd been so successful—and why they'd caught Mr. Williams unaware. He continued to scroll. Before long, the documents were detailing similar activities in Venezuela, Columbia, Vietnam, Korea, and South Africa.

"My God," Pete gasped to himself. About four-fifths of the way through the reel, there it was, in black and white: a GRS-A team had been in Rhodesia, training the communist insurgents and fighting alongside them. Pete's anvil was affecting his breathing now and he could feel his heart rate jump. He closed his eyes and tried to catch his breath.

Opening his eyes, he looked at the film again to confirm he wasn't seeing things, confused, "did I hit my head?" he thought for a moment. But no, it was all there, in black and white, on a TS/SCI microfilm, stamped with the same red square as the GRS-A personnel files.

"My God," he thought, "the communists run the US government." The revelation was almost too much to believe, but multiple pieces were fitting together for the first time. "This is why we can't win wars against the commies. We're not even actually fighting them. I've been doing their counter intel for them." He leaned back in the chair. "My God, these people took my home from me."

It was too much. He had to do something. Removing the film reel from the viewer, he placed the box back where he'd found it, less a single reel. Exiting the first door, he motioned to the guard, with the microfilm in hand.

The guard jumped from his chair. "Sir, nothing can be removed from the SCIF. You must return the item immediately." His voice was stern, his right hand ever so gently brushed up against his sidearm.

"I know, bucko," Pete said calmly. "I need to view this film, but the viewer isn't working. can you give me a hand troubleshooting it?"

The guard looked incredulously at Pete. "Sir, I cannot enter the SCIF under any circumstances, and I believe you know that. Please return the—"

He was cut off by the web of Pete's left hand catching him in the throat so hard he hit the ground and began coughing and sputtering. Pete pinned his right arm and disarmed him, then quickly used the lanyard from the pistol to tie the guard's hands. He was balled over on the floor choking, but Pete knew he had to move quickly, as it would be only seconds before the security team saw the situation on CCTV.

Sprinting through the hall and down the stairs, he hit the exit door trying to look calm and catch his breath. Halfway to his car, he saw the guard booth at the entrance come to life with activity. He heard shouts of "hey, you!" across the parking lot and felt his heart beat in his throat as he sank into the driver's seat. Just as he turned the ignition lights began to jump on across the fourth and fifth floors of the building. He checked his rearview and saw two guards approaching from the guard booth behind him. He smashed the clutch with his left foot and shifted into reverse so hard he thought he'd thrown a gear for a moment, before smashing the gas pedal with both feet and zooming backward across the empty lot. The guards jumped out of the way but were immediately back up and firing at his sedan, with a third radioing from the booth. He blew right through the wooden gate still in reverse, hitting the brake, clutch, and jamming the gear into first while cutting the wheel hard, spinning him onto the street and on his way.

"I have maybe thirty minutes," he thought, unlocking his apartment door. He wasted no time, grabbing his go-bag, which contained three passports, ten thousand USD, and enough clothes to last a few days, along with old Army rations, and a Beretta 9mm pistol. Flipping through the phone book, he phoned four local taxis, all set to pick him up at different locations with different destinations. He popped outside and walked across the street from his apartment where his cab arrived a few minutes later.

"Aeropuerto Sandino, pronto, por favor." He handed the driver a wad of American greenbacks, and they sped off toward the international airport at the edge of town. Arriving at the airport, Pete purchased flights to New York, Cairo, Munich, and Hong Kong, and he shoved the tickets in his bag. He made his way to the bus terminal and purchased a seat on the first available bus, which was leaving shortly for San Pedro, Honduras, then on to Mexico City.

Forty-eight hours later, he stepped off the bus in Mexico City and began a campaign to expose the truth he had learned. From his hotel room, he contacted every major media outlet in the US and internationally where he'd had contacts: ABC, CBS, *The New York Times*, *Der Spiegel*, *The Guardian*, down the list he went. To each he would explain what he had, what it showed, and that it was likely the smoking gun of a silent communist takeover of the West, a revolution without a shot fired or a single paper printed. To Pete, this was media gold, a journalist's wet dream, the kind of story that defined careers. To his shock, none of them were interested. He was willing to go on record, but they didn't care. He had photocopies of official documents and files, exposing the shadowy cabal behind the series of western military, social, and financial failures of the twentieth century, and none of them were even a little curious. He began contacting staffers of Senators, Congressmen, and British MPs he thought might be trusted. They either didn't return his calls at all, or they demanded the original microfilm along with all copies.

Knowing he couldn't stay put for long, he purchased another bus ticket to San Diego and traded tickets with another passenger for a bus headed to Austin. Pete imagined he was likely on a kill/capture list as some sort of rogue terrorist or enemy of the state and resigned himself to waiting it out in the mountains.

In Austin, he met made contact with a local newscaster that had experience with blowing the lid off of stories like this. He handed over the film, knowing it was his only bargaining chip, but also aware that he would likely be disappeared or killed regardless of what happened now. He purchased a beat-up Ford truck, and some winter supplies before setting off from Austin to Townsend, Tennessee, where his uncle had lived for a time years before and had left a mountain cabin to Pete, which he'd never visited until now.

*   *   *

Seventeen years passed, and Pete grew accustomed to his life of solitude. The mountain provided all he needed, and the town of Townsend provided anything he couldn't make for himself. He kept tabs on the news for a while, but that news man never did publish the film. Pete didn't know if he'd been compromised before or after, but his career did take off shortly after, so it didn't much matter. He assumed, at this point, they'd forgotten about him completely, likely classified him as dead and swept him under the rug, like they do with most nuisances. He'd made his peace with that.

PART V

As his magazine ran empty, the creature was on him. It grabbed his rifle, absorbing it and hardening its body to instantly pulverize the weapon into small pieces. Its muddy hands were also somehow like sharpened stones, squeezing Pete's body as he screamed in agony. He pulled the knife from his chest rig, jamming it with all the force he could muster into the creature's head. He watched as the knife simply fell to the ground, as if it had flowed right through its body.

He was squeezed harder still, with more stab-like sensations coming from inside the creatures' hands. He felt as though he were being shredded alive. Resigning himself to death, Pete continued his prayer.

"Jesus Christ," he sputtered. "Son of God," he pulled the crucifix from under his shirt and continued with it in hand, "into . . . your hands . . . I commit my . . . spirit!" Exhaling the final words of the prayer felt like bench pressing a truck.

To his amazement, at those words, this creature made of mud and rock, at once froze its movement, turned completely to stone, and as if struck by lightning, exploded into tiny fragments.

Hitting the ground, Pete began to breathe again but could hardly stand the pain. "Was that . . . ?" he thought to himself, running through what just happened. "Couldn't have been."

Lifting his head slightly, he was able to see what he could already feel: his body had been crushed, and he would likely be dead within minutes. He laid his head back down, coughing up blood he knew he'd soon choke on. He fished through his pockets for the pack of Marlboros. Locating it in his jacket, he could feel it was crushed along with him, and he removed the most intact cigarette from the box that he could feel and placed it between his lips. Lighting the tip, he closed his eyes and suddenly felt warm. As he took a drag from the broken cigarette, the warmth spread throughout his body, the pain dissipated from him, and though his eyes were closed, he saw the softest brightest light he'd ever seen embracing him.

152

The Man Who Picked Up the Crown

Bradford C. Walker

The sun dipped low over Pine Hollow, a sleepy tourist town nestled in the foothills, far from the neon sprawl of the city. It was late March, and the air carried a crisp bite, the kind that made you pull your jacket tighter. Jack Ramsey stood on his porch, a weathered man of forty-two, his hands scarred from years of war—Afghanistan, Iraq, a dozen places he'd rather forget. His family had lived here for generations, stubborn as the pines that gave the town its name. They'd fought as partisans in wars past, against invaders and tyrants, when no one else would. Now, Jack felt that old blood stirring again.

The trouble started six months ago. A wave of foreigners rolled into Pine Hollow—not tourists with cameras and cash, but hard-eyed men with accents Jack couldn't place. They came under some vague legal pretense, sanctioned by the mayor and rubber- stamped by the state. "Refugees," Mayor Hargrove called them, though they didn't act like any refugees Jack had ever seen.

They carried knives, sometimes guns, and they preyed on the town like wolves let loose in a henhouse. Robberies turned to assaults, assaults to bodies left in ditches. The sheriff, a good man but outmatched, couldn't keep up. The state police didn't care—too far, too small, too inconvenient.

Jack lit a cigarette, the ember glowing in the dusk. Down the hill, he could see the flicker of lights in the town square, where Hargrove was holding another meeting. The mayor's voice drifted up, oily and confident, promising safety through cooperation. Hargrove's family had a history too— collaborators, every one of them. His great-grandfather had sold out neighbors to the enemy in '44, and now Hargrove was doing the same, just with better suits and a bigger vocabulary. He'd welcomed the invaders, gave them jobs, houses, even protection. In return, they kept him in power, and the town bled.

Jack's phone buzzed. A text from Ellie, the diner owner: Another girl missing. They're bold now. What do we do? He exhaled smoke, his jaw tightening. Ellie's question wasn't new. It'd been whispered in bars, hissed over fences, asked in quiet corners for weeks. What do we do? The invaders weren't just criminals—they were organized, ruthless, and untouchable under Hargrove's shield. The law was a joke, and the people were scared. Jack's neighbors looked to him sometimes, knowing his past, his family's legacy. He'd ignored it, hoping someone else would step up. But no one had.

He crushed the cigarette under his boot and went inside. The house was sparse, a soldier's habits never fully shaken. On the mantle sat a photo of his grandfather, a wiry man with a rifle, taken after he'd ambushed a patrol in the hills during the war. Next to it, Jack's own medals—Bronze Star, Purple Heart—gathered dust. He'd survived IEDs, firefights, ambushes. He'd killed men who deserved it and some who maybe didn't. Now, here he was, hiding from a fight in his own backyard.

The next morning, Jack drove into town. The streets were quiet, shutters drawn, the usual bustle of spring tourists gone. At Ellie's diner, a handful of locals sat hunched over coffee— Tom the mechanic, Sarah the schoolteacher, old man Carver who'd fought in Vietnam. They looked up as Jack entered, eyes heavy with expectation.

"They took Mary's daughter last night," Ellie said, sliding a mug toward him. "Beat her husband half to death when he tried to stop them. Sheriff's got nothing. Hargrove's saying it's 'cultural differences.'"

Jack sipped the coffee, bitter and black. "Cultural differences don't leave bruises."

"State won't help," Tom muttered. "They're in Hargrove's pocket. Feds don't even know we exist out here."

Carver leaned forward, his voice a rasp. "We've seen this before,

Ramsey. Your granddad didn't wait for permission. Neither should you."

Jack's grip tightened on the mug. He'd spent years burying the part of him that thrived in chaos, the part that could plan a hit and pull a trigger without blinking. But it was waking up now, clawing at him. He thought of the missing girl, the bodies in the ditches, the fear in his neighbors' faces. If not us, who? The question burned.

That night, Jack made a choice. He called a meeting—not in the diner, too public, but in Carver's barn, a mile out of town. Eight showed up: Ellie, Tom, Sarah, Carver, and a few others with spines still stiff enough to stand. Jack laid it out plain—no grand speeches, just facts. The invaders had numbers, weapons, and Hargrove's blessing. The law wouldn't touch them.

Waiting meant more dead, more broken. Action meant blood, maybe theirs.

"We hit them where they sleep," Jack said, spreading a map on a hay bale. "They've got a house on Mill Road—ten, maybe twelve of them. We go in quiet, take them out, send a message."

Sarah paled. "That's murder, Jack."

"It's war," Carver snapped. "They started it."

Tom nodded. "I'm in. They torched my shop last month. I'm done waiting."

Ellie crossed her arms. "What about Hargrove? He'll cover it up, call us the bad guys."

Jack met her gaze. "Hargrove's next. One step at a time."

They planned for two days—scouting, weapons, timing. Jack dug up his old gear from the attic: a suppressed AR-15, a 9mm, a Ka-Bar knife. The others brought what they had—hunting rifles, shotguns, a pistol Tom had carried in the Gulf. It wasn't an army, but it was enough.

The night of the raid was moonless, clouds thick overhead.

They moved through the woods, silent as ghosts, Jack in the lead. The house on Mill Road was a ramshackle two-story, lights dim, laughter spilling out. Jack signaled, and they split—Tom and Carver on the back, Ellie and Sarah on watch, Jack up front with two others. He crept to the porch, peering through a window. Five men inside, drinking, cards on the table, a rifle propped against a chair. The rest were upstairs, he figured.

He picked the lock—old skills never faded—and slipped in. The first man didn't see him coming; the knife went in clean, under the ribs. The second turned, mouth opening, but Jack's hand clamped over it, the blade finishing the job. The others froze as Tom and Carver burst through the back, shotguns barking. It was over in seconds—five down, blood pooling on the floorboards.

Upstairs was messier. Seven more, half-asleep, woke to gunfire and screams. Jack took two with the AR, precise shots through the skull. Tom got another before a knife caught his arm, a shallow gash. Carver ended it, a blast that painted the wall red. They dragged the bodies to the basement, doused the place with gas from Tom's shop, and lit it up. The flames roared as they slipped back into the night.

Word spread fast. Hargrove called it a tragedy, blamed "rogue vigilantes," but the town knew. The invaders pulled back, wary now, their swagger gone. Jack didn't stop. He watched Hargrove, waited. A week later, the mayor's car rolled out of town—fleeing, some said. Jack found him at a gas station twenty miles out, alone, pumping fuel with shaky hands.

"Ramsey," Hargrove stammered, backing up. "You can't—"

Jack didn't speak. The 9mm barked once, and Hargrove slumped against the pump, a hole where his excuses used to be. Jack drove home, the weight of it settling in. He'd acted, and the town breathed easier for it. But the cost—the blood, the sleepless nights, the part of him he couldn't bury again—was his to carry.

Back on his porch, Jack lit another cigarette, staring at the stars. "If not us, who?" The question had an answer now, etched in fire and lead. His granddad would've understood. Maybe even been proud. But Jack just felt tired, the kind of tired that didn't wash away.

Not that it mattered. He—they—were committed now. War came to them, and from here they would bring—and finish—the war there.

Laws without swords do not exist, and now Jack had the swords.

A year later, Jack would be crowned king—and condemned as a threat to "Democracy." But that is a tale for another time.

The Tower

C. Ernest Jäger

It is safe in the lighthouse. The dirt outside is fertilized by seagull droppings or decay. Dry though it may be, better dry than rich in the way of the ensanguined soil of Europe. It does not matter at all to me that the radios ceased their chattering long ago, for the seabirds tweet me a far fairer song. Yes, the harshest thing I must undergo here is a nippy ocean breeze, or maybe, the tempest that passed by a week or two ago now. How glad I am though, that I am not caught up in the blazing fires of London, or Berlin. Perhaps the kindest element of all to me is the fog. So quaintly it does surround my little island! How safely it does shield me from the air attacks. As insurance, I lowered the colors long ago, in case it were to let up. Goodness forbid I be the subject of their onslaught! Yes, the good lads at home carry that burden for us all! Good cheery men they are too, not a fight for me though, I am much better at use here, at my post. I especially wouldn't want to get in their way either, I am feeble for a soldier, there is little I can do.

He set his journal down amongst the radio screens and dials of the control room. A large microphone with its terminal laid bare in front of him. The "lighthouse" had been constructed especially for The Conflict. The control room was dark and streamlined for its purpose. Large screens covered the wall in front of him; terminals littered the whole place. The sound of a radar beeped quietly near to him. It had gone so long without so much as a minor discrepancy in its monotony that he had thought it better to cover it in the excess bedding meant for the station's other operators (that had been conveniently left in the wash), so as not to be driven wholly mad by its noise while working as the sole watchman.

"The Station," "The Tower," "The Lighthouse," everyone had called it something different, the names would be thrown about in conversation constantly. He had taken a liking to them all, there was no urgency to decide; he was the only operator left, the rest had been re-assigned. A team of fifteen men they were, all in their mid-twenties, healthy—full of virility. It had been some years now, he was in his early thirties, the last of the operators. He had never been called to the front and now worked purely under the mere assumption that the tower needed an operator.

The control room was rather quiet, even the static, beeping, and techno-ambiance was rather subdued. A blaring shore-landing alarm shot up like a firework into a pitch-black night. The alarm was meant to warn of any small watercraft beaching itself on the shores of the island; nowadays it was always debris, spewed onto the sand by the open ocean. Sometimes hunks of metal hulls, sometimes pieces of large driftwood, occasionally bunches of trash. It did not matter, the standing protocol was to send out an armed scouting party, regardless of a station's manpower. He took the black rifle hanging from the wall rack by the exit and went down the lift. The lift had always moved with excellent speed, but as time had pushed on the experienced man could note the weary slowing. It brought him down to the exit area; a short, wide hallway with a door at the opposite end, a checkpoint before the lift. Armed and in his black-clad uniform, he walked down the dimly lit hall to the bulkhead. He brought his I.D. card against the door's terminal; the great mass of metal was lifted semi-swiftly into the ceiling. He stepped out onto the gravel; it crunched beneath his sole. The fog was thick; it was practically eternal. The world outside was moist, the air hung noticeably around him. The smell of the sea slipped into his nostrils; he drew the air in until it began to stab at his chest. He turned and briefly looked at the tower; it was such a gargantuan obelisk, fully—metallically—black. Large rectangular panels ran up to its top where glowed a very dim green light, heavily reminiscent of the lighthouses of yore (even with the small metal grate walking platform going around the tower's circumference). One might think that it was a

Herculean task to construct, but the men of these projects always managed to make quick (and quite handsome) work out of the most mythological of tasks. An obelisk, truly.

The entire island was divided up across a grid, three by three. The island itself was of an organic shape, as though two islands adjacent to one another were connected by a land bridge, with one island being somewhat greater than the other. Very simply, the sections were named alphanumerically, Section A1 to C3. Sections A2 and C2 consisted mostly of sea, bordered around the edge by the inner shore of the smaller islands. Section B2 was that of the land bridge. The tower was in Section B1, the alarm had gone off at the right side of C2. A short walk and he would likely see the item of interest with his AdV. (Advanced Vision) Binoculars.

Secretly, (even trying to keep it from himself) he thought of how much he dreaded going outside. In the tower, one could hear naught from even a floor above or below, especially not anything from outside. But outside, he dreaded that he might yet hear the shrill cries of nearing bombardments. There was little trouble with the performance of his duties; he manned the station as necessary, maintained as he could, and there had been no reason to even touch the microphone that sat so forebodingly—ominously, in front of his chair.

The sound of the waves grew to a crescendo as he stood atop the cliff-like terrain on the left part of Section C2. The land bridge leant down like a sort of ramp to the other part of the island, which ran (at its shores) flush with the ocean. He looked down at the spot of grey mass with his AdV. Binoculars, his finger ran up the scroll-wheel, bringing the object close into view. It was (as it often was), debris. It looked to be a part of some old metal hull, perhaps a lifeboat judging by the size. He went through the somewhat considerable march to the other portion of the island. The rifle bounced against his torso as he walked. The cold, soaked grass of the land-bridge squished as he tread on it, icy water filled the depression and came up against the sides of his leather boots' outsoles. He was right, it was the debris of a lifeboat. Odd though, he thought to himself, it was hardly in the condition that much of the other debris was in, that is, very little rust had set in. He could not deny the fear that swelled within him, perhaps the fighting was drawing near and thus the debris, growing fresher. For the sake of putting the thought out of his mind he hastily grabbed hold of whatever part of the debris he could (any part that didn't threaten to cut his hand for the sake of sharp metal edges) and hauled it up. The metal was incredibly cold, and it had that odd feeling that wet metal claims an absolute uniqueness to (oddly porous and gritty). Through shiftings, yankings, and at last a sort of walking the hunk over onto the grassy area, he managed it away from the shore sensors. He brushed his hands off onto his black trousers, tiny pieces of rusty metal bits that dirtied his hands fell away, whatever managed to stick on he picked at individually.

He stood for a moment and looked over to the middle of the little island at a large black metal platform.

It was the station's secondary turret. Another column of metal would arise from the ground when called upon and rain heavy fire upon any target, or even launch the artillery depth charges that had been a piece of firepower unique to these stations. As it was though the turret existed merely as a large octagonal platform somewhat raised above the ground. Somewhere nearby it was a staircase that led to the underground chamber, the "wine cellar" as it was often longingly referred to. Copious amounts of rounds, machinery, and underwater drones in their tubes, ready to be utilized at any moment (all in place of any red). He pridefully clapped together his hands and wrung them, then turned back towards the tower.

The fog had let up only a little as the morning had grown, so from about halfway on the land bridge he could see the old flagpole at the very tip of the tower. The flag had long since been displayed on the walls of his quarters, it hung at his head-board. The station was in some way then protected, by nothing (or rather the absence of something), funny as though it sounded. Though he knew that for all his nothing-assurances, if the enemy were to single him out, then they would do so. That time had not yet come, better to put it off as long as one can, he often thought. Better to get away with life without them knowing, no need to take charge in your own destruction. He smiled. Content.

He went again through the bulkhead, and into the lift. It dragged him back up into the control room. He racked the rifle, and for a brief moment stood, listening for nothing but the standard ambiance. His nothing ensued.

The cafeteria and recreational area were by far the brightest places of the station. The very floor was the light by which one walked. It glowed a cold and stale white. The station had an endless supply of food, if one did not wish to engage in a bit of agriculture, there existed spherical machines out in the open ocean to supplement; connected by thick tubes to a sort of processing machine behind one of the paneled walls of the cafeteria. The machines passively filtered and ensnared edible sea life; kelp, small fish, certain algae. It then pumped it all to a processing unit, wherein it was coagulated and dried all to dispense them as very arid, crunchy food-cylinders. If one wished he could crush them rather easily, combine them with some warm water and have a paste of sorts, or add more water and have a soup. One could even make it into a dough and bake biscuits with it at the manual kitchen station. He had tried it all before when the others were there, but now he was often fine without it. He sat at the black table, ate, and drank. The station, of course, had an endless supply of filtered water, but also a decades-long supply of orange juice (a supplement for the vitamin D one did not receive from the sun), plain ice cream (which tasted purely of milk and sugar, with a chemical in it that made it never melt), and flavorings. The recreational area had decades' worth of watchable content; music from since music had been incepted, and a single book with Digi Paper. One could use the recreational access terminal to download nearly any book in existence straight onto the paper (if one preferred to have a physical copy and not read off of a tablet). He felt well satiated, but for all the amenities he could not rid himself of a cold feeling. It was cold that it itself yearned for warmth, he often described it. Of course, he was missing his brothers, the others who used to man the station with him. A natural thing—yearning, he would say to brush it off.

After some time spent listening to *Wagner's* "Parsifal Overture" and reading at the recreational area, he picked himself up and went again to the lift. If the tower were a body, the lift was its most major artery; down to its beating heart he went. The reactor level was the deepest point of the island, naturally subterranean; he went daily to run routine checks on it. There had never been an issue with the nuclear reactor, it had a constant supply of filtered seawater to cool it. If necessary, the whole lower level could be flooded to prevent a meltdown and drained again later. It was running as normal. The saltwater filters managed themselves, the station would clean and alternate between them as needed. If anything went wrong, he could manage it.

It was nigh on dusk; he collected his journal from his quarters (which was the level directly below the exit) and took the lift all the way up. It spit him out on the "gallery," (as the others had called it) the walkway which ran around the outside of the "spire" (the upmost section of the tower). He could not necessarily see the sunset, but the general hue was visible through the fog. One could watch the fiery sky be extinguished by the frigid sea. He had long since brought a small, stool-like table (with chair) from the cafeteria to the gallery, really the only change that he had made to the tower (aside from the suffocated radar and lack of a flag) that could get him into any trouble if a commanding officer had ever arrived for inspection. He sat—the whole ocean his audience and the kiss of the sun his spotlight. Yes, here, on this spit of land, on this tower, on his tower, the world was there to bear witness to him. The undeniable center of the universe, the true geocentric model. He smirked as he wrote.

Death comes for every man, but life only comes for a few. I think fully, that life came for me when I was assigned this post. I live absolutely fulfilled. There is nothing I lack. Yes, there exist some amenities that I might enjoy that my brothers have on the front, but I am safe; I have food, an eternal shelter, and enough media in the recreational center for even my ghost to stand posted comfortably for another few decades after my body has long turned to dust! My bed is warm, my chair in the command center is comfortable, what an amazing product of ergonomics that thing is! Never have I had even the slightest bit of backache! But yes, life has come for me. I live to my fullest, I truly do. I often wonder how my comrades that were pulled to the front are faring. Good for them! I say, they got out there and did the job! But not me, no, I best serve from this tower. The lighthouse is my life. Life has come for me. Comfortable, so nicely comfortable. I am happy—here.

What little warmth there was left with the sun. The moon cast an eerie blanket of cold light down onto an even colder sea. He was leaning on the railing of the gallery. The waves pushed themselves against the island. Gusts of wind howled in his ears. How the waves did tug on his soul! And they did pull on his very being. Every time the waters drew back and laid bare the sand, how his heart squeezed! Lo! how the chirping of the seabirds tittled the i's and the j's of the word of his existence and too crossed the t's of the sentence of his moonstruck evening. Amidst its great earthly heaving, a breeze would split from the stream and trickle down his uniformed collar. He, the tower, the island, they were no longer something strange to the sea, it had learned not to flow around them, but to flow with them. To sometimes crash with them, and to, in great finality, be cycled down to the depths with them. For all the briskness of the night he was not cold, had the sea splashed upward a massive wave and soaked him in the icy drink, still he would have felt bravely warm for his soul was hot with longing.

Abruptly, he found himself shivering. He stood for another moment, then turned hastily, gathered his things, and went into the mouth of the lift. He was lowered to the living quarters level. The doors slid open, revealing a medium-sized area. Leather chairs, a table, and a synthetic fireplace in the wall were all arranged like a fancy hotel lobby from his youth. Several fake plants and prints adorned the open spaces of wall and floor. He squatted down at the inglenook of the fireplace and brought life back into his hands, they had grown so frigid that it had become difficult to move his fingers. The whole place was dark in the late evening; the only light being from the fire and the under-glow in the hallway. He passed by the long unopened doors. Each one kept a ghost locked away, so he walked (halfway to unknowingly) with a queer sort of reverence and fear down to his room. They were truly odd things, the doors. Had they been accessible to him they would be nothing beyond themselves; it was because they were sealed that he was curiously enamored by them. They meant life, or livelihood at least. Any evidence of human activity was locked in a quantum state behind a keypad.

Memories, artifacts, entire existences neatly numbered one through fifteen down a dimly lit hallway. It filled him with awe and eerie-ness greater than that of the moonlight which bathed the world outside. Ghostly things wailed only in his memory.

He stopped ahead of his door; the keypad dimly glowed at him. He beckoned and the large door gently whizzed to the side with the muted sound of an electromagnet activating from inside the wall, it closed behind him. For a moment there was nothing but blackness, a veil of an impregnable nature. Had any small light come on it may have been wholly consumed by the void. The overhead lights were not so weak however, and with a gentle hum they chased away the dark beast back to the shadows beneath beds and unlit closets. Immediately in his room there was a quaint utilitarian section. A sink, refrigerator, and countertop on the left, and on the right a plain wall bearing a door to the washroom. Straight on through there was a small recreational room, and then the door to his bedroom on an empty wall again to the left. There was no means of cooking in the living quarters. Yes, the refrigerator was there, but only to store drinks and fruits that would be brought by occasionally passing supply ships (which had not come for some time). Meals though, were to be a social event. The getting together and eating of a meal was an essential thing. An ancient bond is recalled at the dinner table as that animalistic part of your mind sees and draws close to those with whom it dines as family. It was a thing always expressed to them in the offhanded or appropriate moments in training, "No matter how bad things get," they would say, "every person should ensure that he dine with the group."

He went straight towards his bedroom. An immense tiredness washed over him as he came to the foot of his perfectly made bed. Undressed he slipped beneath the tightly fixed sheets, his head flat against the pillow. The station's flag hung above him, stuck up and sprawled out against the wall. It did not quite bring him comfort to see, nor reassurance, or anything of the sort. But the sight of it on his wall, it felt like the cold metal of the shorn lifeboat now on the scrap pile. He fell asleep beneath it.

From beyond the great pit of blackness before his eyes, light shone down upon him, what could he do but wake? For a brief moment he lay in bed, listening to the randomly generated string of metallic alerts playing from his room's General Message System (the sound engineers of the tower knew that the same wake-up alarm would eventually fail to motivate after some time). He rose from his bed, washed, and dressed. He left his room for Standard Morning Perimeter Search. The sun poked through the fog better this morning, enough to gently touch his skin. The gravel crunched beneath his boots as he marched toward the minor island, occasionally stopping to observe with his binoculars. Seagulls flew overhead, guffawing loudly. He had read once, that seagulls often gather near whales, perhaps there were whales nearby. The thought half gave him wonder and curiosity pulled from his youth. The waves crashed harshly against the shores; the sea spray kissed his neck.

Clear. The island was, as usual, clear. He looked towards the turret pad and the old heap of trash that lay near it. Perhaps, he might take up some form of sculpting using the old metal, he thought. As he paced back towards the tower the gulls continued on overhead, laughing, crying. He imagined that some fat, voracious gull might land to throw its heavy head back and laugh quite so violently that its stomach might bear out from its mouth. The heavy metal door dragged open, he went again, down the hall, into the lift. He felt at his gut, his belt dug tightly into it, the pain layered over hunger and his stomach gurgled. Perhaps, he could take an earlier breakfast. The lift brought him to the cafeteria. He went straight towards the recreational area and loudly played *Liszt's*

"Les Preludes." He sat at the table bench after having gorged himself on stale bread baked from the food-powder he had made some time earlier. He was thoroughly proud of it; it was not often he got to be proud of something he did; it was not often he did much of anything. He stretched, yawned, and undid his belt a bit as it again dug into him.

"Right, to the control room." He ordained. Walking to the lift, scratching at an itch on the back of his

head and again, yawning, he went up to the control room. It was perfectly warm, the room. Perfectly warm and dimly lit, the screens all having gotten a little bit duller as time went on (a small price to pay for having them draw next to nothing from the station's power). He dropped heavily into the chair; it bounced as he came down upon it. Silence. So, so quiet. So perfectly quiet he could hear the static of his ears like roaring; the muffled sounds might as well have rung like church bells. It was about an hour before his tiredness overcame him. The quietness emphasizing the hypnotic nature of the noises, and the warmth perfectly accenting the well-made chair. Sleep grabbed at his eyelids and pulled them closed. He fought considerably to keep them open, though in the end, it was his own mind saying "Perhaps, I could rest for just a moment," that sent him back to the abyss.

He awoke to an odd noise. His mind felt at first entirely inaccessible, as though it had been cut off from the rest of him. First his body came to, and he could move his hands, then his ears awoke, then lastly, his mind. His brow furred intensely as he zombishly looked around for the source of the odd noise. As though he had been shot, the idea so penetrated him. It burnt his flesh, shattered his bones, had left him feeling cold, weak, and sick. The radar. The discordant beep was slightly muffled, and just beside him. He stood erect, feeling as though he would vomit. The warmth of the control room had totally disappeared, and from within he became so frostbitten and utterly defeated by hypothermia. It had been so long, so long. There wasn't supposed to be anyone, secretly, he thought, yes secretly he wished that the war was over—that they had lost and had not come searching for him. His hand shook as it slowly stretched out towards the pile of sheets atop the radar. He unwrapped it all. His blood was now hot, boiling hot, but his bones and muscles were still of ice. There. There it was, laid bare. A horror of horrors, fate and bad luck laid naked before his eyes. A large vessel, just north of the tower, heading eastward. If it had a soul, he would have seen it so that he might have painted it from memory afterward.

Blankly he stared into the big green dot, his eyes glazed over. But it did have a soul, it had a whole crew of them. He managed to, though still shaking, free himself of the trance, and turned to the main view screen. The details of the vessel came to. It was a Striker-class warship named the *Spoon*, captained by Grand Admiral Warren. Yes! He had heard about this; men of high rank were to be granted captaincies to compensate for the recruiting issues, it had been announced on the private channels. He was staring at the ship's registry when over the speakers came,

"Mayday, mayday. Fortified Outpost Tower thirteen, this is Grand Admiral Warren of the warship *Spoon*. We have sustained significant hull and weapons damage and are requesting immediate support. Enemy vessel in pursuit." Then again, his mind was cut off from him, the minor relief and feeling of control he had attained was simply ripped away from him. It clawed and screamed at him as it was dragged away into oblivion. He looked briefly at the control panel, but then at the radar as another ghastly beep played out of sync over the rest. A much smaller vessel, registering as a submarine, was moving quickly towards the slowly-going *Spoon*.

The message again played over the speakers, "Mayday, mayday, this is . . ." He glared at the control panel, each label over every button shone in his eyes like a welding light, it was impossible to keep watch on one. "READY DRONES - READY PRIMARY TURRET - READY SECONDARY TURRET - READY OUTER - MINEFIELD." Every option crawled into his eye sockets and danced, they leapt together hand-in-hand around his brain—laughing, jeering like gulls. They turned and spun, twirled and box-stepped and leapt, dancing, laughing. He looked again at the ship's registry; every word was suddenly foreign to him. There was nothing but symbols; hieroglyphs poured down in lines on the screen before him. He saw them all, but it was nothing to him. Every word and every symbol there joined in on the dance. These somersaulted through the air, bounced and flipped and rattled his skull. To the calling of the radar, faster, faster, the sub went on unimpeded towards the *Spoon*. One symbol out of the rest became abhorrently clear to him and stood still before his eyes; "442." There were 442 souls aboard the *Spoon*, 442 men, 442 sons, 442 fathers, cousins, uncles. 442 of his countrymen. But, oh, how the dance in his head raged on! Every letter paced faster to the sound of the radar, the sound which played as some discordant sacred drum of pagan sacrifice. They all gathered and with their arms on each other's shoulders beckoned to the fire within his mind. They bowed and rose and bowed again, and began to chant and to hum, and the noise grew faster, faster, and they bowed again. "Mayday, mayday . . . " And faster, faster. And each one began to cross his legs and walk to the side, and spiraled did they all. Spiraling, spiraling round the inferno ablaze in a frozen man. And the shouting! O the crying out of death! How it screamed in his ears! And they ran! Ran into the inferno! And in great screaming and crying they wrung their burning lungs. And they grabbed at his will and cried for he! He that was frozen with blazing hell in his mind!

And the flame itself reared up and laughed! Oh, how it laughed at him! "Ha!" Ablaze! Ablaze! Char your timid soul!

Then, just as it all had come, it went. The radio stopped; the beeping of the *Spoon* stopped. What remained was the quieting beep of the submarine, which quickly fled the radar's range. All was silent. The room was warm again. The warmth embraced him like a mother would her child, only to make him quickly forget the scrapped knee. The radar again beeped slowly, hypnotically. He looked down, his hand hovered motionless above the "READY DRONES" button. He looked up at the main view screen; it was empty again, its standard message slowly panned by. He did not blink; he stared mindlessly at the world in front of him. He fell into the chair. It was so comfortable, the chair, how well it had formed to him. His head fell into his hands; he sat folded over himself. The chair was really very comfortable; it was quite the work of ergonomics. He shook softly, and cried. How perfectly warm the room was.

Some Recollections of a Grave Robber

Daniel Gavilovski

"And what they don't tell you is that the hookers who are legal, like in this country, the hookers who are legal like in this country are a much shittier customer experience than they are in the countries where selling sex is banned. Because she's not afraid of you. When the hooker is afraid of you, she'll do anything to make you happy. You find her online, you message her, and you enter her bedroom. Well with that kind of atmosphere she'll do anything. In these brothels though there's cameras everywhere. There's no element of surprise, and there is no spontaneity. Christ, they won't even give you a kiss."

"Uh-huh."

On an unusually hot summer night I'm standing at Arrivals sharing cigarettes with this young man who is wearing camo pants and a cap bearing, if I remember right, some sort of Lithuanian military insignia on the front. We're waiting for an Uber. He, Jonas, had been to Germany one time before as part of a tour in an amateur orchestral ensemble. He played the tuba. We've been hired to participate in an archaeological excavation of the largest mass grave uncovered in Europe's history.

"Have you worked with skeletons before?"

"No, I say. Does it affect you?"

"Nah, you get used to it quickly."

"That's nice. I was worried."

"But sometimes I guess you do feel something. Like when you're digging the dirt from the eye sockets. Like I did this back in Lithuania, I worked in a lab and when you're digging the dirt from the eye sockets, I guess sometimes I would remember like oh yeah this was a guy once, and he had eyes like me. I don't know."

"Right."

"But mostly it's like geology or something. You start seeing them as just rocks. Especially once they're so old. Where are you from, anyway?"

"Ireland. But my parents are Russian."

"Russian? But, uh—"

Jonas suddenly looks very worried.

—But uh you're not a . . . um, I dunno. And there's a lot here in Germany but, uh . . . well, I don't want to be rude. But there's a lot of . . . *vatniki.*"

"I'm not a *vatnik.*"

"Oh, thank God, says Jonas and he lights another cigarette. Jonas would later be very impressed by the cig dispensers which are stapled to walls across the city."

Our Uber arrives and opens the trunk."

"Are you Russians?" the driver asks to my surprise.

"I am. He isn't."

Jonas hides his bag between his knees which are now quivering.

"God this place is a shithole, says the driver. *Nichivo yesli ya po kuryu?*"

"*Po kuryi.*"

*   *   *

I am living in a modern apartment with vinyl flooring in a mid-sized German city, in a building inhabited mostly by Turks, Slavs, and Germans of a suspicious variety. When I first enter the place after having spent the night on a bench because neither Jonas nor I have a key and no one is awake to tell us our apartment number I choose the bed placed awkwardly in the living area next to a table and I'm glad I do because the bunk which Jonas has picked gets unbearably hot in the nights. I can't stand hot nights. All my life I've slept with open windows even in winter. Into the room where Jonas resides are

172

crammed three Lithuanians (I am the only non-Lithuanian of my roommates) like sardines into two bunk beds.

Then there's another gentleman a meter or so to my right side. The whole thing is a tiny space and it's a marvel of Eastern European ingenuity to have turned a bachelor's Ikea lebensraum into barracks for six grown men. There are two mini fridges which are always packed to the roof because we are all *economizing* by not eating out. Any food that doesn't belong in the fridge we keep in clear plastic containers so that the roaches don't reach them, of which there are magnitudes. I never asked and never found out why exactly the toilet seat was fragmented and sitting in a pile behind the toilet but you come to realize how little you really need a toilet seat. This is a common motif of my time in Germany: there is little you can't do without. I have two pairs of footwear for example, steel toed work boots provided by the company (these are for the job), and rubber lined brown faux loafers (these are for everything and every time else). Still, it's annoying when I flush the toilet and, once in a while, for seemingly no reason, my fear and loathing bubbles up the sinkhole in the adjacent bathtub. I think it's something to do with the piping, or maybe it's the sand that invariably coats every nook and surface of the apartment and lines all the piping of that apartment forevermore, like milk lines your intestines before a night of teenage drinking. You can feel the medieval sand on your bare feet as you walk the Brazilian chipboard. Every day we import a seaside's worth circa the dig where the skeletons are drowned in the stuff. At the point of my arrival there have been around three thousand bodies exhumed and we discover maybe ten new ones every day. Men, women, children. The first thing that strikes you is that they are all colored a luminescent aqua-green, like the statue of liberty.

"There was a copper refinery here in the 19th century. The waste trickled down into the soil and gave them that color. It's called a patina."

This I'm informed by a girl in glasses and tattoos who has been here for a few months before me. Klara is Swedish and pretty in a bookish sort of way, and has an ass that's round enough, which isn't surprising since the job is physically intensive enough that a nice ass becomes a natural development. The Swedes are the second most common nationality on the dig after Lithuanians and after a while I grow quite fond of them, and psychologically begin to think of myself as one of them, ending up even resenting my Baltic neighbors. After Swedes there are a handful of Italians and then maybe two Germans.

All in all, archaeology in Europe is the best kept secret of our time. At any given moment in any country there are digs happening (though most of them don't feature one of the largest mass burials uncovered), and the realities of the profession are such that recruiters either can't or won't check if you have all the necessary credentials, if you have a degree, or previous experience. If you don't mind back-breaking labor which is equivalent to a construction gig but with lower pay then, well – I was going to say the pay can be good, but like I just said, it's lower than that of a construction worker. Then again, construction workers don't get flights paid for them.

"They're not just bubonic plague, a lot of these are soldiers from the Thirty Years War. That's right; there might be some Swedes here."

"Wow."

"Have you worked on a medieval site before?"

"No, just bronze age."

"Was that interesting?"

"No. Just rocks."

"So I hear!"

I don't want to give the impression that this is an operation of a massive scope. In fact, were you to stumble into this quarry of ours on a workday, and many did, including schizophrenics from the nearby mental ward, journalists, and simply curious passersby (tall fencing was later erected to prevent unwanted attention), if you were to stumble in then you'd hardly think it was an operation any more complex than a class exercise. There's not a lot of us, and we are all fairly young. I don't think there's more than a person or two over thirty. There is an interesting thing that happens on a dig where individuals like this are thrown into a hotbed *Massengrab* and are given almost free reign and in thirty-degree Celsius heat to beat. Let me explain. My Swedes—I can't help but forever think of them as "my Swedes," especially since I ended up commanding some of them—are archaeologists. They're well-educated and eager, though a bit bereft of hope in the way that all Zoomers are. Almost without exception the men are short, sometimes with bushy beards which make them seem like the Seven Dwarves. They're nebbish, meek, have a modern American sense of humor, and are autistic about history. One girl whom I work with is a germaphobe. If you put me on the spot and asked me a worse career option to pursue as a hater of germs I could not give you an answer, and not only that but she is our tent's only osteologist—that is, the only one officially qualified to point out which bone is which and so we often come to her to identify if a toe is a finger, or if a tibia is an ulna. But anyway, back to my point, Lithuanians, on the other hand, are a different story. If you'd like to for a second imagine what the archaeology industry of a nation that does not even have a developed tech sector is like, you're probably not far off. A Lithuanian archaeologist is just about any sewer dwelling vagabond willing to shovel World War 2 corpses for a penny a pound.

Interest in "history" is optional. Usually, one takes up the job because he is strapped for cash, and has outdoors experience. They're chain smokers and drinkers with mysterious scarred physiognomies and elusive backgrounds. What is required for this job is a strong stomach. But I don't want to sound too harsh here; Between the two cohorts I know exactly who would win in a hole digging competition. Some funny skirmishes happen when you pit them against each other. But then, some peace on Earth, as well: one time my colleague Sven was lecturing to thin air about how fifty-one percent of penises lean left and surly Benas, who has no ability for small talk and usually doesn't so much as crack a smile, explodes into a raucous howl.

I'm using a trowel to spoon sand from the inside of a crushed cranium. Craniums are the most delicate part. A lot of times they've imploded from the pressure, or fragmented like what you see at the bottom of a Pringles can. But even after four hundred years this one retains a cap of hair. I'm so lucky they don't smell, I think. If they smelled this would be so much worse. We brush down layer after layer, taking photos, sketching, and measuring each body in a pit that seems to be endlessly deep. In my tent there are a lot of children and sickly individuals. Basically, you get acclimated to the sight of cadavers after a week or so. Jonas was right, I think, it's like geology. But every once in a while, you discover a creature so inhuman and twisted that it snaps you straight out of your trance. One day Benas uncovers a man with legs like parentheses and arms like spaghetti. He stops to admire his work with arms on his hips on the landing over the trench and so do I and Sven since if one person does something usually the rest mirror, involuntarily. Word spreads and soon a parade of colleagues from the other tents are sticking their heads in one after the other to see the "something" like it's all a circus show.

"I hear you have something for me."

"Rickets. Not enough Vitamin D."

"How old do you think he was? Judging by the stature twelve or thirteen, no? Poor guy can't catch a break even in the afterlife."

Molesting corpses all day is not as psychologically pleasant as you might suspect, but the malfunctions from doing it enter you quietly through the backdoor, in a trench coat, without you noticing. In the same way that working in construction predisposes you to a takeaway and a lazy beer after work, if an archaeologist does not acquire some sort of release, take that word in the broadest possible sense, then he'll start to act out. Something becomes pent up in a man, and if he's *economizing* then it's even worse. The more we exist here the more we become antsy, quick to anger, irritated at the slightest triviality. One day I come home after having worked overtime and find a head of garlic on my bed. I and everyone here is highly territorial about their personal quarters precisely because we have so little of it. Privacy is nonexistent. If someone wishes to masturbate, even the bathroom is not exactly a fortress of solitude. That reminds me that one time I got the idea in my head to solicit the patronage of an older woman. I had no one in particular in mind, but, I think, why not? If not now, then when.

If I had an older woman, preferably a wealthy and lonely one then not only could I have a place all to myself, but also I could quit this miserable lonely gig and focus on more important things. It's hard to describe just what opium just the *possibility* of a good fuck is when you're neck-deep in a peasant's *hüfte*. So on my day off, I buy a tube of glue and print some A4 posters from a Turk. *Seeking Patron and Lover* it reads in bold font. *Achtung: Ich Suche Liebhaberin und Mäzenin. Because devotion to my craft and vocation does not allow me the time to hold a normal job, I am looking for a woman to support me as I write. In exchange, I will have sex and accompany you socially.* I make sure to stick them around the upper-crust hotels and the art galleries. As I'm doing this, to my surprise, I find that I've wandered into the city's red-light district. The cobblestone street is sandwiched by brothel after brothel after brothel illuminated by, yes, red light LEDs. Girls of all sorts are sticking their heads out; Brown girls, fat black girls, duck-lipped girls, sad girls, happy girls, bouncers, empty windows. Something about me feels that "I'm on the clock," so I do nothing more than admire the ladies like chimps in a zoo. One in particular catches my eye: a Slavic looking girl on floor three. It's a full body window so I can see that she's wearing black lingerie and a purple robe.

She has her knuckles on her *hüfte*. There's something mesmerizing about her, like she doesn't belong here. I like your bob cut, I think. It's a blonde bob cut and you have a round innocent face that as far as I can see from down here is unfixed. You know you've got a Marylin Monroe type of corpus? I'm staring at her for so long right now and she's staring back. She gives a wink and a "come here" type of gesticulation and from the cobblestone I shrug my shoulders and with my posters walk away. But anyway, I've gotten away from the point. Like I was saying, I come home and there's this head of garlic on my bed. Ordinarily I would not care or notice it but now it throws me into a fit of rage. I already know who did this.

"Jonas, did you do this?"

He's on the balcony in a tank top and underwear, smoking a cigarette.

"Yeah . . . because—"

"Well, don't do it again."

"I will if I want. You are *always* leaving your stuff. The butter you leave on the counter," he says. "The garlic," he adds.

"People leave butter on the counter. So it's soft and spreadable."

"There's no space. I tell you: there would be consequences," says Jonas.

"Okay, there's no space, so where do you want me to leave this? In the fridge? It's garlic."

"I don't know."

Now Jonas is hiding his face and gets out of the chair and walks into the kitchen to escape me.

"You don't know? Well fucking think of something. Fucking think of something before you throw my garlic over where I sleep. Where am I meant to put it?"

"Well, I don't know! It's your food. Why should I be responsible?"

Then I'm so overcome with rage that I go back to the balcony, throw open the fridge door, and start taking out one by one the large bacterial yogurt cartons which he buys and clogs the fridges with. They're spatially overlarge for their caloric content and have an awkward shape so they're impossible to stack.

"What are you doing?"

Then I start throwing the cartons over the balcony and onto the pavement below.

"How's this for space for your fucking yogurts!" I yell. "How's this for space? You touch my garlic, I touch your yogurts! How's this, you fucking gimp? You're lucky I don't throw them over your bed!"

*　　*　　*

For as long as I can remember I've wanted to hear Wagner live. So on no particular occasion, I find that a production of Tannhauser is playing at the *Nationaltheater* in the not-too-distant Munich. The opera is playing on a Sunday so I book a ticket amounting to one week's wages and on my day off take a well- deserved trip. Since this is a once-in-a-lifetime experience and I know one must dress up for a "night at the opera" I decide to buy a nice white shirt. Apart from that I'm dressed in the nicest clothes I own, which is my pair of jeans, and my brown shoes. The train there is inhumanly packed and there seems to be no air conditioning even though it's a boiling summer day. There are Americans sitting on the steps leading between carriages, tanned Spaniards or maybe Portuguese leaning on seats, and a fridge-faced Asian lady in the seat next to me. Whatever happened to those Victorian compartment trains you see in Westerns, I think. Oh well, I have *the* Wagner to look forward to! I wouldn't trade all the compartment trains in the world for a Wagner show.

The *Nationaltheater* was commissioned in 1810, four years after the dissolution of the Holy Roman Empire, by King Maximilian I of Bavaria. But Napoleon's assault on Russia siphoned state finances, and the complex, with its Corinthian colonnades, was not to open until 1818.

A hanging chandelier hangs above and an immaculate marble staircase to the left. I graze around for a while. All around are cohorts standing around and gossiping with champagne glasses in hand like bison at a watering hole, affluent physiognomies, mustached faces. At intermission I scan these faces methodically (when they notice me staring, I quickly look away) in an effort to play a character who is so wealthy and bored that the whole thing of a Wagner opera is blasé. My parents would drag me here as a kid, see, I've involuntarily memorized the lines and frankly they're unrefined, see. But still, I feel like an alien. These people come from a different world than me. They're born into money. Born into opera. Outside they were parking Porches. I feel like a working class LARPer goddammit. I'm singlehandedly diluting the integrity of the conserved arts by my gracelessness, my provinciality, my inborn illiteracy, and, at the end of it all, my very presence. Just when my self-doubt starts to overflow a voice beckons me.

"Young man. Young man."

"Yeah?"

A grey-haired man is leaning on the marble ledging and is hemmed by concubines dressed in exotica who are absolutely fixated on me.

"Why jeans?" he asks. "If you are at opera, you must wear something—what is it—*nice*. It is an opera. It is Wagner. It is not a supermarket."

Some of his girls are breaking into giggles. He is holding a flute glass. Anyway, I say to him the first thing that comes to my mind which in retrospect does not make too much sense but at the time elicits the desired reaction and it's this: "I have to wear jeans because I'm a playwright."

"You are a playwright?"

"Yes."

"I see. I am sorry."

In fact, I've written absolutely nothing except for some diary entries in five months. It's summer and summer is my best season. My worst season is winter. I buy myself a double gin and tonic to cheer myself up. Y'know what, I think. I'm no intruder. I'm the most valuable guest this venue could ask for. If anyone here knew who I truly was, they'd be starstruck and feel like spies in my presence. *They're* the intruders! I'm an aesthete. I'm more cultured than these nobodies. They're nobodies. All their life they've grown soft and flabby in their coddled milieu. Hell, I'll probably end up earning more money than them too. Are there any artists in the building? Any artists? I'll earn more money than *you* too. You are a nematode—a nektonic lifeform—a statistical obligato. My thinking of this turn of phrase cheers me up and returns to me my confidence, and I feel content to graze the bars and the foyer as clandestine, unbothered and undisturbed. Thank God I have the freedom to dress so shabbily. One day it won't be an option. I leave the gin and tonic half drank on a random tray. I don't even need to finish it. I've sampled.

Tannhauser itself lasts four and a half hours broken up by three short intermissions during which I get consistently drunker. My production is off to a great start because for the first ten or twenty—or who knows how many—minutes, I'm treated to a procession of white girls naked from the waist up, nymphs with bows and arrows stretched all across the stage like vaudeville firing arrow after arrow to the zing of the string sections. Each girl expertly and with precision contracts her dainty deltoids and *fwing*! *Fwing*! *Fwing*! The arrows stick the wood in a giant eyeball over the stage. They kneel down in a wave-back to the audience, resting their bows on their lap and their ass on their heels. I imagine the suspension of blood flow in a million cellular vessels, each hemisphere turning white around the heel, only for their liberation once the girl rises, heels on the ground, and once more cocks the bow. I am rapturous. Only briefly now and then does my trance break and I notice the guys opposite and in front of me. Sure is nice having a boner in your pants while all the while bearing the pretext of participating in high culture. The next scene is even better. the lustful warden Venus is a massive ugly obese creature, straight from a Cronenberg or a Brian Yuzna picture, dripping with lube and beckoning to noble Tannhauser. He's enraptured with her and they duet in what's an affectingly gruesome sequence before he finally breaks free of her lair.

But soon the knight's beloved is elegizing and I'm thinking this is going on for too long but I don't want to check my phone because it might be rude. Now there is a triptych over the stage bearing words like *hundert*, *Jahre*, and *später* approximately in that order and my eyes are drooping. What do those words mean? Now it's saying *Hunderttausend Jahre später* and then *eine Million Millionen Jahre später*. Oh, I get it, these are years passing. Years later. This has an unfortunate effect on me tantamount to counting sheep. One Million Years Later. That's a worthwhile technique, I think. Now Tannhauser is glottalizing over a pedestal bearing the skull and bones of his beloved Elisabeth. Now they are turning to ash. Now I doze off and dream of the girl with a bob on floor three.

*   *   *

"Catch."
"Don't throw it."

181

"Catch it."

"Don't throw the femur, Benas. Ah! I told you not to throw it."

It's been a month or so, and when I first came here, I was barely pretending to know what I was doing, but now there have been enough changeups that I'm the person who's known my tent the longest, and so I know the most about what's going on, what to do next, and how to handle it. As de facto leader of the tent I have executed to have an early lunch.

It's a hot, lazy day. Most of the crew has been transferred offsite because of some construction that's meant to take place. The grave was discovered, after all, because a new high rise is being built. So, we're taking it easy, cracking jokes. Jonas is down there in the trench corner browsing Instagram shorts with one hand and forking macaroni out of a lunchbox with the other next to a pair of toddlers who look to be embracing each other. I wish I had drawn it. Once you draw something you struggle to remember it. But it was a pretty image, and it's one of those rare times I think to myself: it's good to be alive. Torbjörn is whistling "You Never Give Me Your Money" while sprawled in the sand because it's a bit cooler down in the trench. Overhead, every now and then, you can hear a plane pass by. I'm falling asleep with my cheek on my knuckle because it's so hot, trying to read an article by Alexander Dugin. It's about the necessity of Russia decoupling from Western ideals, and from Latin-based linguistics. Every nation has a right to cultural sovereignty, he's writing. It's alright, I think. A bit old. Sven has, unprompted, begun reciting the tragedy of Darth Plagueis the Wise. Sven's an endearing personality and good at making me laugh. When we first met and I told him that I'm from Ireland his first words to me were: is it pronounced Cú *Kull*-ainn or Cú *Chuh*-lainn?

"Actually, it's Cú *hull*-ainn because in Irish a C and an H make that sound."

"Ah. Fascinating."

Every time Sven starts reciting his fun facts Torbjörn, also under my command, looks as if he's going to kill himself. Like another day when we're de-anchoring a tent and carrying it to a new spot like the Amish do with their barns. It's way too hot for this—this heatwave doesn't let up. It's midday and the sun is nuclear. And I don't understand why I have to do this. I sure as hell didn't sign up for *this.*

Suddenly Torbjörn scratches his calf on a rusty rebar sticking out of the ground and starts bleeding.

We look for a first aid box but find only some gauze and nothing else. Torbjörn is dismissive of the whole thing.

"It's not a big deal. It'll stop by itself," he says.

But I'm pissed off and there's no boss around and I leave the site right there. What if Torbjörn catches tetanus or something? He has his whole life ahead of him. I go to find the nearest pharmacy and soon I'm panicking that they'll bandage Tor's leg dry which is just no good at all and I start running and by the

time I find a shop I'm out of breath.

"Antiseptic?"

"Ja."

"Is it good for open wounds?"

I didn't ask *Sprechen sie Englisch* first so she's a bit disoriented.

"Oh. Uh, ja. I mean, uh, *yes.*"

I pay, and back on site Torbjörn disinfects his gash and wraps it up neatlike. All is well.

"Thanks."

"No problem. See, now you won't die of the Black Death."

But then is it a sin to admit that, after the fact, once we get back to work, all I could think was *was it really necessary I spend €9.50 on that bottle?* Why did I do that? No one gets sick anymore. This asshole wouldn't even offer me food if I was a guest.

*   *   *

One day a storm blows in over the city. It starts with a light drizzle, but pretty soon we can't hear each other talk over the clamor of rain. The tent's roof inflates like a ferocious balloon, then subsides and inflates again, pulsating. One of the legs of our tent collapses into the recess, and me and Benas scramble to lift it out without falling in ourselves. The immense construction crane is spinning over our heads like the second hand of a clock. Then we hear a scream from the neighboring tent. The little Italian girl Gia is directing orders. Hold this bucket here! Sven, catch this leak! Don't let the water touch the finds. But the rain is biblical and the back tarp is overflowing. All the rain is flowing down into our quarry from the adjacent roads and concrete.

"Shouldn't we cover the bones with a tarp?" I ask.

"Sure, but what's it gonna do?"

Sven and I are holding buckets over our heads and we exchange a look that's like *yep, here we are.* Gia returns saying Tent 3B is in trouble, and I run over with Jonas and that's when I see it: a waterfall like Niagara is flooding my trench, enveloping every single biofact in mud, cutting the walls and crashing ledges of dirt into the deadly rapids below. No less than six feet of mud and shit filling the dig like a crockpot. Gia has run off God-knows-where and eventually all I hear is *alright folks. That's it. Day's done.* All that work—washed away in an instant.

"I'm thinking of switching vocations."

"Me too."

"I think I'm done."

The next night I booked the first flight out.

The First and the Last

Evgeny Volkov

My father-in-law once told me, during one of our many car rides together, that a man—a husband—is both the first and the last line of defense for his family and all that he holds dear.

Should he falter, it is not only he who sinks, but also those who love and depend on him, their lives pulled into the same dark undertow. At the time, I was in my early twenties, more a boy than a man, though I was already married to the love of my life.

His words struck me with a weight I could not yet fully comprehend, but they lingered in my mind like the echo of a distant bell, tolling a truth I would one day have to face.

My father-in-law was a man worthy of deep respect, a figure who had weathered storms I could scarcely imagine. He had lived through the collapse of the USSR, endured the anti-Russian sentiments that swept through Uzbekistan, and then, with nothing but twenty dollars in his pocket, had moved his family to Russia and built a life from the ashes. His was a story of resilience, of a man who had stared into the abyss and refused to blink. In comparison, I felt like nothing—a young man who had only recently moved to Russia from America, chasing the promise of a better life for my wife and myself. We had decided, together, that Russia would be the soil in which we would plant our roots, despite its struggles and imperfections.

At first, life seemed to unfold as if scripted by a benevolent hand. I had a good job teaching English, a modest apartment, and a wife whose happiness was my greatest pride. What more could a man ask for? Yet, looming in the background, like a storm cloud gathering on the horizon, was the Special Military Operation (SMO)—a new chapter in the long and brutal war in Ukraine. The SMO has irrevocably altered the modern world, and it has changed my life in ways I am still struggling to understand. It was because of the SMO that I married my wife when I did, and it is because of the SMO that I am here today, writing these words.

Why, then, did I put my life on hold and sign a contract to fight in the SMO? Why not sit patiently, letting others bear the brunt of the suffering while my family and I remained safe? The answer is simple, though it carries a weight that presses heavily on my soul: I went to fulfill my duty as a man—a real man—to protect what I love.

I had studied the history of the war in Ukraine since its inception in 2014. I knew of its brutality, of the atrocities committed by the Ukrainian government with Western support against the Russian people in Donbass. I supported the resistance and the actions of the Russian army, yet for the longest time, I told myself I would never go. Why risk it, I thought, when my family is safe here? That was my refrain, my excuse, until the day the Crocus City massacre shattered my complacency.

The massacre was a crime of such unspeakable horror that it seemed to stain the very air. A group of men, driven by hatred for the Russian people, slaughtered hundreds of innocents and burned a theater to the ground. It was an act that echoed the Chechen terror of the early 2000s, a reminder that evil, when left unchecked, will always return. This atrocity, aided and abetted by the Ukrainian state and the broader West, was the spark that ignited something within me. It could have been someone I loved who died that day. And if they could do it once, they would do it again.

In that moment, I knew what I had to do. I had to fight— not for glory, not for politics, but to protect the people I love from those who would see them harmed. I had to fight for those who could not protect themselves. Every day, I think of what might happen if Russia were to give up, if we were to falter.

Millions have already died in this long war, and terror has taken root in many cities. But if we do not fight, hundreds of thousands more will be killed or driven from their homes, guilty only of being Russian.

This I cannot abide. I cannot let my future children grow up in a world where such monsters roam freely, where the price of safety is paid in the blood of the innocent. It is for them—for my wife, for my family, for all those who cannot fight—that I raise my hand and take up arms.

The first and the last line of defense. My father-in-law's words ring in my ears, a reminder of the weight I now carry. It is a burden I did not choose, but one I will bear, for as long as I must.

The Muck

Jake Leone

I

The lake was the last.

A crystal body, overflowing with nature's grace. For years, onlookers watched the others surrounding it die in rapid succession, suffocated by sludge, poisoned until no life remained.

They had seen the waterways blacken, damning once vibrant streams to practical death, and they certainly smelled the thick scent of putrefaction that hung heavy in the neighboring regions. Oh, but how they shook their heads and whispered of tragedy, carrying on in too low of a murmur to truly enact change.

But there it was: pure.

It stood untouched and pristine, gleefully mirroring the boundless heavens day and night.

The smooth stones that had been polished under Orion's watchful gaze lay perfectly visible below the rippling glass. Fish darted beneath the surface like living silver, their scales effortlessly catching the warmth of the day. Species of all kinds were drawn to the lakes edge where salvation could be found in nature's cradle and interactions were steeped in respectful mutualism.

Those that lived by its shores and ate from its depths took comfort in its comparably steady nature, where homeostasis was found through the connection with the order provided at conception. They told themselves that all would be well as long as this lake retained its vigor. Regardless of surrounding turmoil. These foolish stewards were convinced that this lake was theirs, opening the door for a delineation unrecognized by nature. Fueled by such absurdities, they watched on unbothered as others pleaded for assistance from the prevailing pestilence which was enveloping their legacies.

"This is ours. That is theirs. Ours is strong and will stand true in the face of foreign winds!" Mammon said through his biological puppets.

And so, when the first warning signs came, they were ignored as inconsequential.

An almost imperceptible change in the air, a hint of dampness that galloped through the natural order, an unrecognized forewarning of the pale horse which was sure to follow. The reeds once stood tall and green at the lake's edges, their roots melding with the earth, finding harmony in the organic balance offered to all. Ever so slightly these roots loosened leaving the reeds to fall one by one. Such is the corrupting pestilence that seeks disunity and the destruction of the divinely established order. A disappointed fisherman pulled up his net revealing an unhealthily dull catch, void of the signature sheen he had come to expect.

"Just a bad season," they said.

Then came the first piece of plastic. No one knew where it had come from, for the community lived without such products. Perhaps it was carried into what was once salvation by a gust of wind originating in a far-off land. An ignorant youth picked it up and attempted to distinguish what it was as it clearly did not belong. He tossed it back into the lake, watching as it floated through the gentle ripples until it had disappeared from sight. A single piece of litter in the very body that sustains the many. It was out of sight but one would be foolish to claim that it stopped existing at that moment. What a reckless ignorance the youth is cursed with, only to be overcome through vivisection and deliberation, allowing for the ancestral grail to be handed down to those worthy of such inclusion.

No one was worried.

So naturally, nothing was done.

II

The lake had survived for centuries, in a way that seemed effortless. It had withstood countless years of storms, droughts and floods, surely it could handle such a small amount of pollution.

Pollution is a fatal poison to the pure, one which is not confined to what is permitted by the living corpse who has yet to feel ill.

Right on cue, as all lay ignorant the skies blackened, the air grew damp and carried a charge that pushed the wildlife deep into the woods. The downpour eroded the soil, crafting deep trenches leading directly to the lake. The wind, fierce and unrelenting, tore through the trees that guarded the lake's shores.

For the first time in history, the lake did not dance with the morning sun.

A thin film blotted the surface of the lake; clearly a byproduct of the awful storm. The residents weren't worried as the lake had stood the test of time and would surely right itself as it sees fit.

It wasn't long before the reeds which graced the bank began to sag, their tips turning more yellow by the day.

With the rising sun, a fisherman trolled through the dull water as he had done for as long as he could remember. He came to a slow stop near his most lucrative fishing hole and made his way to the stern of his humble vessel, steaming coffee mug in hand. While preparing his bait he happened to see a small silver fish floating past.

Bloated.

Rotting in the open for all to see.

Fish die. All is well.

The town's annual festival grew near. Many flocked to the lake from surrounding regions, hoping to enjoy what they themselves had been deprived of by nature and the unhygienic behavioral patterns of those who came before. Voices filled the air as boats lazily drifted by, their wakes gently rippling outwards toward the congested shoreline. Children joyfully kicked around in the water, their feet stirring up plumes of silt that refused to settle.

The inconsiderate outsiders had brought in much more than they had left with. This was a completely foreign concept to the local inhabitants who had spent generations rejecting such products that refused to degrade. It had been so long since the threat posed by this refuse was recognized that it simply became a way of life avoiding such, over time lowering the guard of the people, spelling out certain demise. A single wrapper cast into salvation has become an element of desensitization, leading to the acceptance of bottles bobbing in the shallows and wrappers piling on top of one another, fighting for the chance to smother the reeds out of existence.

Nothing was done, and so the lake swallowed it in silence.

Seasons passed, and with them came gradual changes which unfolded slowly enough to go unnoticed by those who sought to remain blind and happy. The same fish that once reflected a beautiful bouquet of silver, had been denied such an honor by the sun which does not afford such luxuries to that which fails to maintain its character. The sun will not burn hotter simply because a fish has failed to find an adequate habitat to fend off the decline of its being. Likewise, the wind will not blow harder to lift the dying bird, stopping its final descent. Nature is not so kind. It allows the fish to be poisoned and die just as it allows the unwell bird to plummet to its death.

Nature does not hear your pleas and knows nothing more than strength or weakness. It is the enforcer of the binary of existence which does not allow for a state of being outside of life or death.

III

What is to be said to those inhabitants whose fate is inseparably linked to this once beautiful lake?

Now you see. It took a migrating bird falling onto your lap for you to look around at this muck?

You didn't see them losing their feathers? You didn't smell the stench of the rotting life being paraded directly under your nose? You didn't feel the sun turn its back on you, denying you its warm embrace?

You were slowly boiled like a frog. You allowed what you now must endure. That which is taking its final position to devour you whole, leaving not even a drop of blood for your descendants that you have killed.

The lake did not die in a single moment.

It slowly and quietly drowned.

Maybe there were muffled calls that fell on deaf ears, or an unfamiliar gurgle upon reaching its breaking point. Maybe it is simply abnormal for such a pure and noble thing to cry out while being asphyxiated. Regardless, a grounded man would surely have felt the disturbed soil below his feet, calling for his attention. Such would require a man who has not willingly insulated his soul from the harmony that nature offers, which would have allowed him to hear the divine struggling to draw breath.

The algae sprawled across the lake's surface like the pestilence it is, offered a home through the accidental alteration of the state of being offered at conception. Fertilizers from distant farms and industrial waste trickled down hill, inviting themselves into the lake's depths through the most convenient points of entry. They all found their way into the very heart of the lake, not through conquest, but rather neglect.

Of course, the residents had to recognize such a change now! Nothing that can't be solved through disingenuous didactics, where the casually malevolent can mask the problem in excuses, decorating the death rattle of purity with a pretty bow.

"The lake will find balance."

Of course it will! The forest being scorched by wildfire will also find balance, even if it means the destruction of its very being. Such does not bode well for the critters of the forest, just as the fish of the lake, or those who rely on its cleanliness to quench their thirst. They clung to such foolish assertions as homeostasis, not because they understood what it meant, but rather because it sounded like a promise that no action was required on their part. At best, this is akin to a man tired of life without the emotional strength to fend off a knife-wielding attacker, wishing only for his demise to come quickly, with minimal suffering.

The algae consumed the oxygen first. It became greedy and

voracious in the sunlight, ripping life from the gills of the dullest first. The world slowed beneath the dark green sky, where fish began to drown, mouths fluttering, begging with desperation for assistance in a world that is no longer capable of sustaining their needs.

It was not a clean death.

They spasmed and twitched as they drifted toward the surface, their bloated bellies dotting the invasive surface. It wasn't long before they ruptured, discharging foul odors that repelled all.

The birds stopped landing.

At one time they had dipped their beaks into the lake, feeding on the variety of fish and insects that had remained constant for all of time as we know it. But these insects were changing; adapting to the muck.

The stillness brought about a new order, free of the natural balance that kept all satiated.

Then came the mosquitoes in Biblical proportions. They grew in the murky shallows, facing no birds who sought to feast on the young larvae, and no dragonflies to chase down those who escaped. The muck fostered them by the thousands. Unpleasant. Then tens of thousands.

Terrible. Then millions. Unbearable. Citronella candles and curses were no match for the dense clouds of hunger that now lay like a diseased fog over the town. Hovering over what could at one point be called a lake, the mosquitoes angrily awaited those who passed by, pouring down the sickly reeds that remained while waiting.

It became impossible to even approach the lake without being devoured. They coated every square inch of exposed skin. They unrelentingly screamed into the villagers' ears as they searched for orifices to invade, eventually finding their way into nostrils or the mouth of a trespasser. The dogs knew not to approach this living tombstone even when their master commanded. It only took one encounter with the swarm to know it would end in painful thrashing, and whimpers.

The dogs understood how to keep their lake clean.

The birds understood how to keep their lake clean.

The well-meaning villagers did not understand how to keep their lake clean and now the lake is little more than a vibrating mass, emanating a hellish hum.

The last reeds fell. The locals retreated into their boarded-up homes, others abandoned the region entirely in search of something that even remotely resembled what they allowed to die, but none took action. The brave men who would have picked up a shovel and gotten to work were quiet and blind. The intelligent men who recognized threats such as these were immediately imposed with a moral duty to throw themselves into the fire, in the hopes that strong men would hear their final plea for service and be persuaded to keep this eternal flame of duty lit through the burning of their own flesh.

Where are these intelligent men who bear the torch of blood?

They have only looked within and have grown pathetic!

These cowardly worms muttered about balance, cycles, and natural resilience as they were too afraid to see their own bones turn to charcoal.

In the end, regret is a quiet disease.

The lake had nothing more to give. No fish to feed the locals. No water to drink. No place to swim. The sky could no longer be convened with through the divine mirror that had now been shattered and left to break down and rot, becoming one with all that imposed. It was little more than a stagnant, wheezing reminder of the delicate nature of purity.

Life went on regardless. A different form of life, but nonetheless life. Is this a consolation for the locals? Who in good faith can tell a man who stands as one of the few left out of a dying body:

"At least the bugs are happy. Life goes on."

I would sooner squash them under heel than allow for my brother to be swarmed!

The insects multiplied, regardless of the polite wishes of the town. The frogs croaked happily with bloated throats filled with an unnatural bounty. Beetles emerged in numbers never known to the region to dine on the decay offered by the prevailing muck. A new cycle of unbalance developed, offered through cascading circumstances originating in neglect and comfort.

The cradle of life had become a coffin. It calls all who had once sprung from its depths, and in that thick mud, under the putrid surface lay the graves of those who will never carry on as was intended.

The perfectly clear lake that had once offered the promise of life, now offers only death to those who are too foolish or too ignorantly faithful to draw near. There was no exchange, simply death.

The animals learned this lesson quickly. Those that braved the swarms found a soft bank, slick with the dark bile of decomposition. Their hooves and paws sunk in the muck, only a few inches at first, getting deeper the longer they remained. Some thrashed about, only realizing the awful circumstance they were faced with too late.

The stench grew unbearable as the earth festered, drifting through now desolate fields.

The crops began to fail, as the water had been tainted for some time now and few remained to tend to the eroding fields. Leaves curled. Fruit rotted on the branch.

Then came the strangers. No, they were not pilgrims or refugees, but rather the worst sort of opportunist. Perhaps they came to see how their own stench rivaled that of the muck, or perhaps they simply came to rip the piping and wires out of walls, jewels out of homes or the decency from what few women remained.

What was there to take? Everything had been packed up or sold months ago, leaving only family mementos that were now worthless. There was no family, as those pictures failed to carry on the spirit like only the lake could! This lifeblood was fluid and trickled through the centuries, very rarely being accompanied by such shallow things as names or photographs.

The town had died.

This was irrelevant to the brave who had been stirred up by fleeting recognition. They decided that action must be taken, and set out toward the muck with shovel in hand, and rifle slung over shoulder. It was decided that they would live on in blood, and if not, in spirit.

They stepped into the rot with a slow and deliberate gait that a man only finds when he understands the price of his own apathy. Some men began to shovel, while others just stood

motionless looking toward the horizon. It wasn't long at all before the tree line began to fill with foreign witnesses, arriving to watch the final spectacle that these men could offer.

Sinking.

They did not cry out for help. They looked on at those who would replace them on the very land for which they had remained stewards for all of history. They would occupy the very houses once filled with the spirit of life. Generations of beauty and kindness offered up to the first vile animal to make a demand!

None panicked, for they had died long ago with the lake and were only facing their own biological death.

Such things are discovered to be inconsequential when the time draws near.

No monuments would be erected. No eulogies will be spoken. Not even a bird will sing its praises to the fallen men who stepped into the depths, agitated by the ancestral strength that they had only found when the Rubicon had been passed.

No. They will be simply bones in mud, forever incarcerated in putrid earth, watched over by the ever-changing guard of humming insects.

Here lies purity, now muck.

A Father's Regret

Jesse Poe Holiday

In the small English village of Wethersfield in the state of Essex lives an inconsequential man named Edward Oldham. There's hardly a thing about him that is unusual and certainly nothing about him that is extraordinary. To describe him as regimental while adding fifty buttressing adjectives, still wouldn't do the man justice for he does everything the exact same every day, seemingly down to the minute. He never intentionally causes any problems—always avoiding potentially disputatious or controversial issues in conversation in an effort to never offend. As a result, rarely were any of his preferences or wishes fulfilled but it was worth it to him, for he never sought to "rock the boat."

Edward is also traditional in the sense that he holds conservative values—at least what is considered conservative for the time. He, of course, respects the law of the land (even if it violates his personal beliefs), values hierarchy and unquestionably obeys authority. Therefore, since childhood he was always obedient to his parents and loathed any fellow classmate who showed the slightest recalcitrant behavior. This trait is displayed through his obsequious grey eyes and congenial face notably during the times when his workplace superior unfairly ladens him with more work than warranted and the compliant Edward accepts the responsibility alacritously.

Moreover, Edward embraces what all good conservatives in the post-modern Western sphere are expected to embrace, the perceived virtue that all men were created equal and all should have the right to seek their own fortunes and happiness, irrespective of ethnicity and culture. As long as a person is (or promises to become) ideologically

British, then British they shall be, through and through, Edward believes and often pontificates.

He provides for his family of three (his wife, his son, and himself) by way of a decent salary working as a software engineer for a large company in Southend-on-Sea, the largest city in Essex. He joined a nascent company in the early 2000s and has been with them ever since. He has made the long commute daily to his job for over twenty years now—never has he been late and rarely does he miss a day. Throughout his tenure, his superiors noticed his natural talent and offered him on several occasions a leadership position yet he has kindly denied all of them.

Edward has never thought of himself as the Napoleon or Caesar type; he instead fancies himself as filling a pivotal ancillary role in the company—an exceptional archer on the right flank of Caesar's army— esteemed by his generals and crucial to the battle but never a leader.

Edward met his wife Mary at a pub through mutual friends in Southend-on-Sea when the couple were nearing the age when mothers, nervously biting their nails, are pressuring their offspring to give them grandchildren. Mary was working in public relations at a large firm and opted to change careers once married and pregnant. She now is a consultant for a smaller company working from home, a position on which she places more significance than warranted.

If Edward is governed by fear, Mary is governed by self-interest. She had learned a protocol of conceit and authoritativeness from her single mother which proved to be a perfect match for her meek husband. If Mary were less laconic and indolent, she would be an unmitigated and merciless tyrant. Nonetheless, she still rules the nest in the Oldham household with her biting and pernicious words and her ability to manipulate. Edward serves as the idle chess pieces and Mary the chess player. The arrangement defies the laws of nature and places the husband in pathetic situation, but it works for them.

As a consequence of marrying near middle-aged, Edward and Mary had just enough time to have one child (a boy) eleven years ago—a year after their marriage. That boy's name is Albert. Being the precocious child that he is, Albert's higher-than-average intelligence propelled him up a grade in school; he's an eleven-year-old seventh grader.

It would be safe to suggest that Albert, being the product of a pusillanimous father and assertive mother, would turn out to be an amenable weakling, making him a life servant to the opposite sex. However, this was not the case. Albert emerged from the fetal womb a being of his own, an independent thinker, a warrior for the divergent creatures of civilization—an agitator. Invariably, since he was old enough to form cogent ideas, he'd have ideological battles with his parents and contradict his mother for its own sake. Curiously, outside the home, he'd be more receptive to the opinions of others and would conduct himself a bit more reservedly—he did push the boundaries at times though when coaxed.

Daily life is quiet in the Oldham household. Edward leaves for his job in the early morning with Albert whom he drops off at his exclusive private school in Southend-on-Sea and Mary remains in the home, conducting her important business and doing as little housework as possible. All's well, it seems; however, recent events in Great Britain have greatly impacted the lives of the common people of England, including the Oldham family. For the greater part of a decade, the UK government has been importing migrants from India and countries in north Africa. These "asylum seekers" are mostly men, have a penchant for crime, and hold traditions and values that are diametrically opposed to those of the English. Moreover, their birth rates have been quickly eclipsing those of the native whites. Forecasts say that by 2040, native English will be a minority in their own country.

Wethersfield is not yet a victim of this invasion of the outsiders but Southend-on-Sea is. The city has taken on thousands of these non-whites. It has changed drastically as a result. The overall atmosphere of the city—the feeling one gets walking downtown—is a less English one.

Storefronts look foreign. Strange languages are spoken. Crime is high. Trust is low. Taboos that were once strictly regulated by English elders are now wholly accepted.

What's more, this invasion has altered the economic landscape. Companies that hire the cheap labor which the migrants provide (and that displaces white labor) are rewarded with the ability to undercut their competition. Migrants occupy rentals and, in some cases, manage to cram several families into single-family homes and apartments, which drives up housing costs. The children of these people pour into local schools, forcing down the educational standards and frustrating the native English children.

This brings us to one particular night at the Oldham home. Edward and Albert had arrived at the house in the evening to an expectant Mary.

"Hello, dears. How was your day? Mine was exhausting. Flood of paperwork came across my desk."

"It was fine mom," little Albert said as he walked through the door while his tristful father followed slowly behind him.

"Supper is about ready," mentioned Mary, completely ignorant of her husband's sullenness. "I wasn't able to fix anything so it's microwaved Chinese food again."

The three Oldhams sat quietly together at the dinner table. The mood was dismal. Mother and son shared a few niceties. Mary then prattled on with a slight air of importance about mundane aspects of her job. Edward stayed silent. He leaned his head on his fork-wielding hand and stared blankly at his plate.

"Dear, is everything alright," Mary asked austerely while eyeing her full plate, more so out of obligation than of empathy.

"I'm sorry, Mary," began Edward after which he cleared his throat, "something happened at the office today—" His voice faded.

"What happened," Mary inquired. Her mood changed with great haste and her attention went wholly on her husband.

"Well, you know that Indian executive that's been making my life a living hell for the past year?"

"Yes?"

"Well, now instead of hiring other Indians for the lower-end positions, he's now starting to lay off whites in skilled positions for other

Indians. You know Charlie? His wife is Liz, whom you met a few times before—he's gone. And Rich? Him too. Five engineers and a manager were let go today. That makes ten native English men in two months. A lot of them have been there for a decade or more."

"Ed." Mary's facial expression sharpened.

"I know, Mary." His voice drifts off again.

There was another prolonged silence. Mary tensed her shoulders and face. The inevitable question must be asked. Edward watched Mary from under his eyebrows which shaded his eyes like umbrellas from the coruscating glare of his wife. He held his breath in dreadful anticipation.

"Your job is safe, right Edward?" Mary said—more as a statement than a question, as if an answer of "yes" is all that she will accept.

"I'm not sure, Mary," Edward confessed, letting out a drawn-out breath. He said this as if the response had been rehearsed.

Her trenchant words that followed impacted Edward like knives to his chest. "You should have taken that promotion like I said. You foolishly turned them down and now look at the mess you're in. We can't afford for you lose your job."

"I know, I know," Edward said plaintively.

"We have a mortgage and Albert's tuition . . . I'll have to go graveling back for my old position at the firm. I wonder what the others will do? How will that look for us? What will others say?"

Meanwhile, while his mother prattles on about how the youth of the country are displacing the older workers (missing the point entirely), Albert had been absorbing all this. He had been speciously looking as if his thoughts were assiduously focused on the task of consuming his chicken but he couldn't help indulging in his youthful curiosity.

He felt sorry for his father, despite his lack of respect for him. So often does he acquiesce to the domineering force conjured by the imperious female of the house. This is the way it is however; there is no slaying the indefatigable dragon that is her ego and placation is the only defense to soothe the beast.

"I didn't speak up, Mary," Edward began, looking pensive, "I was too cowardly. I have the clout and seniority to at least make the other executives listen. I didn't want to do make myself a mark for the next round of layoffs." The Oldham patriarch looked pathetically at his wife.

"You did the right thing," Mary confidently remarked as she raised her ladened fork to meet her mouth. "God, don't be growing a conscience now when your job might be on the chopping block. Keep your head down and do your job. Our budget is tight now as it is."

"Yeah . . ." Edward was fondling his food with his utensil and muttered quietly, "I just feel that I failed to do what should have been done—like I didn't do the right thing."

"Dad, you still can." Albert jumped in the conversation.

"No, Alby, your father should stay quiet. There's no need to rock the boat."

"No way. Dad, it's bad enough that the Africans and Indians are taking over the city. You can't let them put out your friends. It's not right."

"Now, Albert, don't make this about race again" Mary said in a shaming tone.

"It's wrong, Mum. It was created as a white company and with all white workers," remarked an emotive Albert. He is now without his fork and emphasizing his points with his hands. "Not to mention, this is a white country!"

"I don't want to hear this right now," muttered Mary through a mouthful of food, shaking her head.

"Now Albert, there is where you are wrong," his father said half-way sternly. "Those men came here legally. The ones at my office are hard workers and have earned their right to be here—they are legal citizens, after all. It's not their fault the government allowed them here. The illegal ones—now that's a different issue altogether. I'd be inclined to agree with you then."

"But Dad, is our country not white? Wasn't it founded by white English?"

"Yes of course, lad, but times are different. We have a shrinking population. Our government is trying to inflate the number, otherwise there wouldn't be enough people to work. I just wish they were a bit more discriminating about who they let in."

"But, when is enough, enough?" Albert's voice is now cracking as he tries so desperately to sway his father. "It's like what happening at my school. If they keep doing this, there won't be any white students left. Same goes for your job—and for the country."

"Alby, please." Mary's monotone voice was nearly lost amongst the series of clangs of her fork stabbing her food.

"Well . . ." Edward's voice lingered while letting out an audible sign as he contemplates his next words. "They are pushing for diversity, which is just a synonym for white replacement."

His eyes furtively hid under the umbrellas again in anticipation of the glaring sun which came like a rising phoenix, burning what's left of his charred dignity.

"Edward, why are you feeding our boy's fantasies?" Mary said vehemently, dropping both elbows on the table, frustrated that she has to interrupt her dinner. "Didn't he already get in trouble at school for this type of talk? And you are fueling it with comments like that."

"Your mother's right," Edward reiterated, nodding his head and morphing his face into one of a concerned parent, while turning his attention to Albert. "We pulled a lot of strings to get you into that school and I don't want you to have another incident like last time. Let's talk about something else."

"Dad, can you not see it?"

Not much was said heretofore. The family cleaned up the table and Albert went straight to bed agitated. Once in his dim room, the boy laid supine in his bed and looked pensively at the dark ceiling about what transpired that evening. It's the same song and dance every time. He manages, after some coaxing, to break through the wall of propaganda that has been built around his father since his childhood, only for the process to be interrupted by his mother or the ghost of his progressive school teachers or whatever it may be that buttresses his modern thinking. His father invariably reverts back—all progress lost.

"If he only could understand," the boy whispered to himself," what went on at school, then they would be on my side."

Flashes of school yard memories filtered through his mind like a film reel in a projector. He can recall only snapshots—soles of shoes propelled at his head, tightly rolled ashy fists thrown, youthful scrums of bellicosity.

This was the reality at Southend-on-Sea Academy. A private school with a rich history, infiltration by the "Browns" starting in the 1980s—Indians at first, then later (in the 2010s) Africans. Its demographic makeup currently stands at roughly half-white, the other half comprising a diverse range of non-white ethnicities.

These new peoples have a penchant for preferring those in their own group and antipathy for those who are not, a feature not demonstrated by the native English children. Couple this with their violent tendencies, persecution against the white students commenced.

As the numbers of foreigners grew, ethnic gangs formed. They roam the school yard during recess, harassing the timid and peaceful white students. A particular cadre, an Ethiopian gang, has targeted Albert's small friend group due to their physical inadequacies. Nearly every day for months, this gang of bellicose nine-year-old dark-skinned reprobates has accosted Albert and his chums. Initially it began with teasing and threats. Then things escalated into outright violence.

The members of this African gang are unusually large and strong for being in primary school. They dwarf Albert's friends all of whom have thin frames and are shorter than the Ethiopians. Fights between the two groups often erupt and are instigated invariably by the Blacks. The White kids rarely fare well in these melees. As for Albert, he has been punched, kicked, scratched, and pushed to the ground too many times to count. His mother rarely would ask about the injuries.

His father did but Albert lied about their origins—no further investigation occurred.

The next day came. Albert could hardly sleep the night before. He was quiet the entire car ride to school, partially due to his frustration from last evening's conversation. The defiant eleven-year-old, however, was up to something—something big. He figured that circumstances must change. Enough gumption and gallantry had accumulated from the night previous that he thought today was the optimal day for it before he loses the nerve.

It took no time to finalize his plan.

The car pulled up to the school's campus; hordes of obstreperous children littered the yard. The ethnic landscape was a progressive's utopia—shades of brown, black, beige and white flooded the eye. This diverse scene served as the foreground to an ancient school, a veritable castle. It's a beautiful building, a four-story masterpiece of architecture, that has a tall tower at its middle with two spires flanking it. The windows on it are grand and prodigious. It's reddish exterior starkly contrasts with the light powdering of snow which lays lazily on the rooftop and the surrounding pine trees; the scenery is like a Christmas card almost year-round. Girding the complex is a stone wall with a grand gate that guards the opening. Within the robust partition are two statues and a grand fountain. The statues are of two historical figures, Dr. James Murie an explorer and Sir Charles Nicholson, Southend-on-Sea's most significant architect. What a stark contrast! The children of tribal savages lethargically trapsing the campus grounds of a place defined by loftiness and assiduousness is akin to mixing oil and water.

Albert left the car and scurried past his nemeses, the Nigerian gang who was loitering around one of the statues. He went directly to his friends and other white students who were loosely associated with his friend group to tell him of his plan. Given that those particular students endure the most persecution from the foreign dark-skinned gangs, they were more amenable.

Albert was a boy motivated and ambitious. He found himself in an almost possessed state when persuading his fellow students of his idea. It was like a ghost from the past, a persuasive and infectiously virulent speaker, had inhabited his body. His rhetoric was breviloquent and soaked with motivating speech. He approached clique and clique of white students, between classes and even during classes when he could, arousing a spirit of action. Some weren't responsive and others even castigated his efforts; those students were obviously steeped in the modern ethos of racial liberalism. These small intervals of vituperative remarks and rejection did not sway Albert. His resolve marched on.

The time came. Recess had begun. Students alacritously disembogued from the school halls onto the playground in a disorderly and tumultuous mass to then chaotically organizing into their little atomized groups, some by gender, some by social class, and most by race. Albert's group also met at their usual recess meeting spot, a particularly tall jungle gym.

The mood was different than most days; a nervous anxiousness resonated through the group. They all looked at Albert for direction. He was resting at the apex of the playground equipment, his face pallid and breathing heavily. There was no doubt that he was nervous. His usual modus operandi is causing controversy in the classroom, not starting a school-ground revolution. Albert had a reputation for challenging his instructors on historical truths and facts that were regarded as gospel in the zeitgeist. He was never officially reprimanded only tacitly admonished by his instructors until last year when he vehemently denounced in a history class England's importation of non-whites. The school as a result of his actions deemed it necessary to suspend him from school for a month and they nearly expelled him. This event drove a wedge further between his father and him.

At last, Albert beckoned his fellow comrades to scale the jungle gym. The leader surreptitiously peered over the bars at a particular area of the playground. His followers bewilderingly but sycophantically mimicked him. They waited.

Not long after, the Ethiopian gang coalesced near a big pine tree, a short distance away. Glittering in the sunlight was an oppressive sheen on the sable skin of the Ethiopians—Albert's clan could clearly see them. Soon they moved as one toward them. Their intentions were manifest. Their de facto leader, the oldest amongst them, yelled out in broken English to Albert and his friends—an obvious threat. The white students didn't move. He repeated it again more aggressively. Again, no movement. The Ethiopian leader advanced toward the barn and his cadre followed. Some began to climb the gym. This engendered the white boys to ascend higher to the top of the equipment. Annoyed, the dark-skinned boys impulsively spit invectives at their prey.

Of a sudden, the white boys in unison slipped between the bars and descended onto the Ethiopians in a coordinated attack. Juvenile fists flew. The white boys who have had enough of the daily torment unleashed their anger upon their enemies and a scrum of violence formed. It was a chaotic maelstrom of screaming and flailing children. This quickly grabbed the attention of the instructors—all six of them rushed to the scene. As they attempted to break up the scrum, Albert furtively fled.

He ran to the center of the playground where a particularly large slide stood. It was once a popular attraction before the invaders arrived. The native English children freely utilized it and the equipment yielded much joy. This changed when the migrants came and the area around the slide was frequently being occupied by vagrant loiterers, dark-skinned slipshod who initially used the spot for exchanging illegal substances but it has become a matter of spite for they enjoy barring white students, especially the younger ones, from being able to use the playground equipment. This is where Albert resolved he should make his stand.

Albert postured himself before several blacks, around ten of them, stationed at the slide. They each donned the white dress-shirt and brown khaki pants that the school required all male students to wear. It looked dreadfully out-of-place in them, contrasting luridly with their near-blue complexion. A wolf in sheep's clothing seems more natural.

The black students looked at him expectantly with their dark eyes. An air of bewilderment washed over them. "What is this fool doing," possibly ran through their minds.

"This is stupid," Albert thought as he trembled. "If they don't come and I'll be running for my life in a few short seconds."

"What do you want cracker," boomed in a thick accent one of the large Africans, his large lips smacking as he spoke.

At that moment, three male white students approached stridently. Then, a few more arrived. More filtered in until there was a sudden surge of them, rising like a steady tide. There had to have been three dozen of them, maybe four when all was said and done. They finally came to rest behind Albert and glared collectively at the Africans; they said nothing but their harsh stares conveyed enough.

This struck fear in the very souls of the blacks, a fear that was most primal as if it was inherited from their ancient ancestors who once roamed freely on the savannahs until one day a boat arrived on a distant shore and its pale occupants disembarked and showed them the meaning of civilization. Though they lacked the reasoning skills their white contemporaries possess, the black students were quite astute in the art of intimidation and violence, therefore they knew they had two choices—fight or flee.

"We want you to once and for all leave this slide alone and allow us to use it again." A robust voice catapulted from deep within Albert's chest, his head was head high and his neck was erect. "And to let you know this is our school. We will no longer tolerate bullying of any kind against our own. Is that clear?"

There must have been a signal or an inaudible call of some kind for a contingent of black students coming to the other's aid, rushed upon the crowd in an effort to intimidate and distract. A few at a time would come from behind the group of whites and swing an open hand at their heads, only to retreat and a few more would repeat the process. It was an odd sight, one not foreign to an animal enclosure at a zoo. The white students ducked and swung at the assailants like a farmer swatting flies in the hot sun.

This continued for some time until a white student punched a black antagonist, knocking him flat on the ground. A frenzied scrum ensued. There were shrieks and cries summoned from within the young students; bellicose cries of war which could only come from an ancestral calling—an ancient instinct. It was a primal display of primitive survival.

Albert had a thrilling sensation stream through his body from head to foot. There was an element of fear but a fear that reminded him of his mortality and consciousness; it was exhilarating. He had no knowledge of how to fight yet he knew what to do. He swung his small fists at vulnerable areas of his enemies. He'd draw blood then his enemies would. All reason and thought were lost in the frenetic blurry skein of black, white and red.

*   *   *

A blue sedan pulled into a parking spot of the school and out came Edward, clad in a suit and tie, armed with a rejuvenated spirit. All morning, he had ruminated at his work desk about the conversation at the dinner table the night before. He realized his irrational position on the issue and considered his son's cogent protests; he also admired his courage to confront his wife and him. So, he decided to visit his son for lunch and extend an olive branch in hopes to mend their strained relationship.

Edward, ebullient and refreshed, walked gayly to the building, one hand in his pocket, the other swinging to and fro. He heard a general tumult of shouting students from the recess grounds behind the school and thought nothing of it—children being children. As the father moved closer, the noise sounded more like a cacophony of distress and rage. His pace increasingly quickened and made his way to the locus of the uproar.

Rounding the building, he descried a large group of students and instructors, gathered in one place, a scene looking like the aftermath of some kind of accident or tragedy. There were students nursing their wounds, others standing confoundedly, still more being separated or held to the ground by campus police and male instructors.

What looked more alarming was a small contingency grouped around a supine boy, a few kneeling by his side and others standing looking down at him. Edward got closer and saw that their faces were sullen; there were those who were lachrymose, their faces drenched with tears, female students and adults alike. Two men looked to be holding pressure on the chest of the boy. Near the cluster, a black student had been subdued by older students and a sanguine knife was lying in the ground close by.

"What happened?" Edward asked aloud to whomever would answer.

Then Edward recognized the shoes worn by the boy being tended to; they belonged to Albert. He rushed to him and came upon a bloody mess of a scene. There was hardly a dry, bloodless spot on his son and the two aides besides Albert's face which was white as the vestiges of snow leftover from winter on the pine trees. Edward hardly knew what to do, or how to process the situation.

"My boy, my boy." The father fell to his knees and reflexively cleared out with outstretched arms the men who were rendering aid to the boy. The father's hands then took up the task of trying to stop the bleeding.

"W-what happened?" Edward repeated in a half-crying, half-incredulous manner.

"He was stabbed," one man said, while searching the horizon for first responders. "Ambulance is on the way."

"Why, who?" Edward was trembling. He peered down at his son and his eyes welled with tears.

"I was," started Albert trying to catch his breath, "I was fighting the immigration. I was fighting them and one of them stabbed me."

"Fighting? The immigrants? You don't fight. That's not you, Alby."

"I did it because of you, Dad."

"Me?" Edward wiped his face with his sleeve. Though the claim was cryptic, he almost knew what his son was insinuating.

"You—" whispered Albert, "I had to do it because you failed to do anything." Albert choked and coughed.

"Alby." The distraught father cried out and stroked his son's hair with one hand and caressed his cheek with the other, smearing blood on the boy's face. "I'm sorry, my boy. Please forgive me.

Please forgive me."

"I always loved you, Dad. I forgive you . . . I forgive you."

"Help," shouted Edward in an unrestrained howl to whomever will listen. "We need help here."

Albert's eyes closed softly and he seemed to have drifted to sleep, his face suspended in a wistful manner. Before he left this world, the boy briefly dreamt of the open field behind his house, this idyllic landscape of greens, browns and yellows, rolling hills, tall grasses and waving trees. The dream was of a particular day when he was younger, his father and he, hand in hand, walked amongst the whipping grasses. He could hardly see over the vegetation. The boy was giggling and frolicking, pulling on his father's grip as young ones do. Edward beamed. He watched his son's playful innocence.

"Daddy," little Albert looked up at his father, "you won't ever forget me, will you?"

In Black and White

Ndabaningi

The little body was twisted about, back upon itself, impaled in three places on the same stake. The head and limbs were missing. The plump abdomen was all that remained, almost dry now in the glare of the sun. Robert stared morosely at the pathetic tableau, the little scene of cruelty and murder. He wondered if there was a greater lesson to be drawn. *Sic transit vita mundi,* and all that. He let his focus relax a little, and took in the boundary line that stretched out into the distance—a three-strand barbed wire fence that neither deviated, nor, it seemed, ended. On the other side lay the stubble of the neighbor's harvested maize-fields, on this side his father's pasture.

The sun-blackened corpse was only one of a number of other unfortunate victims. The wire barbs made perfect little stakes and the impaler had made good use of them. Robert didn't look too closely. A fat, headless locust was one thing, but fluffy chicks, striped field mice and harmless little shrews on the gallows always depressed him. He felt himself being watched. He knew that the perpetrator was keeping a dark, beady eye on him from the shade of a thorn tree next to the old milking-shed. If he'd been in the sunlight, the murderer would have been resplendent in his little tail-coat of black and white. His name itself was derived from the uniform of money-managing clerks of former times: the Fiscal Shrike. His cruel ways had lent him his more popular names: Jackie Hangman, Butcher Bird. He perched in the type of tree his race had been using for millennia—before becoming enthusiastic adopters of the White man's fence—and observed. If the man had presented any threat to his gruesome larder he would have dive-bombed and harassed him until he had relinquished the notion.

Robert sighed. Black-and-bloody-White. It was always Black-and-White in this country, yet seldom ever simply black-and-white. He let his eyes wander to the east, past the sheds, the stable, past the rondavels, the house and towards the long dirt driveway that led to the tar road to town. The hint of red dust still hung in the hot air, the trail of the vehicle that had just left.

He felt anger. It could not be focused. It would have been unfair to blame his parents, making their way to town at that very moment. Could he blame his grandparents? Yes. Perhaps. But then again, how could they have known? They should have known; they could not have known. Things were different then. His parents had finished school in the mid-80s. They were too young. But his grandparents' generation? They'd built the tennis club, the bowling club, the agricultural hall. Private funds for common causes. There had been years of prosperity—the fifties, sixties, seventies. Even the sanctions of the eighties hadn't dampened the returns as agriculture and its attendant service industries had come into their own. They should've bought the bloody school. Less money on bigger tractors (overpowered for local soils, no less a sign of wealth than the luxury personal vehicles), more money pooled to privatize the school.

Robert knew he was being unfair. They all thought it would never end, it wouldn't "happen here." Sure, as the wry joke went, Great Rhodesia had become 'the Zimbabwe Ruins' and, before that, Portuguese Mozambique and British Kenya had returned to Africa. But that was unthinkable in South Africa, with its huge economy, its developed infrastructure, its formidable defense force, its fiercely determined government. And there was the rub. Apartheid's success had made its downfall less manageable. The frog had found itself in very tepid water indeed. Most South African Whites had no idea, no experience, of living in Africa at all. The segregation had, for all intents and purposes, meant that they lived in a Europe under sunny skies.

Only the most far-sighted would have been aware of the warning signs. The winds of change might have slowed down as they crossed the Limpopo River, but they were blowing nonetheless. The burgeoning African population—thanks to European hygiene, medicine, agriculture

—made that inevitable. But hindsight was always twenty-twenty. The few who had spent time up north, in the 'real Africa' beyond, or who had drifted in from Mozambique after 1974 or Rhodesia after 1980 had always been seen as somewhat eccentric with their talk of Black majority rule, "Uhuru" and ruined lands. Things were good. They wouldn't change.

And the schools? Why would anyone turn down the generous government subsidies that kept the fees so low? Who would be so haughty and arrogant to want to privatize a rural school in the 1980s? Of course, there were private schools—many quite famous ones—but they were the products of unique historical circumstances. Most government schools were more than adequate, some of them even out-competing the expensive private ones, both academically and, more often than not, on the sports fields. Both Robert's parents had gone to the local school, as had his paternal grandparents and great-grandparents. His father had admittedly won a rugby scholarship and had spent his final four years at a private school in the city. The neighbors had gone to the local school too, generations of them. Along with the three local churches, it had been a fixture of the little town for over a century.

Along with any number of South African schools it had sprung from rudimentary beginnings. While missionaries from a number of European missionary societies built schools for the children of African tribesmen, the settlers were left to their own devices. At first a few of the women held lessons under the trees. On wet days, all the classes were crowded together in a single-roomed wattle-and-daub building that also served as a community hall. In time the farmers clubbed together to pay the salaries of a pastor who doubled as a schoolmaster. The humble hall gave way to new brick buildings. Sports fields were laid out. As the country developed, provincial departments of education came into being, matters were regularized, standards were imposed. Funds became available. The government's shilling was welcomed; facilities could be improved, expanded.

Decisions weren't made. Decisions that Robert would have made in a heartbeat. Things were too good. Why privatize a school? Whatever for? And so, when the government changed, when the unthinkable happened, they were less dependent on the new regime than tied to it. The school had been rapidly integrated and the community had been left with very little say over how that would be implemented. Over the years they had increasingly lost what little say they had over the place. It was still a 'good' school, thanks to the efforts of the farmers who maintained the grounds and buildings and to the larger White community who supplemented the teachers' government wages in order to attract the better sort of educator. But things had gone downhill nonetheless.

Robert had spent the first five years at the school, his sister Elizabeth three. Their younger brother Edward had spent no time there at all. As soon as he was of school age all three had been bundled off to boarding schools in the city. The same was the case for many on the surrounding farms and in the town. The number of White children had dwindled. And yet the community had continued to contribute, endeavoring to keep the school functioning. The Governing Body, comprising farmers and businessmen, was still involved. What for?

Robert felt bitter. It wasn't as though the school would magically turn back into the place his parents and grandparents were nostalgic about. It was gone. The thought depressed him as much as it angered him. He had been happy there. Most of his friends had been from farming families and the ones who weren't had parents that were still somehow involved in agriculture. All the children were "on the same page," although the literal page seldom held their attention. They were outdoors as often as not. Barefoot and energetic they spent breaks hunting birds with catties—Y-shaped slingshots strung with tire tube rubber—fishing or catching frogs in the school dam or generally getting up to inventive mischief. There never seemed to be a dull moment, a boring day.

He hoped he had forged friendships that would last a lifetime and he resented the fact that those friends were now prematurely scattered to the winds. It was difficult to keep in touch. Some had even been sent to different provinces and were only ever around for the Christmas and winter holidays. Edward didn't get to experience any of that. And his future children? What would it be like for them? Plans would have to be made.

Perhaps a sort of collectivized homeschooling . . . ?

He sighed again. One thing was as sure as nuts. He wouldn't be rushing off to town to mediate yet another bullshit "racial incident." He felt himself old enough to tell his parents not to bother. But, while they hadn't punished him for his cheek, they hadn't taken his advice. Duty had called them away. He wondered what it would be this time. What would have set off the permanently offended, the fragile thin-skinned "learners"? What would it take to smooth things over?

"Not my *ndaba*," he said out loud and turned towards the house. He had promised to help Elizabeth in the kitchen and Edward needed persuading to get into the bath.

*   *   *

He felt it, before he heard it. In a matter of seconds, he was wide awake. Something was wrong. Something, *someone*, was out there—in the dark, moving. He rolled out of bed and onto his feet in a single fluid cat-like motion. He cocked his head towards the window and listened. Silence. A silence that seemed to conceal something. And then he heard it, properly this time—not just intuitively. A low scrape and a sort of rattle. He cursed under his breath. *They were trying to break a lock. But which one? The rattle . . . a chain . . . The cowshed? The workshop? Where the hell were the dogs?*

Robert moved along the passage and into the lounge. He paused to listen. He could hear the rattle again. Then it stopped. His breath suddenly caught in his throat. *He was not alone.* He willed himself to breathe out noiselessly. Goosebumps spread up his arms and shoulders. A presence emanated from the darkest part of the room. *He was not alone.* He stared until his eyes burned and ran his fingers across the bar counter that separated the lounge from his father's little pub. His hands closed around a solid, heavy object. He knew it, this piece of stone. It was a chunk of fossilized wood that his parents had brought back from Namibia before he was even born. It would have to do. He gripped it tightly and hoped his opponent was less impressively armed. His entire body tightened and

216

converged on the makeshift club in his hand while his senses stretched into the shadows, probing. "Robert?" the darkness whispered at him. It was quiet and reedy but seemed at that moment to be deafening. The tension dissipated in a sudden spasm and he dropped the rock. A wash of relief suffused him. "Edward? What the hell are you doing here?"

"There's someone out there," his brother replied.

They moved closer to the window and strained their ears. It was there again. *Scrape. Rattle.* Robert put his hand on Edward's shoulder and led him quietly out of the room and into the kitchen. They spoke in low tones. The dogs must have been poisoned. It would be up to them. They would have to act now. Mum and Dad were spending the night with friends in town. The meeting had gone on too long. Robert had suggested they stay, decompress; assured them that he would look after his siblings. He felt gratified that they had taken his advice. He sensed that his brother knew what was expected.

Silently they moved along the passage to their parents' room. From the wardrobe Robert extracted a shotgun and a revolver. From a bedside table he lifted a heavy torch. He handed torch and revolver to Edward and crept into Elizabeth's room. She too was awake and was clutching the hand-held farm radio and a cellphone in tense hands. She looked up at Robert with wide eyes. He shook his head and held his finger to his lips. The three of them conferred in low sibilant whispers. She knew what to do, whom to contact and locked herself in. Robert cycled a cartridge into the chamber and checked the safety on the shotgun. Then the boys sneaked out through the back door.

The night was surprisingly warm and yet they felt a chill as they left the house. They carefully and noiselessly circled round the house to come up behind the workshop and the cowshed. They paused. There was no sign of the dogs. They knew what that meant. Robert felt his anger rise. *Scrape. Scrape. Rattle.* It was coming from the workshop. Between them and the building lay a vegetable garden planted to potatoes. There were some dried stalks of maize too. That would give them cover. Although cloud hid the moon it was not as dark as it had seemed before. They moved across the open area stooped low and found themselves up against the maize. Now the sound was loud and unmistakable. They had clearly not been heard themselves. The intruders were too busy—*scrape! rattle!*—to have noticed them. It seemed as though they were having trouble sawing through the reinforced steel of the chain.

Robert looked at his brother who was steadying the revolver on the wrist that held the torch. He slid the safety off and curled the tip of his index finger onto the trigger. He nodded and Edward turned on the torch. As the burst of light exploded ahead of them, everything seemed to happen all at once.

Afterwards, it appeared that everything had happened in slow motion. The scraping stopped instantly, the rattling rose to a crescendo as a wall of spikes, black-and-white rose towards them from far closer than they had expected. They had both been so focused on the workshop door that they had been staring over the potato field and it was from there that the intruder rushed them. At full speed, in reverse. Robert pulled the trigger, sending a blast of buckshot through the workshop door. Edward dropped the torch but thankfully resisted the urge to fire the revolver. In the crazily dancing light of the rolling flashlight they saw their adversary, disturbed by the shot roaring overhead, turn and make a run for it. They caught a glimpse of a little piggy eye, a determined expression and a cavalcade of quills as the potato thief made good his escape. Robert reached down to retrieve the pump-action and winced. A number of quills had pierced his forearms. He heard Edward swear and saw him gingerly fingering an array of spikes bristling from his thigh. Robert laughed involuntarily. It was a good thing his brother had turned instinctively at the last minute. *One wouldn't want a load of the pretty spikes boring through the crotch.* Edward seemed to understand and grinned broadly. It was at this moment that two large, boisterous Rhodesian Ridgebacks and a wire-haired terrier turned up. The boys cuffed them gently, pleased to see them in spite of their dereliction of duty. The dogs had obviously heard the scrape of holes being dug, the rattle of quills and known exactly what was going on. They had then, rather wisely, decided that caution was the better part of canine velour.

Robert firmly grasped his brother's shoulder and turned him back towards the house. They'd have to get Elizabeth to call in the all-clear before the farm watch was at the gate. They had done their duty and, though slightly punctured, had at least manfully saved Mum's potatoes. Behind them a scattering of porcupine quills, black-and-white gleamed in the newly returned moon's light.

Lepanto, 1571

Nick Griffin

The wind had dropped after midnight, leaving the sea calm, flat and grey as beaten lead in the cold light of a moon waxing towards full. Here and there the still water caught the glow of a lantern from one of the galleys, scattered all across the wide bay where the Holy League fleet was at anchor.

More than two hundred ships, waiting out the last few hours before the battle every captain had told the men would decide the fate not only of Christendom, but their own families.

The men aboard the Santa Catalina were silent now, or close to it. Some—the oldest of old hands and exhausted new oarsmen—snored. A few spoke together in hushed voices, most sat or lay silent, stomachs churning as their minds kept returning to visions of the horrors the day would quickly bring.

Somewhere out there to the east lay an even bigger host of warships: The gigantic fleet put together by Selim the Sot, the drunkard son of Suleiman, who the Turks called "Magnificent" and despairing Christians had called a blood- soaked monster.

It was now more than a year since the young Ottoman Sultan had unleashed his navy on Cyprus, where the Muslim horde they carried to war slaughtered scores of thousands of Christians. Every man on the Catalina had heard the lurid accounts of the horror. Fear and the thirst for vengeance vied to keep them awake.

It was the same on all the other Spanish, papal and city state ships. If the rumors were true, the new day would decide whether Cyprus would be avenged, or whether the Turkish infidels would turn the Mediterranean into a Mohammadan lake and fill it with the blood of every Christian still living on its shores.

Word was that the Sultan himself had sworn to raze Rome itself to the ground. The Spaniards and southern Italians especially knew exactly what another Mohammadan victory would mean back home.

On the deck of this Spanish galley, a small group of men huddled beneath a canvas awning stretched between the gunwale and the mainmast. They sat close against the chill of the October night, their backs pressed to crates of shot and coiled lines.

The smell of the sea, tar, and old sweat clung to everything. Pedro clutched his woolen cloak tighter about him and shifted on the smooth-worn planks of the deck. He was a soldier, not a sailor, from the mountains, not the coast, but he had already grown accustomed to life at sea.

Partly to keep warm, partly to be ready for action, each man was already wearing his brigandine. The metal plates sewn between the rough wool outer and the scratchy linen inner weren't exactly comfortable, but the weight was reassuring and it was better than having your teeth chatter and the other think you were shivering from fear.

Their helmets—some morions, others simple iron caps—sat beside them, ready. They were *infantería de galera*, supposedly seasoned shipborne soldiers trained to fight on cramped, blood-slicked decks or storm the narrow streets of enemy ports with sword and pike.

Pedro's own steel cap sat heavy in his lap, his short boarding sword hung from a wide leather belt alongside a dagger. He wasn't seasoned at all; the only blood he had seen at sea was on the backs of the men flogged for infringing the iron discipline of the fleet.

"Cold, lad?" came a voice beside him.

Pedro looked up. Martin, they called him. No one knew if it was his real name. Whispers had it that he had killed his wife and another man, and joined the *infantería* to disappear, but no one dared to ask him if this was true. Martin was as wiry as his temper was short. Leather-skinned, his hair the color of ash, with a beard to match. He'd been rowing and fighting since before Pedro was born, but there wasn't a scar on his face.

"Don't be scared of a man with scars," he had told Pedro one evening, when a saved-up wine ration had briefly put him in a kindly mood. "Worry about

meeting the man who gave them to him."

Was he cold? "No, I mean—yes. A little. Not too much."

Martin chuckled softly. "Your cloak's as thin as my patience." A long pause.

"Wish you were back in the hills tonight?"

"Guadix," said Pedro, absent-mindedly hearing the question as a query as to where he came from. "Near the Sierra."

"No mountains here. Though we'll be scrambling over piles of spilled guts and severed heads in a few hours. Maybe one of your arms or legs. Or your cock."

There was a low murmur of laughter. The little band sat in the half-light like ghosts, faces etched with toil, eyes gleaming in the glow of the charcoal in the small brazier between them.

"Leave the boy alone," said Esteban, a broad-shouldered Galician with scarred knuckles and a voice like gravel under nailed boots.

"He's tough enough," sneered Martin. "He's seen more battle at home than plenty of men out there tonight. The Morisco revolt was no child's tale."

Pedro nodded, remembering it vividly: the night his uncle's house burned, the screams in the gorge, the injured rebel he'd finished off in a red-mist madness of terror, grief and boundless hate.

"Still, this is different," said Juan, a lanky Catalan musketeer, who kept his beard tidy, his boots polished and his weapon spotless. He flicked his fingers toward the eastern sky, where there was perhaps a hint of false dawn. "That's where they'll come from. And it'll be like nothing you've ever seen. They were fighting treacherous peasants in Granada, not Janissaries."

Martin spat. "Janissaries. They're tough. Christian flesh and blood, with the damned souls of infidels. But slash their bellies and they spill their guts and squeal like the pigs they really are."

Pedro said nothing. He'd sharpened his sword three times that evening, then said his prayers twice. And still the fear gnawed his innards.

Silence fell again. Someone stirred the embers with a stick. Sparks danced upward like souls flying up to heaven and judgement.

"Were you snoring, or did you see it?" Martin asked suddenly. Pedro frowned. "See what?"

"The comet," said Esteban. "Last night. Split the sky like the edge of a blade."

Juan crossed himself. "It was no comet. It was a sign. The tail forked in three, like the Trinity."

Martín spat into the brazier. "Then let's hope that's how we fight— three parts, one cause. If the grand Almirantes don't work together, this will be another Los Gelves and we'll all be feeding the fish by next nightfall."

No one argued. They knew it was true; any weakness or mistakes and the Turks and Moors would smash this, the last Christian fleet, as they had destroyed so many ships off the coast of Tunisia a decade earlier. Even the Genoese and Venetians had kept their quarrels in check these last two days, knowing what lay ahead.

Pedro swallowed, and strove to keep his voice steady and low. "Do you think we can win?"

Martín leaned back and scratched his chin. The fire glow just showed the angles of his face, like an old carving on a church wall by candlelight. "Lad, I've seen battles lost that we should've won, and battles won by fools with luck and saints on their side. But this . . . this is different."

He pointed toward the blackness where the Ottoman fleet waited.

"They've got more ships. More men." He gave a sour chuckle. "But they're stretched thin. And they think we'll scatter. They don't reckon on us standing fast. Not the Venetians. Not the Pope's men. And certainly not Spain."

He paused, then added, more quietly, "And they don't reckon on the fury that burns in this fleet. Not after Cyprus."

A hush settled again. A faint gust of breeze came from the west, where the outline of the coast showed as a darker line higher than the horizon. A light gust, a mere hint of a night-time land breeze, stirred the sea. The ripples slapped gently on the hull, but nothing else broke the silence. Even the galley seemed to have stopped its incessant creaking.

Pedro had heard the stories, like everyone. Of Nicosia, where the defenders had been slaughtered. Of Famagusta, where they'd surrendered under promise of mercy—and been butchered. Of Bragadino, skinned alive and stuffed for a trophy. Of the girls hauled off to slavery. Of the dozens of boys who died to make one eunuch to sell in the market in occupied Constantinople.

Of how Joseph Nasi, the Sultan's advisor, moneybags and purveyor of fine wine, had manipulated his drunken master into slaughtering the Christians of Cyprus, in order to have the empty land for his own tribe of Christ-killing infidels.

He thought of the village priest who'd wept as he gave him absolution, and of his mother's pale face when he boarded the galley in Málaga. Then of his father, his eyes gouged out and throat slit at the very start of the Morisco rising.

Esteban broke the silence. "They think they can do the same to our people, one port at a time."

Juan nodded. "Christ's blood. That's what we're here to stop."

Pedro felt a strange calm fall over him. These men, weathered and foul- mouthed and scarred, were not frightened. Or if they were, they carried it as a familiar burden, one to which they would never admit. He only had to do the same.

Martin, still gazing out into the darkness, which was now something less than dark, spoke again. "If not us, then who?"

It wasn't meant to be profound. He said it as if he were commenting on the weather. But it struck Pedro hard. He sat still, the words repeating in his head.

If not us, then who? Then another question sprang up unbidden to join it. "If not today, when?"

The brazier hissed as Juan tossed in a scrap of salted cod skin he'd spotted on the deck in the now fast-growing light. Smoke curled upwards. Normally, the smell would have made Pedro hungry, but not now.

Esteban reached into the neck of his brigandine and pulled something out. "You must take this," he said, holding it out to Pedro.

Pedro blinked and stared hard to confirm what it was. A little wooden cross, which he'd seen the man take out and kiss when an autumn storm had hit them a few days earlier. He'd seen then that it was darkened with age and sweat.

"But it's yours. You need . . ."

"An old soldier gave it to me just before we sailed to relieve Malta. It's brought me through worse than a scuffle on the briny. You wear it today. Pray with it. Fight with it."

Pedro took it, clumsy with surprise. The little cross was warm from Esteban's chest.

"Thank you," he whispered, dropping his head lest the others see the tears in his eyes.

"Don't thank me yet," Esteban muttered. "Just give it back tonight."

Martin gave a low snort. "Stupid boy! He's planning to die gloriously. I, on the other hand, intend to crawl back to Cartagena, drunk, and find myself two plump, talented, whores."

Laughter again. Softer this time. Not because the joke was better, but because, in their own very different ways, they were all picturing the same things: return, home, and a future.

A bell clanged across the water. Then another. And another. The bell of their own ship answered. The watch changed; cold, weary men grumbling in the night. The stars wheeled slightly in the sky and the moon sank even further towards the west. The brazier was dying now, the warmth ebbing and the glow fading in the growing light of this most dreadful day.

Footsteps approached. A young voice, sharper than needed, rang out from beside the mast.

"*¡Carajo!* What in God's name is this lousy mess? Who tied a line across the deck like that? Get it clear, you fools. Now. And that awning

—down. You want men breaking their Goddamned legs before the Turks so much as show themselves? If we had time, I'd have you flogged."

The group stiffened. The voice belonged to the Alférez, barely older than Pedro, his breastplate already buckled, his tone wavering between command and fear. A green boy, but a green boy who could have a man whipped half to death for a hint of defiance, or for hesitating to obey some damn-fool order.

He stepped closer, spotted the dying brazier, and swore again. "*¡Hostia!* And put that bloody fire out—do you want us to go up in smoke before we even weigh anchor?"

"Someone can't sleep," muttered Martin, though he was careful to do so low enough that he wouldn't be heard. "Louse-ridden pup."

Juan smirked and began folding back the awning. Esteban moved to untie the rope and coil it away into his knapsack. No one complained. But, all too soon, the job was done and each was left still and alone with his thoughts. Juan leant against the mast, the others sat down again, though no-one bothered to lie down and go back to trying or pretending to sleep.

Out over the bay, trumpets sounded. Drum beats began to float over the water. From below deck came the first crack and creak of timber: the groan of men shifting in the rowing benches, and the muffled voice of an overseer.

A command rang out. From the bow came creaking of the windlass and rattling of chain on the deck as the anchor was hauled up. A rope hissed across wet wood. Then another shout of command, followed by a powerful drum beat. The ship lurched forward.

The drum beat again, and again. Slow at first, then faster. The Santa Catalina trembled as the oars dipped and pulled. They were under way.

The whole fleet was, the noise spreading like a waking city. Across the bay, sails began to shake out where the wind allowed it. Not many —not yet.

Galley sails, with their great lateen yards, could move these mighty warships at a seemingly irresistible speed. Once the sea breeze picked up later in the day, it surely would again, but for now the power had to come from the banks of oars.

Pedro sought to calm his churning guts with the thought that, however bad it was to be a soldier, it was better than being a convict down below the deck, chained to an oar, governed by a whip, and doomed to drown like an unwanted kitten in a sack if an Ottoman ram caught the Catalina amidships. He shuddered, and gripped his sword for reassurance that he did at least have a hand in his own fate.

The huge Venetian galleasses further out to sea were raising their spars in the hope of catching a breeze. The great masts on the Real, Don John's flagship, loomed above the others, but the flags at their mastheads barely moved. The crosses under which her crew would fight and die were still hidden from view.

Pedro looked out with growing awe. He could make out more ships every moment as morning put the last stars to flight. Their hulls, dark in the half- light, began to show flashes of color: red and gold—the colors of their Spain—then green and white, with heraldic beasts on painted shields and streamers. The sea reflected the pageantry in broken shards. Banks of oars rose and fell in perfect rhythm.

They were going to war. But, for now, the action was for the oarsmen. All the soldiers could do was to wait. Or to saunter up to the heads and squat over the holes over the sea, pretending that it was just a matter of morning routine, rather than an urgent need as their guts turned to water.

Then they stood in their little knots of special comradeship, stretching aching limbs and rubbing their arms. Pedro remained sitting, the cross in his hand. Martín stayed beside him.

Eventually, Pedro spoke again. "Were you afraid? In your first battle?"

Martín didn't answer at once. Then, softly: "I pissed myself halfway to the boarding rope."

Pedro grinned despite himself.

"But I went over," Martin added. "And I'll do it again today. And you will too. There's nothing wrong with being scared. A man's not a coward because he's frightened, but only if he lets fear unman him. Which you won't, even if you do shit yourself. Stay close to me. You'll be fine once it starts."

They sat in companionable silence once more. It wasn't just the eastern sky which was light now. It was, indeed, the day.

"Get yourselves ready. Break your fast. Prayers and blessings at the next bell. Sunday mass early today, we've got God's work to do." Even the Alférez sounded reasonable for once and Martin didn't mutter his usual contempt. Instead, he simply stood and stretched his back, joints popping.

"Well, that's that. Time to die, or to earn a little more pay and a bit of extra wine. Remember Cyprus if you want, I'll remember those two plump whores."

Pedro followed him to his feet, hoping that Martin—tough, dauntless Martin—wouldn't see he was trembling. His sword was ready at his side. Esteban's cross was in his hand.

More ships were sliding ahead now, cutting the glassy water like sharp knives through meat. Officers barked orders; the thudding of the drums kept time, the beating giant heart of a fleet which nothing could resist—unless it was the even bigger one which rumor said had been assembled by the Turks.

The infidel fleet, whose masts Pedro was suddenly sure he could make out to the east. Hundreds of them. God, what was he doing here? The boy crossed himself. Martín clapped him on the shoulder.

"Remember Cyprus, lad. And the ones back home. Keep your head low. And your faith high."

Pedro nodded. Took a breath. And eased his sword an inch in its scabbard.

"If not us . . ."

". . . then who?"

Lepanto, Its Consequences—and an age-old question

Our Pedro and his equally nervous comrades represent the 60,000 or more men who served in the fleet mobilized in the Holy League effort to check the rampant aggression of the Ottoman Sultan. Worries about Muslim expansionism had been brought to a head by the invasion of Cyprus, where the Greek defenders and civilians had been massacred by the scores of thousands.

Lepanto, known today as Naupactus, is a coastal town in western Greece, situated on the northern shore of the Gulf of Corinth. It lies near the narrow entrance to the Gulf of Patras, a strategic chokepoint for fleets entering or leaving the eastern Mediterranean.

The Christian fleet which challenged the Turks at Lepanto was made up of some 40,000 oarsmen and sailors. Most were free men, convicts promised freedom, or volunteers. The Ottoman ships were rowed by slaves, including thousands of Christian prisoners.

Pedro would have been one of roughly 25,000 soldiers. Mainly Spanish tercios—pikemen and musketeers—Italian infantry, papal troops, and volunteers from across Europe, they were stationed on the galleys for boarding actions.

The Holy League commanders were so worried about the engagement that, shortly before the fighting began, the order was given to unchain the convicts and arm them, so they could join in the fight to repel Turkish boarding parties.

The clash, on Sunday October 7th, 1571, ended in a decisive victory for the Holy League. The Turks lost 180 of their 250 ships. Christian casualties were about 7,500 dead, while the Ottomans lost an estimated 25,000 to 30,000 men, with 12,000 to 15,000 Christian galley slaves freed.

Most of the Christian dead fell in the Venetian ships, so the chances are that Pedro would have been able to give Estaban back his cross, and that Martin made it back to Cartagena.

All Christendom rejoiced as news of the victory spread. Lepanto marked the end of Ottoman naval dominance in the western Mediterranean. It was the largest naval battle of the age of oared warships, it was a turning point in the history of the Mediterranean— and beyond.

Its long-term importance lay not in territorial change—Cyprus remained lost to the Ottomans—but in the psychological and strategic check it placed on the great Muslim power of the age. The myth of Ottoman supremacy at sea was shattered.

Though the Holy League dissolved soon after, and the Ottomans quickly rebuilt their fleet, they never again attempted large-scale naval offensives into the western Mediterranean. The victory secured Christian control of key sea lanes and gave breathing room to vulnerable states like Venice, the Papal States, and southern Italy.

Had Lepanto gone the other way, the whole of the central Mediterranean would have been at the mercy of the victorious Ottoman fleet. This would not have reversed the Reconquista of Spain, which had been sealed by the crushing of the Morisco revolt, but Malta, Sicily and the coastal settlements of Italy would have been threatened.

More important still, Lepanto gave Europe time. The battle did not end the Ottoman threat, but it stalled its momentum at sea—buying time that Christendom used to transform itself. Over the following century, Christian states—especially Spain, the Dutch Republic, and England—invested in new naval technologies: ocean-going sailing warships, improved artillery, and better logistics.

Europe surged ahead militarily and scientifically, reinforcing the maritime dominance that would shape the early modern world. The Ottomans, by contrast, remained committed to galley warfare and failed to keep pace with Western naval innovation.

Indeed, they fell steadily behind in terms of technology in general. Even the great Ottoman army which besieged Vienna in 1683, relied on artillery supplied by Louis XIV of France, as part of his broader policy of undermining the Habsburgs, his chief rivals.

This reminder of the long-standing problem of elite treachery brings us to the final consequence of the victory won by the courage and sacrifice of the men who fought at Lepanto: It severely weakened the power of Joseph Nasi, who for some years previously had been perhaps the most dangerous enemy of Christendom in general, and Spain and Portugal in particular.

Originally João Mendes, his Portugal-based family had feigned conversion to Christianity and taken the surname Miques. Nasi was a Sephardic Jew who took refuge in Ottoman Constantinople after being expelled from Iberia. He rose to high influence at the Ottoman court, first under Suleiman and later under his son.

Described by contemporaries as "the Sultan's favorite," Nasi harbored a deep hatred not only of the Hapsburgs who had expelled his family from Spain, but also of Venice, which had confiscated some of his aunt's assets and expelled his agents from Cyprus in 1568 when it was discovered that Nasi was plotting with local Jews to bring about an Ottoman takeover.

Nasi saw himself as the future king of Cyprus, which he aimed to turn into a Jewish colony, although both he and his aunt—the hugely wealthy and powerful spice merchant and money-lender Gracia Mendes Nasi—also funded Jewish settlements in Palestine.

Joseph Nasi became notorious across the whole of Catholic Europe as the man behind the invasion of Cyprus. It is also clear from Selim's reaction to the disaster at Lepanto that he had also played a big part in persuading the Sultan to go to war against the Christian alliance which had been brought together by the Pope.

According to a report by Don Cesare Carafa to the Duke of Urbino, Venetian spies had informed him that on learning of the fleet's destruction, Selim had reportedly sighed "so, these treacherous Jews have deceived me!"

Nasi managed to survive the crisis, though on Selim's death three years later his wealth was seized by the new Sultan, Murad III. Nasi was permitted to keep his titles and his pension, but his hopes of establishing a Jewish kingdom in the eastern Mediterranean were gone.

His effort to incite Islam against the hated Christians were not, of course, an isolated quirk. The phenomenon was already more than eight hundred years old, having been seen when Jewish leaders in Spain invited the Moorish invasion and opened the gates of key cities, including the capital, Toledo.

Nor was it to end with Nasi. To give just one example, Dönmeh

Jews—the Islamic equivalent of the fake conversos of Iberia—dominated the so-called Young Turk revolution. This not only overthrew the Ottomans, but also led directly to the 1915 genocide of the Christian Armenians, Greeks and Assyrians. Coming right up to the present day, we see the unholy alliance between Zionists and the Sunni fundamentalists of Al Qaeda and Islamic State.

The uneasy but deadly relationship between fanatics and schemers among the two other "Peoples of the Book" is one of the oldest, though least known, factors in the history of Christendom, Europe and the Near and Middle East.

Fortunately, however, it has always been countered by something even older:

The willingness of young men to stand up to such hatred, and to resist the tyranny and genocidal impulses which it unleashes. It has been seen from the first blows of the Reconquista at Covadonga, through the great victory at Lepanto, the charge that saved Vienna, and on through the liberation revolts and wars which restored freedom and European civilization to the Balkans.

Unlike the Ottoman galley slaves and the kidnapped Christian boys who became brainwashed Janissaries, the vast majority of the defenders of Europe and Christendom at Lepanto were there of their own free will. It was their choice; they volunteered to fight.

Why? A few were no doubt escaping from something even worse; some were surely there for adventure, glory or the hope of personal enrichment. But surely, for most of them, it was the same small but burning question that has motivated freedom fighters and rebels throughout history.

The question that is once again set to become the most important of all as the men of the West face a new version of an ancient peril. "If not us, who?"

The Bridge

Paul Dempsey

That evening, Ilya Nikolayevich had a spectacular dinner at his favorite restaurant, where he went every Saturday, always at the same time. Completely satisfied with his four-course meal (once in two weeks he indulged in a dessert) as well as beer during the meal and brandy afterwards, the man was now walking down the *Leninsky prospekt*, observing the street in the dusk and savoring the memories of the meal.

He started with an exquisite Olivier salad, followed by hot borscht with *pampushky*. His favorite dish of sausages with sauerkraut and potatoes came next—all accompanied by a crisp lager beer. After the main course settled comfortably, Ilya Nikolayevich decided he still had room for a honey cake and some tea. To top it all off in a respectable manner, a glass of brandy called "Old Königsberg" was put on top as a cherry.

Feeling warmed up and braver than usual, Ilya Nikolayevich complimented the waitress, whom he had known since their university days.

"You look wonderful today, Ira," Ilya Nikolayevich said, turning red as a beet.

Ira gave a brief, tired smile, looking at the short, plump man with a bald spot on his head.

"You too," she said coolly and returned to her work.

Ira's smile reminded Ilya Nikolayevich of his magnetic charm— even irresistibility—but he wouldn't act on it this time. He'd liked Ira for years but resolved—after serious consideration—that he would leave her for someone else. She was too old for the man now, with her wrinkles and her tired face, and the same tired hairstyle week after week, month after month. He wanted someone younger, fresher. Still, that smile totally gave away her feelings for him. Ilya Nikolayevich chuckled, remembering it. Indeed, he knew his way around women.

Meanwhile, the man walked down the *Leninsky prospekt*. Half-expecting to see the House of Soviets, he looked up and to the left at the place where it had to stand, gloomy, dead. There was no House of Soviets anymore. Remembering that they had torn it down a few weeks earlier and simultaneously seeing the empty space, Ilya Nikolayevich grinned and felt a pleasant, ticklish feeling in his stomach. He had wanted it brought down for a long time, although in secret, as he did not want to initiate any arguments at work. He knew that the views differed on that matter.

Ilya Nikolayevich stepped on the grey concrete of the enormous Estacade Bridge sprawling over Kant Island, reminding him of the dry crust of bread he had played with when he was a child. Once he pretended it was a bridge for his soldiers to march over, and the adults yelled at him, "Don't play with food!" It was unclear why he couldn't play with it, but Ilya was an obedient boy, so he didn't play with food anymore, and a sensitive boy, so he didn't play with his toy soldiers anymore as well. Sometimes, when there was no one at home, he would open the box with his toys and play a little bit, right in that box, to be able to close it quickly should anyone come home. Most of all he feared to be yelled at, and he feared he might play with the toys in some wrong way again, with someone noticing it, and yelling. But that was long ago.

The concrete of the bridge was full of holes and patches of fresh asphalt, and the cars moved quickly in four lanes, with the tram track in the middle. Years ago, that tram carried Ilya Nikolayevich to the university almost every day. The view from its windows had changed over the years. A new hotel-and-apartment block sprang up on the right bank of the river, reminding one of old German warehouses stamped onto souvenir marzipan bars. As a true native to the city, Ilya Nikolayevich disliked the tourists that had flooded it in the past few years, but personally, he found that warehouse-like building quite agreeable.

On the left side the trees of Kant Island opened into an alley leading toward the cathedral. Ilya Nikolayevich was old enough to remember it being ruined, and later, in his "hungry student years," he watched it being restored out of the tram window, looking like a gingerbread house one could bite the tower off of.

It was getting late, but the bridge was well-lit and the nights were warm, even though it was late September.

"Climatic change, for all you know," Ilya Nikolayevich explained the phenomenon.

There was no one else on the bridge now. Even cars, it seemed, passed less frequently. He recalled that in German times, two smaller bridges and a road had once crossed Kant Island. Now this massive structure spanned it directly, casting a filthy, dark, urine-soaked wasteland beneath—one he had always hated.

He remembered when his classmates had nearly tossed him into the Pregolya there.

"Ilyuh, there's a secret German bunker under the water. You need to explore it!" they had laughed, dangling him halfway over the edge. A passerby—an old man with a thick walking cane—had intervened, threatening to shove the cane up their asses. The boys scattered.

"You better get yourself a thing like this," the old man told Ilya. "Never know when you'll need it."

Ilya Nikolayevich shook his head. Sour memories. He wanted nothing to do with them.

Now, beneath his feet, the Pregolya flowed—its waters murky, half-lit by the bridge's orange sodium lamps. The surface stirred in all directions, as if the river couldn't decide on a course. On its bank stood the DKM, a stately old building with lions at the entrance. It had been a stock exchange in German times, a concert venue in the Soviet era, and now served as an art gallery.

He had been to an exhibition there dedicated to the siege and fall of Königsberg. There were many photos from that time and a small room deep down in the building where they played the historical footage. Ilya Nikolayevich must have spent several hours there—the room was so quiet, secluded, as if buried in the basement of the gallery. It felt nice being there, just the siege footage, old brick, dim yellow light, stillness, and him, Ilya Nikolayevich.

The man went on, now descending from the bridge. On the left there was a newly-built park square with evergreen trees and small artificial hills—deserted at this hour. On the right, a construction site with a tall crane towering over it.

"New blocks of flats, no doubt," Ilya Nikolayevich thought disgruntledly. He resented the steady stream of people from all over Russia moving to his city. The man would like it to be smaller, quieter, safer, like he remembered it from his childhood.

Suddenly, Ilya Nikolayevich heard a voice.

"What are you doing?"

It was the voice of a young woman. It came from under the bridge, some ten meters below the place he was standing on. There the square ended in a dark underpass leading to the construction site.

"Go away!" the girl screamed.

Ilya Nikolayevich stopped and listened intensely. He didn't want to look.

"Come here, don't be afraid." That was a man's voice.

"Help!"

Girl again, now muffled. There were sounds of a fight.

"What can that be?" Ilya Nikolayevich thought. He knew what that could be but stopped himself from making conclusions to not have to. . . . He didn't have to. He was just a man crossing a bridge. He could just continue walking.

There were sounds of a struggle—now on the ground, it seemed. The girl screamed, briefly. Ilya Nikolayevich almost said "Quiet" out loud. He wanted nothing to be happening. He wanted to tell himself, *Oh, it's just nothing.* The sounds from the girl again became muffled, less intense now.

"Couples sometimes fight. They sure do. They must be a couple," the man told himself, but he didn't believe it.

He heard the man under the bridge panting and growling. There was a rustle. Ilya Nikolayevich didn't want to recognize it but he recognized the faint rustle of fabric—the noise jeans made when someone undressed, only louder. The fabric rustled three times. "Waist, knees, and legs," the back of his mind told him.

"I could intervene, but by the time I run down the bridge it might be over, and if it's just a couple fighting, I'll look a fool. I could shout, but I have no voice for it—they won't hear me over the cars. Call the police? And say what? They'd laugh. Just noise under the bridge. Or I could fight him, but I don't run—I haven't run since childhood—and he'd beat me easily. And the laws—so easy to breach, so easy to land in prison for years. I've never fought in my life. Better to believe it's nothing. Pure imagination, like the noises in the kitchen when I was alone at home. Tomorrow I'll laugh at myself," Ilya Nikolayevich thought in just half a second.

He heard short muffled sobs and rhythmic thrusts. There were no cars to drown out the sounds. Another half-second—and he continued walking down the bridge, quickly, down the road, then across the road, and home by a different, lengthier way, to get farther from the bridge, to not hear it, to not know.

"That was nothing. Just nothing. Nothing. Laugh at myself tomorrow," he kept repeating to himself over and over again.

Ilya Nikolayevich moved farther from the bridge. Cars passed. Stop lights blinked. Some people walked by occasionally. It was easier now to become one with them, the people, the cars, the blinking stop lights —to walk in their shade, pretending to be part of that sane, ordinary, Saturday-night life, and not the other life—that under the bridge.

At home, Ilya Nikolayevich went to bed at once, without undressing, and shivered himself to sleep under as many blankets as he could find.

*   *   *

The morning came. It was sunny. Ilya Nikolayevich woke up.

Picking up his phone, he opened the first local news website he could find. His worst fears, which he knew would get confirmed but hoped they wouldn't, got confirmed. Eighteen-year–old girl. Forty-year-old man. Father of two children. Two children. Ilya Nikolayevich broke into tears for the first time since childhood. It seemed to the man that such things couldn't happen, must not happen and therefore could not happen, but there it happened and it happened in his presence and he had to do something, but he hadn't ever done anything—how could they demand he did something now? No one demanded anything from him, but Ilya Nikolayevich felt that he had obligations he did not know about, and he failed miserably, not just the evening before, but in life.

Ilya Nikolayevich hurried out of his house into the sun-filled, as if mocking, street. He took the taxi. When the car was crossing the bridge, he shut his eyes very firmly. First he went to the theater. The taxi driver frowned—he didn't want to wait for the man.

"Pay you double. Wait," Ilya Nikolayevich said.

The man was back in five minutes, and the taxi carried on. In five minutes, finally, he arrived at the restaurant, which had just opened. In the cool depths of the main hall, the man saw Ira, who was very pretty with her careless (was it careless?) bun, smiling, talking with another waitress. She did not expect to see him.

"What a surprise," Ira said, her smile shining at him now. "I never saw you at this time of day."

"I'm sorry, Ira," Ilya Nikolayevich said, not knowing what he was asking forgiveness for. "I'm so sorry. I like you. Do please come with me to the theater, it's going to be good. I know. I have two tickets. Here."

"Erm, yes, I guess. It's rather unexpected . . . I never thought. . . . Is it you?" Ira said, her cheeks turning red.

*　　*　　*

Ilya Nikolayevich had another place he had to go that day. The police station was located on the first floor of a rather dilapidated

German building. The man entered it quickly, the air straining his lungs.

"I would like to report a crime!" Ilya Nikolayevich said outright, in a high-pitched voice.

"I'm just a security guard," said the old man at the entrance, baffled.

"Who can I talk to?"

"Sergeant Nepokoyev, I guess."

"Where can I meet him?"

"Further down the hall, to the right. Room 1."

Ilya Nikolayevich knocked on the door and opened it at once. A short, stout, balding man by the table raised his tired eyes at the man.

"Yes?" he said.

"I would like to report a crime." "What crime?"

"I was on the Estacade Bridge yesterday and I heard what was going on and I didn't call you. I didn't do anything. I just went home."

"Why?"

"I was afraid."

"Of what?"

"I don't know."

"Did you see it all happen?"

"No, I only heard it."

"Leave your details and go away, you idiot. You'll be a witness. We'll call you. Think about what you have—haven't—done. Happens ever again—I'll hold you responsible."

"It will never happen again."

"It better not."

Ilya Nikolayevich closed the door and left his details with the secretary in Room 8. Everything took much less time than he had thought it would—it was even, in a way, unsatisfactory. When he was back in the street, Ilya Nikolayevich looked around. For a few seconds, he observed the yet green trees and overgrown grass and crumbling plaster on the building across the road. Then the thoughts entered his mind. Painful, breath-taking. He felt as if he would not be able to hold them in his head—they would rip it open, killing him. The man wondered if they would ever go away. He didn't know. Gasping, he went down the street, to the bus stop, to go home. But his flat now lacked walls—he knew it. When he gets there, he would find it entirely transparent, penetrable. *And that room in the art gallery?* Ilya Nikolayevich asked himself. That would be even worse, he felt, being there alone, buried there under the ground with those thoughts. He had nowhere to go now, nowhere to hide. Suddenly, the air gained gravity. The city pulsated with blood.

Corn and Circumstance

Peter J. Peckinpah

PART 1: THE BEGINNINGS OF THE END

The half-light of morning gave way to a sherbet hue; how he wished to stay in, comforted by his bed for two more hours. Not one, but two.

Six days a week he worked a double-header, two jobs to support two kids. He thanked his lucky stars he had but only one wife. Her side of the bed was empty. She was about downstairs, so with a groan he propelled himself upwards and sat hugging his knees, gazing out the window upon an untidy back patio. *Chores, so many chores. So much wasted space.* With a grunted lurch he launched out of bed and proceeded to shower while fried potatoes wafted up from the kitchen. Not all was bad.

He patted his hair down with a towel soaked with hot water. Droplets fell onto his shirt, wet splotches on brown cotton. Below, Malcolm was crying, but he seemed to be the only one making noise. Willy was still sleeping, which was a dream come true. His nightmares had kept everyone up for months. Running down the stairs he welcomed Sara with a kiss and softly took the fussing Malcolm from her arms.

"Good morning, love," he drawled, smooching on her cheek again. The baby was squealing and squirmy, but after holding him for a few minutes in between gulps of coffee, the little man resembled his father more and more, and a general silence reigned in the household, punctuated only by gasps from the coffee machine as it wheezed through its second oblation that morning, and hisses from the pan as grease bounced off mounds of potatoes.

Joseph's eyes were still a bit murky, his contact prescription was outdated, and a new appointment would charge too much, so he'd have to make due by stretching out the remaining pairs over the remainder of the year, or by returning to glasses. Even then, the pile of opened mail was quite visibly clear, a veritable litany of expenses and deadlines: electrical bills, property taxes, water taxes, heating and air-conditioning, storage space, boat storage, the mortgage . . .

Only two rays of light penetrated that awful mound of malevolence. Today, he was quitting his main job. Secondly, potatoes and another round of coffee were placed in front of him. It was, of course, a bland blend, hardly worth buying, and his gut hated him after he drank it. However, Malcolm was in his arms, William still lay asleep in bed, and Sara, depleted yet loving, was more than enough to counterbalance the effects of a troubled gut. He was only frustrated he had clung on as long as he had to rat races and contests of appearances leading headlong into an early death of joyless apathy.

He handed Malcolm over to Sara and slouched against the chair with a loud sigh.

"We're gonna have to tighten the belt. We can start by selling the boat. Clean out the storage unit in a couple of days, sell the ATV." He paused to shovel a freighter of taters into his mouth, happy to take his time with such measures, "Besides that, not much else we can do to keep costs down. It's not as if we eat out."

"Not even on our anniversary." Her eyes were drifting off onto the ground. She had said it so resignedly.

"Hey, Sara, we don't have to go through with this. I don't have to quit today." She met his gaze across the table and the fires of devotion were lit in her eyes.

"Joey, the kids don't care how many jobs you work, how much you make, but they're affected when you're gone too long. When you're here, they want to avoid you. It's taken courage even for me some days, the moods you bring into the house."

They sat in silence, eating and thinking of solutions to issues they once had believed to be essential in the conquest of life. After a while, Sara rose and placed Malcolm in the crib, his little fingers toying with dangling stars hanging above him. Joseph finished breakfast, said his grace after meals, wiped his face, washed his hands, and kissed his wife goodbye.

"It's D-Day, dear! Say a prayer it all works out." He gave her a toothsome smile and left for work. "Someone's excited," Sara murmured to herself. She prayed all that day.

*   *   *

Beads of salty sweat snaked and plopped from his knitted brow, onto boxes of various shapes and sizes. The conveyor belt jolted and traveled with an obscene reliability. Many had been the day he had wished, let alone prayed, for a jam or a malfunction, but the thing was more reliable than those working it. But today a smile was on his face, and the floor manager, Desh, had noticed. Desh was a frowning man, who officiated above them in a well-cooled room of white walls and mini-fridges. To know him, was to hate him; to hate him was a sacrosanct bylaw for the sorting crew. Although he was efficient, nevertheless it was efficiency for efficiency's sake; personal emergencies for his underlings were denied with bitter zeal. He also disliked supervisors who mingled and assisted with the floor caste. By those standards, Joseph was not winning any employee of the month bonus.

But today, Joseph was smiling for Desh, at Desh, into Desh. The rest of his crew were too busy sorting the boxes by size into trucks to even notice the act of resistance from their supervisor. To them, he was mister happy-go-lucky, and to work with him made their crippling workplace hate abideable for a few hours.

The hours crawled by, and the clock read 2:30 p.m. They were ahead of schedule, trucks were full, and the break had been due half an hour earlier, yet still, they were driven on. No break bell had rung. *Why not give it a go? It's your last day.* Joseph's mind was a whirligig of possibilities. *Should I turn in my resignation quietly, normally, or should I punch Desh and vandalize his desk with today's breakfast, leave without a word, and never come back?* Regardless, he was never coming back.

When the shift ended, Joseph nearly bolted up the stairs, backpack in hand, locker cleared and cleaned. Desh was waiting, and so was his second commute.

*   *   *

He whistled happily, a half-organic creation mixed with a bastardized church hymn. He hadn't even bothered with putting in his 2 weeks' notice. Loyalty to Desh? He had quit on the spot. Traffic was now light, and the afternoon sun was waxing. The better job awaited, the one he was keeping. He had to drive a distance for it, but these people weren't the Deshes' of the world, but scions of polite society, and his personal friends as well.

It took him thirty minutes to reach the Butler Estate, but when he did, he found they had yet to return from Vancouver, only the shed keys under the tiger lily pot remained. It was a vast property of nearly five hundred acres, mostly covered by pine pasture, with some clearings for a fire pit, several gardens, a miniature orchard of struggling quality, and a sumptuous patio. The pasture areas were fenced off for the thirty head of cattle grazing thereupon, kept here to avoid the noose of property tax. It was comforting to find that loopholes existed for law-abiding folks and not just for criminals.

He unlocked the shed, grabbed the chainsaw, oil, and gas, and then foisted himself upon the Kubota tractor and was off to eradicate a grove of pines that the bark beetles had killed. He worked till an hour after dark and found himself back on the road home after recording his hours. Starting tomorrow, this would be his full-time duty. Ed and Vera were beautiful people, allowing him to keep his Angus cattle here. He almost winced as he saw them mournfully munching on the drying grass. *So scrawny. That'll change soon.*

It was past ten when he arrived home and stepped out of his sedan. Sara's jeep was leaking oil again. Now he should have the time to finally fix that. No one was out and about in the whole neighborhood, but he could see several TVs through windows flashing frenetic figures of various shows and programs. He remembered ruefully when his friends had played basketball with him by the light of the moon until midnight during the summer.

His thoughts happily evaporated by the opening of the front door and the wheezing of the slammed screen.

"Dad! Mommy, Dad's home!" William came at him at an impressive pace for such little legs, jumping into his outstretched arms.

"Well good evening my little prince," Joseph said as he held his son and spun him in his arms. "Past your bedtime, but the king is home, and he is happy. Want lemonade?"

"Yes!" William screamed. Joseph put him down and the pajamaed five-year-old pranced around him as his father strode through the front door. Sara was in the kitchen bothering a frying pan of chicken, singing to Gordon Lightfoot.

"Hullo beautiful!" He threw his backpack with gusto down upon the floor and kissed her face.

"Now, now, brown cow, you smell like one," Sara laughed, "wait . . . did you do IT?" Joseph nodded and tapped her nose playfully before continuing.

"Yes, I am Desh-less, footloose, fun, and fancy-free. We are in motion dear, or free fall. Tell you all about it in a jiffy. I'm gonna wash up real quick and be down in a few minutes."

"I am timing you, mister! We have a big day tomorrow. I borrowed the rototiller from the Brooke's. We are all set."

"Halleluiah! Okay, I'll be right down." He ran upstairs and found himself singing along to the music player down below as he tore off sweaty clothes and threw himself into the shower, not minding that it was cold. He leaned against the shower wall and closed his eyes, sending up a prayer of thanksgiving for how easy the most dreaded part of the day had been. Still, greater work lay ahead, and they hadn't tried living on a single job income since they had dated. Tomorrow was the beginning of things, a trimming of the budget, financial burdens to unload, and a lawn to tear up.

PART 2: FIRSTFRUITS

The soil had been churned, and bits and bobs of mangled grass were still sticking out like the ragged survivors of an artillery barrage. The rototiller had done its work well, and he had made sure to clean it off and fill its tank back up before returning it to Josh. He remembered the look of shock and then dawning approval when Josh realized what he had done with his equipment.

"You did what with it? I thought you told me it was for a small garden."

"Well, the lawn is small, so I tore up the entire backyard."

"All of it? What? Why?"

"What good does it do, Josh? How many people complain when grass gets slightly brown? That's why they fertilize it and poke holes in it—so it breathes better. It gets more doctoring than most people can afford for themselves! I quit at UPS, and the budget is tightening now, so we are growing as much food as we can. We are even using hay bales with fish emulsion for the tomatoes. Sara planted the Czechoslovakian Reds already on the sides of the house."

"So you're putting in a farm? What's next? Chickens and pigs?"

"First two, yes, but no pigs. Too far. I've lived next to pig farmers before. Well, anyway, Josh, the lawn is going to host corn. Obviously potatoes, zucchini, squash, carrots, cucumbers, tomatoes, jalapenos for me and my eldest, and a coterie of herbs that Sara's got planned out. We would do the front lawn but the HOA would say something about that."

"Speaking of them—you gotta hear this. I took my tires off my truck last week, and for one day I left them over there by the side of the garage, when one of those busybodies saw them, took a picture, and messaged the neighborhood website insisting we remove them. Do these people have no shame?"

"No, they don't! Neither should we. Our property is our business and there is nothing they can do about mass disobedience. I'm tempted to till up the front yard. Lord knows we'll need more ground."

*   *   *

After he had returned from a full shift on the Butler's estate, husband and wife were sitting by the electric fireplace. He was reading, devouring page after page covering the Reconquista of the Iberian Peninsula and Sara was working on Sudoku. Malcolm was sleeping between them, his three-month-old whisps protruding out from under a white baby beanie. Joseph reached the end of the chapter before she had finished her "brain food."

"Well, I ran the estimate for our future budget while in the truck this afternoon." Sara put down her pencil and furrowed her brow at him.

"So, are we boiling leaves for soup or is it a losing baby weight-style recession?"

"The latter, I hope. With my projected hours, with the storage unit cleared out, with the boat to be sold, and with our shed and dock space soon to be relinquished, we'll be able to tuck away several thousand into savings."

"Oh, that's better than expected. But wait, you haven't finished?"

"Oh, baby I haven't, grocery bills we can manage until we get our first yields out back. Frankly, we have to expect the worst but work for the best here. Cattle alert: the price of feed has gone up, so we'll have to butcher Dutton. Remember him?"

"Yeah, he's the one with the lazy eye, right?"

"Yup. Well, he's getting butchered, and that'll cost us. But that'll be our meat. Anyway, I am lost, where was I? Oh yes . . . expenses. After a few months, we'll be barely cutting even, and lest we forget those two growing boys who eat more than their pop."

247

"And perhaps more soon, God willing, and provided that you're willing?"

He snorted at her challenge.

"God, I love you woman, and I am more than willing."

"Well, hold your horses. Keep business on the brain—for now."

"Right, right. Well, I am planning to eat one meal a day to save us some money. No dissension on my behalf. We're already spending plenty on gas and the essentials, so, If I only eat at dinner, and pack coffee with me for the road before I leave for work, that'll be good. And no more beer, or liquor in general for me unless it's a feast day or some kind of celebration."

"I cannot tell if I married a monk or a puritan, but this is good. So skinny you'll be, wow. Hm, but if this makes you grumpy all the time, you promise me you'll quit?"

"It's only temporary, because when our situation stabilizes, I can scale up the groundskeeping business, and there will be room for a little more splendor and a few more kids in our lives."

"I am proud of you, Joseph. I mean it." He never had learned to handle love bites like these; it was like being tickled to death. "For a time, I was worried. You know that. who you were, the family we were—it wasn't just you. This whole obsession with green lawns, white picket fences, and new vehicles—the so-called American Dream —was hurting us. You can't make that work and live family life the way God intended."

"You can't serve two masters," he whispered.

"You were working two jobs, hardly getting any sleep, yelling at William for merely existing, hardly saying a word to me. What was it you eventually said?"

"Kids don't care about how much you make, how much you work, and how hard it all is, they notice how long dad's gone and they want me to be their dad when I'm home."

"Exactly." Sara reached over and grabbed his hand. "I know it took a sacrifice to admit that and to act upon it. You were on a track at UPS. A few more years, and you'd have been in the managerial caste, pun intended."

"I would rather be homeless than work with a dozen Deshes, let alone under that one. Mom and Dad think I am losing my mind, as do yours, but you know who doesn't? Josh, Ashley, Shaun, and the others. Our generation gets it. There is no surplus waiting for people like us, and if there is, one must sell their soul to get it. And that's not what will get us to heaven, or even to conditions amenable for our people to live holily and wholesomely. Here we stand, a sign of contradiction to the fatted calves of yesteryear and to the unholy hustlers of today."

"Cotton Mather couldn't have said it better himself." He slapped her hand playfully away. "You are an intemperate wench, woman—a sinner in the hands of an angry God."

He lunged from his chair and began chasing her up the stairs, forgetting that her playful screams might awaken the kids.

PART THREE: SCORCHED EARTH

The neighborhood was at war, one which had broken out first on Joseph's, then Josh Brooke's property, then on a few other houses on the cul-de-sac, until finally all around the circuit of the community as if it were gospel truth. Joseph, true to his words, had torn up his front lawn and planted corn. The soil, long fertilized, promised a thick and strong yield for such a small plot. Others, following suit, banded together in rejection of the HOA's rules, giving their moral support, but far more were voicing vituperative disapproval against them and even threats.

"They're complaining about everything," Josh said to Joseph at a block party, pausing for a sip of dark beer.

Joseph eyed him jealously. He remembered that the drinks were free tonight, so he grabbed one and joined him. It was his first in a long while.

"They start with the property values—*as if*. It's always the fogeys and the divorcees saying that crap. Anyone with a functioning family gets the picture, even if they don't want to join us. That takes work, after all."

"Right. Few of us grew up on a farm, but I do not excuse them. The right to complain about food being too expensive does not exist if you can grow it yourself. Nope."

"Get this Joe, in the last meeting the board brought up the 'degradation of community standards and values,' and how this is all because of the transplants from out of state."

"More like the natives who sold us the land willingly with a smile." There were about hundred people at the barbecue, and all of them were crowded onto the sidewalks and street, huddled near portable fire pits and ice chests packed with beverages and sausages. Some were from church, most from the neighborhood. The first stars were twinkling overhead, and the nearby ridgeline was bathed fire-red in the dying light of the departing summer sun, illuminating the Rhode Island Red hens roosting upon their perch in Joseph's pen.

"Andrew Lytle said that a farm is not a place to grow wealthy, it is a place to grow corn. He was right, for his time, I think. But not all of us can move out to where the grass is green and the land is cheap. For the good grass is federally owned and the remaining land is not cheap. So we make do with what we have. We brought the farm to us."

Josh nodded and pointed at him: "And you brought the beef to us. Thank you, Joseph, but most importantly, thank you, Dutton. He sure smells delicious. If only all of us could be so lucky in our friends as you."

"Well, Ed and Vera are fine people. On a more serious note, Josh, we need to move ahead with the election prep. If we can win that board, hell, who knows where we could go with it, we'd be able to plant a co-op farm in the park."

"If."

*   *   *

Josh had said the quiet part out loud. The elections had been close, but most of the people in their neighborhood had voted for the "Save Our Community" slate of candidates. Joseph and Josh had both run and lost. Now, as the first weeks after election day filtered on by, notices, both physical and digital, were arriving by mail to the dissident residential farmers of Glistening Creek Homes.

And to think life had been going well. He had trimmed off twenty-five pounds and was sleeping qualitatively, and enough savings were available to purchase a work van for his upcoming, actualized sole proprietorship. The paperwork had been approved by the state, yet storm clouds loomed overhead. His stand, or, as he sometimes deemed it, his hubris, had placed them all at risk. Fines and penalties were incoming, and behind them the heavy artillery: lawsuits. Back to the Land is a dead and vacuous thing if one has no land to go back to. They would have to lawyer up, and that would cost them. *Was it all worth it?* Doubts persisted, but the family had never been happier. Other allies relayed similar stories. Folks were engaged and interested in maintaining and expanding their gardens. There was even a promise of a neighborhood farmers market springing up in the middle of Glistening Park, next to the volleyball court. It was heartening for him to see that many of his people were steeling their nerves to find tangible means of casting themselves off the hamster wheel.

*   *   *

These thoughts raced through his mind as he parked the tractor under the lean-to and spotted the elderly couple approaching from the main house. They were always smiling, and they had good reason to be. As they got closer, Ed Butler spoke but the meaning was lost in the space between.

"Hello, Butlers!" Joseph shouted. "You caught me just in time. I was nearly about to be off. Dinner is in the oven and big dog's gotta to eat."

"My, you look as thin as a rail. It's good to hear you're still eating at all. We love what you've done to the place, Joe," Ed said with a voice

251

well acquainted with tobacco.

"You get in yesterday?"

"Yes, the city has gone to hell. If I wanted to visit China, I'd go there. I am selling our place there soon. It's a damn shame."

"Ed tells me you're in legal trouble? Vera was not one for small talk, or Vancouver, definitely not small talk about Vancouver.

"Yes ma'am. The HOA is trying to shut us down—or worse, drive us off. We are already being fined, with lawsuits coming next. With the elections lost, the best thing we can do is fight this in court. I've spoken about it with Josh Brooke and Shaun Murray. They're interested in pitching together for a legal defense. We can't just up and leave, but at the same time, it might be more expensive to stay."

"You can't run from this fight, Joe. It'll follow you," Ed said with a sudden feeling. "Many people move to a neighborhood like yours because they want to be around folks that look like and believe as they do, but many are also red diaper-babies or retirees, and most of the times both. They'd disown their own son if it meant one more cruise in the Caribbean."

"Couldn't have said it better myself, Ed."

There was a brief silence between them before Joseph checked his watch.

"I must be going sir. The best part of the day awaits, and it goes quickly whether I'm there to enjoy it or not. Take care, Ed. Goodbye, Vera."

Shaking their hands, he turned to leave.

"Joe, one last little thing." He turned back around and saw their expressions redden with embarrassment as they approached, almost bashfully. "Vera and I discussed something on the ride home. After all, what else do you talk about at our age?"

The couple exchanged glances and Ed fidgeted, a rare display of awkwardness.

"Excuse me? Not sure I exactly follow," Joseph stuttered.

For a moment he thought he was getting let go. A vision of a foreclosure sign on the house and a once verdant garden dried and blasted, of chickens dead and decapitated, of pawned wedding rings, flashed across his mind.

"We have decided to cover the expenses of hiring a lawyer for your imminent legal battle. The best lawyer we can find, except he does not require finding. He's *our* lawyer. And he thinks you have a solid case already. But he will need lots of details, so hide nothing from him."

Joseph could hardly believe his ears and nearly had to steady himself on his guardian angel to keep from tottering over like a felled tree.

"Thanks be to God," he finally sighed, "but I'm not even family, let alone a member of your church. I mean, you—" he trailed off, not knowing if any thanks would suffice for the magnanimity of such kindness.

Vera stepped forward and clasped his hands.

"You can thank us by winning. What else were we going to spend our money on? We could never have children. We didn't know we wanted them before it was too late. Vacation homes cannot fill that void, Joe, but the building of a better future means we leave behind a legacy our grandfathers' grandfathers would be proud of. And that is sufficient for us."

he released his hand, and he almost wept at what he had just heard.

"Now, now," said Ed, "Go home to your wife. Tomorrow he'll be here to discuss the battle plan. Here's his card. His name is Lloyd Reisner, and he has a bone or two to pick with HOAs and diaper doper babies. You'll get a kick. Now get."

*   *   *

The miles sped by under his heavy foot, and as the last familiar right turn into the community loomed expectantly, something caught the corner of his eye. Illuminating the sky were red lights, directly over the position of his house. He nearly rammed the gate—such was the impression of death and violence done upon his family. His fingers quickly tapped the code on the keys, and with a chime, the gate jerkily opened.

The lights of houses were on, and people were on the sidewalks, curiously eyeing the scene of certain criminality some blocks away. Joseph hardly spared them a glance—his attention was fixed forward as he rounded the last curve and swung the vehicle right. Sure enough, two fire trucks were present, and flames—an utter blaze of fire—were nearly consuming the entire house except for the front. He left the vehicle running and sprinted past the firemen, who shouted something he couldn't hear. A chicken was loose, and he smelled something awfully close to burning flesh. He hoped that it was only chicken.

Sara's voice slapped him back into focus. Twisting around, he saw her behind the juniper tree, holding Malcolm. William was beside her, trembling but oddly calm, a Rhode Island Red hen clutched between his arms. Joseph reached them and collided into a desperate, all-encompassing embrace, wrapping his family in a grip of wild, mad relief.

"Oh babe, oh God, thank God. I was—thank God you're here." She was struggling to keep her voice from warbling. He kissed the screaming infant in her arms and remembered vaguely that he might be squeezing the life out of them.

He was dimly aware of Josh and Ashley's family, and a few others, huddling closer to offer their words, but he could not even look—he would not. Just knowing they were there for his family was enough for now.

Sara moved in his embrace, and it took Joseph several days to fully understand what she then spoke to him, almost too softly to be heard, for the sake of William's ears.

"Sometimes I used to feel like we are the chickens in the pen, vulnerable to be the dinner at any time one chooses."

He wiped her tear-flecked eyes and found it odd that he was once again master of his emotions. They were safe, and the relief of that fact turned outward toward the enemies who had done this.

"The same goes for them. And we have a ratcatcher now."

Sara nodded in a guessing prescience. He would confirm her discerning look about the implied lawyer later—for now, they just wanted to hold their family tight and watch the show. Popped corn was probably not too difficult to find, although most likely half-charred.

William tugged on his sleeve. It amused Joseph to see him so calm and chipper now that his father was here. He wasn't much of a talker, even for a five-year-old, but he was smiling at Joseph in a way that made his dad's heart melt.

"Dad, Mom said ash is good for the dirt."

Universe 25

S. Strix

Life is a wheel.

Runners on a track turn a wheel each rung they climb, their motion spinning the wheel clockwise. For hours on end, the runners maintain a continuous pace in the same fixed position on this treadmill while the wheel cycles endlessly below them. Today, however, one runner had other things on her mind that pulled her attention away from this monotonous activity.

Only a few more turns of the wheel before I can clock out from a job that gets me nowhere, Renee thought bleakly. After work, she had reservations with her mother for dinner in the central district of the city. Seldom did she frequent this bustling borough, for she preferred her quieter comforts in the outskirts of the city, but her mother insisted on spoiling her only daughter by introducing her to a newly unveiled eatery.

Renee made her final stride on the wheel and stepped off, experiencing a brief wave of vertigo and unsettling nausea as she adjusted to solid ground.

"Only a couple more weeks before I can get my body back to myself," she murmured half-heartedly, touching her tumid stomach.

Rubbing her eyes and tidying her snug coat, she gradually regained her bearings as the nausea subsided.

She hastily shuffled into the public transport tunnels to begin her transit to the city center. Traffic was heavy, even in this less populous sector of the city. Most of the crowd had white coats akin to Renee's since most members of this population were loosely related. Yet despite this shared ancestry, every face felt like that of a stranger. Nearly all pedestrians traveled in silence with their eyes kept downcast, hunkered into their coats in an unconscious attempt to appear as small and unassuming as possible in order to avoid potential confrontations, especially from certain population segments that did not practice this silent passage.

As Renee approached the heart of the city, the number of her relatives dwindled as they turned down corridors that lead to their own homes. However, for every bashful cousin that meekly slipped off into his or her hole, a horde of individuals donning colorful coats swarmed the public transport, dissolving the once orderly, homogenous queue into a mongrelized mass. A wave of nausea washed over Renee once again as the newcomers flooded the route with their exotic smells, shrill voices, vulgar babble, and lack of personal space.

The tunnel passages became increasingly dingy as she reached the city's core. Renee found herself stepping over scraps, trash, and even fresh feces as she navigated around bodies sleeping atop shredded cardboard. A disheveled, crazed male with a ragged black coat, reeking of urine, staggered up and down the walkway, mumbling to himself and occasionally shouting obscenities into the void. As Renee passed, she felt his vacant stare follow her. Shuddering, she searched the faces of nearby commuters for reassurance, but she could only find that they were utterly oblivious to the vile scene before them. *They are totally blind to this filth*, she observed with shock.

Renee reached the dining place before her mother and decided to seat herself while she waited for her arrival, dwelling on her disturbing recent experiences. The fact that her mother was over a half hour late by the time she arrived did nothing to abate her stress.

"Renee! I'm so sorry for—" Her mother called out as she hurried over, stopping short after she had become close enough to fully see her daughter. She gasped and then let out a short gleeful squeal, scurrying over to her daughter to enthusiastically embrace her.

"I'm going to have grandbabies!" she exclaimed. But after releasing her daughter from the constricting hug and more thoughtfully considering her figure, she pouted, "Why didn't you tell me earlier?

You're so far along."

A shadow crossed Renee's face as she mournfully recollected the secret funerals for the little ones that never made it to term. The explanations for her failures spun in her head: *stress, overexertion, geriatrics, malnourishment, dysgenics* . . . The causes were countless, and her suffering was endless.

"I just wanted to be sure, I guess."

Unaware of her daughter's buried sorrows, her mother resumed her elated mood and overwhelmed Renee with conversation about the big news as they began to eat from the endless buffet.

This food is slop, just like what is served everywhere else, Renee thought gloomily. Like most denizens of the city, her mother was obese due to this limitless access to highly processed food. In the past, Renee had tried to offer gentle diet advice, but her mother would melt into tears if it was even implied that she did not naturally embody beauty standards without any effort, so Renee avoided that topic and powerlessly watched her mother slowly eat herself to death.

In between bites, her mother asked, "So, how does Samson feel about becoming a dad?"

"He might even be more excited than I am," Renee answered with a smile, though the smile slightly faded as she recalled how late it was becoming and how her husband had made her promise to be home before dusk, away from the city before the ruffians became most active. "But he might be even more nervous than I am, too."

Renee's mother had mixed feelings about her daughter's husband. While his optimistic, enterprising demeaner was a refreshing contrast to her daughter's pessimistic, brooding disposition, she bemoaned how he allured her daughter to move to the outskirts of the city, away from her.

"Well, he probably wouldn't feel so nervous if he had just chosen to live in the city limits so his amazing mother-in-law could come to the rescue," she teased. Despite Renee's efforts to explain her reasons for moving away from the city, her mother refused to understand why her daughter and son-in-law would willfully forego the opportunities available in the city in favor of a rustic, uneventful life.

Recalling again the hour, Renee opened her mouth to begin commencing the farewell ritual when she heard a ditzy squeal behind her. Turning around, she saw two males—an older, fatter fellow with a white coat and a younger, lankier one with a brown mink coat—scurrying over to their location. Renee could feel bile rise in her esophagus before the two even said their first words.

"Well, well, well, if it isn't our favorite little ally, what a fabulous surprise to run into you this evening," lisped the fat one as he gave Renee's mother a peck on the cheek. Turning to Renee, he dramatically gasped, "And this must be your gorgeous daughter. It's so exciting to finally meet you! Your mother can't stop sharing wonderful news about you."

Noticing her swollen belly, he gasped again and cooed, "But she obviously has been keeping secrets."

Then he sighed, "We've been desperately trying to find a surrogate, but it's almost like no folks assigned female at birth want to carry a little bundle of joy anymore." His eyes watered, and his partner, sensing his melancholy and desiring to cheer him up, embraced him from behind and began kissing the old one's neck and sensually nibbling at his ear. Squirming with delight at the suggestive attention, he seemed to forget all about his earlier complaint.

"But at least we have each other," he giggled, then continued in a loud, theatrical whisper, winking at Renee, "But we're here to meet some new fellows to spice things up a little too."

The couple and Renee's mother began catching up while Renee sat at the edge of the discussion, her twitching nose betraying her feigned geniality, for being in the vicinity of these two effeminate males conjured feelings of nausea, akin to viewing maggots squirm in a decaying carcass, especially when they began to publicly fondle each other. *These freaks should never so much as be in the same room as a 'little bundle of joy,'* thought Renee in disgust.

She needed to leave, but she could not muster the will to express this; her desire to remain agreeable was stronger. Finally, the couple bid farewell because their party had arrived, so Renee and her mother also departed the booth.

"When the babies are born, you and Samson should drop by so I can meet my grandbabies," Renee's mother implored. Pausing uncomfortably, she added in a labored tone, "Make sure to visit your father too, if he isn't too busy with his new wife."

Resuming her cheeriness, Renee's mother concluded, "Just come over after you've settled in; I don't want to get in the way. I just want you to be happy, and I would do anything for that."

You would not be obtrusive. You are my mom. I want to be with you, and I want your help, Renee wistfully thought.

Mother and daughter hugged goodbye and began to walk their separate ways back home.

Renee had a long commute, and it was well into the witching hour. She knew that her husband would be terribly worried by her tardiness, and she could imagine him pacing about the house, regularly peeking out the window, hoping to find her.

Though she let her mind wander to her devoted husband, she remained wary of her surroundings during her travels. Ahead, a lone figure staggered down the path, ranting incoherently into the empty passage. As she approached, she recognized him as the same homeless individual in a shabby black coat she had passed earlier. Renee considered taking a different exit to avoid this unstable individual, but the next exit would lead her down an unfamiliar path in the dark. She also contemplated turning around and going to her mother's apartment to ask to stay the night. However, she stubbornly clung to this idea that she had the inalienable right to travel, unmolested, in what she still believed to be her own society. *After all, he was only talking to himself earlier and did not seem violent,* she reasoned. Deciding to maintain her route, she continued onward, averting her gaze and shrinking into her coat, hoping to slip past unnoticed.

Never relax, she told herself.

The unintelligible raving continued as Renee walked by, but just as she thought she might pass unnoticed, the vagrant suddenly turned and lunged at her.

Already tense, Renee dodged the attack on instinct.

Without hesitation, she turned to run. At her peak, she had been one of the fastest runners in the city—thanks to her practice powering the wheel—but not in her current condition. That handicap was all it took for the deranged drifter to catch her.

He overtook her and began pummeling her head, clawing at her face and eyes with his verminous nails. Renee screeched in fear and pain, thrashing wildly in an effort to land a solid blow. She struck him repeatedly—hits that would have driven off a sane man—but the attacker seemed to feel no pain. Her resistance only enraged him further.

They grappled on the ground as he maintained control of the skirmish. He slammed her head into the pavement, battered her stomach, and bit at her flesh. The assault ended as his sharp yellow teeth clamped down around her throat. Suffocating in his jaws, Renee felt as if she were drowning. Her mind slipped beneath a wave of darkness as she sank into unconsciousness.

*   *   *

There is an incessant vibration.

The denizens of the city had subconsciously repressed this muffled buzzing sound from a young age, as if it was simply a given state of the atmosphere. However, an occasional inhabitant of the city might become briefly aware of the tone during a specific natural episode when a piece of the sky recedes and a blinding light from the heavens pours from the opening. During such events, the buzzing intensifies until the sky is restored and the sound is muted again. But even then, the hum often goes unnoticed; a low-pitched background noise is often overlooked when the hands of colossal gods enter the realm during these events, stirring a primal, instinctual fear in the heart of every individual. Even the boldest soul will run and hide while the hands of the gods manipulate the world, for every fiber of their being senses immeasurable danger from these powerful prime movers.

While peeking from the window of his apartment on the night of Renee's death, Samson saw the sky part, flooding the dark world with light and that intense, static buzzing. From afar, he could see the god's hands dismantle a section of the tunnel transit system. One hand of the god then tilted the tunnel over its other hand, and out tumbled a stiff, small scrap into its palm. The hands then lifted the section of road and the unresponsive bundle out of the world and into the light. There was no body to mourn, for every lifeless body was taken away by the gods' hands while it was still warm.

Samson stared numbly at the opening of missing sky for what seemed like hours before the hands emerged once again from the light with the segment of road it had previously removed. The hands reconstructed the highway in a matter of seconds so that it appeared as if it had never been altered, then they withdrew from the universe. The piece of the sky was restored, and the world was darker than it ever was before.

Since that night, the oppressive, low-pitched buzz still reverberated in Samson's ears. Even now, as he stood within a crowded, chattering meeting hall reserved for Renee's funeral several days after that night, the only sound he could hear was that supernatural vibration.

The crowd quieted as Renee's mother with glossy red eyes began to address the assembly in a wavering tone.

"We gather here today in the heavy shadow of grief, yet amidst the unyielding light of love, to remember Renee, a beloved daughter, wife, and mother," she said, choking back tears at the last title. "Renee was a beacon of light. She always had a beaming smile, and she loved everyone equally. She held no hate in her heart."

She spoke for several minutes about her daughter's virtues, putting disproportionate emphasis on examples of her compassion, patience, temperance, and humility. Samson, deaf to her words, could focus only on the omnipresent humming, but he abruptly awoke from his stupor to catch the last words of his mother-in-law's speech.

"I wish that my daughter, Renee, was killed by a male with a white coat."

A hushed murmur swelled through the crowd. Samson's eyes widened in disbelief.

"I bet you never thought anyone would ever say something so blunt," she continued. "But if that guy had killed my daughter, then our family wouldn't feel so much guilt for causing pain among a healing, marginalized community."

"To clear the air," she went on, "my daughter was not murdered; she was accidentally killed. We forgive our brother because he is also a victim: a victim of the mental health crisis. It is not our place to punish those who need help, for they know not what they do. Our only duty is to love all of our brothers and sisters equally."

Clearing her voice, she finished, "This tragedy has touched everyone in this city, but don't turn towards hate. In order to live like Renee, you need to accept everyone, choose to shine, make a difference, lead the way, and be an inspiration."

At its conclusion, the crowd earnestly applauded the bold speech, and the consensus among the audience was that Renee's mother was saintly.

By this point, Samson realized that he had been clenching his jaw so firmly that he chipped his incisor. As the masses praised his mother-in-law, he rose from his seat and stormed out of the gathering place without a word. Unconcerned with the congregation's disapproval for his impropriety, he took off alone into the city alleyways.

My Soul has left me. My conscience no longer exists in this world, for it now lies in a small heap in the hands of the gods.

While he weaved aimlessly down forgotten paths of the city for hours unbeknownst to him, Samson picked up an undesirable scent. Stalking forward several paces, he lurked behind a wall to covertly observe the source of this odor.

"Momma, I'm hungry," whined a young boy with a dusty black coat as he slumped next to a pile of shredded fabric, rubbing his dewy eyes. His three siblings noticed their brother's respite and also began complaining of hunger.

Meanwhile, their mother with an ashy black coat unhurriedly

rummaged through a mound of shredded newspaper, scavenging for hidden treasures.

"Shut yo' asses up," she barked, flicking away one of her children that tried to suckle at her teat. "Y'all don't eat until we find somethin' good."

The brood pouted and reluctantly returned to their salvaging, apart from one young girl with a ragged black coat, tears forming in the corner of her eyes.

"I wanna see my daddy," she cried.

The mother paused her ransacking in annoyance and muttered aloud, "Which one is he again?" After a brief moment of thought, she nodded in sudden remembrance. "He killed some knocked-up girl with a white coat the other week who was probably disrespecting him. They'll kick him out of the looney bin and back out on the streets any day now. Now get back to it, or I'll give you somethin' to really cry about."

Samson's heart raced. He remained still behind his cover, waiting until the mother and her brood found the treat they were looking for and moved on from the location. He stealthily followed them as they made their way to a dilapidated apartment. Watching from the shadows, he saw them enter the dwelling. He waited silently, his mind only occupied by the oppressive, ever-present buzzing, until the onset of dusk before approaching their home.

Beside the threshold of the apartment, Samson could hear a jingling sound as the children kicked around a ball with a bell inside. In their play, the children accidentally kicked the ball outside the entryway, rolling right to Samson's feet. Giggling mirthfully, the young boy with the dusty black coat skipped after the ball that had rolled out of the apartment. With his nose to the ground, he picked up the ball and then looked up. His small, murky black eyes met Samson's vivid red eyes. The muted jingle of the ball as it dropped to the floor was the only sound that returned to the apartment dwellers.

After a few moments, the playing children realized their brother had never reappeared from retrieving the ball. Two boys, growing impatient with their brother's delay, scampered out of the apartment to investigate. Upon turning the corner, they both felt their bodies become momentarily paralyzed by fear as they processed the scene before them. Letting out a squeak of horror, the two boys clamored over one another as they tried to retreat to their mother. But Samson had been prepared for their arrival. They never returned to their mother.

The last child, the little girl, heard her brothers' terrified squeaks before silence fell. She could sense a terrible danger just outside of the apartment as the metallic scent of blood seeped into her nose. Tugging on her mother's coat in distress, she began to cry uncontrollably. The mother, preoccupied with eating a morsel she had found earlier, initially ignored her bawling child, but the scent of blood eventually reached her nose. Turning towards the entryway, she unconsciously dropped her meal in shock as she confronted the dead bodies of her three sons stacked by the entrance and a male with a white coat stained with blood beside them.

"Oh, my babies," she sobbed.

She aggressively lunged a few inches towards Samson, howling in grief and rage, but immediately withdrew her attack and fell back to the wall when she quickly noticed that Samson did not flinch at her advances.

"I ain't never hurt nobody," she vigorously insisted.

Samson was unmoved by her implicit pleas. *She could never possibly recognize that her existence, in itself, implies that she must violently impose herself on others. In order for one to exist, another must not exist. For her and her offspring to live, another must die. This is the law of scarcity to which every beast adheres. She is her kin and race, and her kin and race are she. She and her offspring bear the burdens of their race. She and her breed must die for my breed to live.*

Darting forward, Samson cuffed the mother's head before she could react, temporarily stunning her. In her dazed state, Samson locked his jaws on her throat. She feebly flailed in his grasp until she went limp. Tossing her lifeless body down, he then turned to the screaming little girl in the corner of the room, quieting her forever. All was silent now, except for the static, pervasive otherworldly buzz.

Samson knew the mother was right about one thing: Renee's murderer would be released in a matter of days due to overcrowding in the facilities he was kept and the lack of perceived severity of his crime in the climate of this society. The death of one individual was meaningless and impersonal to the overpopulated, overstimulated, oversocialized masses. After his discharge, Samson knew his enemy would pay the apartment a visit, and Samson wanted to be the first one to welcome him.

The apartment was a slaughterhouse, and hands of the gods would soon arrive to guide the slain to the great beyond. *These vermin should not be bestowed the same voyage to the afterlife as my own Soul,* thought Samson.

Looking down to the young daughter of Renee's murderer that he had butchered last, he began to tear the meat from her flesh and devour her remains. *There will be no body to offer the gods.*

The sound of nearing conversation could be heard approaching.

". . . I don't know what came over him. I was so shocked to see my own son-in-law disappear from the funeral for his own wife. But I suppose we all cope with trauma in our own ways, and everyone is valid," said a familiar feminine voice, wistfully.

"You're so right about trauma responses; you're such an angel," lisped one of her two effeminate male companions.

"Thank you both so much for coming with me today as emotional support. I just want to heal with a family that needs even more prayers than I do during these unfortunate times."

Rounding the corner of the threshold to the apartment, initially oblivious to the blood- stained floor beside the entryway due to their desensitization to soiled surroundings, the three visitors felt terror claw at their throats as they grasped the reality of the carnage before them. The chatty fat male companion with a white coat fainted in shock at the scene and his male partner with a brown mink coat scurried away in panic. The female in a white coat stood at the threshold, petrified in fear.

"S-Samson," she stammered while cold tears streamed down her quivering cheeks. "What have you done?"

Samson looked up from the carcass with blood dripping from his jaws, his radiant red eyes reflecting a newly ignited fire that blazed within him.

His mother-in-law shuddered and shrank back. "I don't even know you. The son-in-law that I knew was good. You—you're evil."

Samson sneered, "To you, goodness is everything that is weak and passive while evilness is everything that is strength and active. You exalt the victim and celebrate suffering, justifying your lack of power and inactivity as meekness, mercy, compassion, and humility."

Trembling, she beseeched him through sorrowful tears, "You have no right to punish innocent babies for the mistakes of their father. Yes, their father made mistakes, but we are all sinners. We are not called to be executioners; we are called to forgive our brothers and sisters, or else we destroy ourselves from our wrath."

"Just look at you," she continued, "you let hatred control you, and now you've become a monster justifying his violence and revenge under this guise of righteous strength. You speak of strength, but true strength is in love and mercy. We can't right a wrong with another wrong. If we do, we lose our very souls."

Sinking to the ground in despair, she grieved, "You can't bring back my daughter—the hands of the gods took her away forever—so you can only forgive because that is all that we can do."

Samson looked down at her as she prostrated herself before him. He felt no pity for his helpless mother-in-law but rather disgust at her relinquishment of her will to act: a surrender to suffering.

"We can still save future daughters from the clutches of savages, but only if we are cruel
today."

"This litter," and motioned to the deceased, "will mature to be savages like their father before them because that is their nature. They are not our brothers and sisters."

He continued in a piercing tone, "I do not forgive because I do not need to. I act. Inaction is the only sin, for it is the only thing that destroys our lives and decays our souls. The grief you feel is the consequence of inaction. If we had only acted when the threat first invaded our society rather than submitting to those that see us as nothing more than a servant of their own will, then our family would still exist. Our inaction has killed our progeny—our future—and we are nothing without our kin."

Samson's gaze sharpened and he snarled in contempt, "You never loved your daughter, because if you loved her, then you would never have betrayed her, sacrificing her in worship of victimhood. You cannot feel love if you cannot feel hate towards those that threaten your beloved."

She wept with outstretched limbs and did not resist as Samson dispatched her. *A martyr for nothing.*

Next, Samson executed the fat effeminate one that had fainted. Grimacing, Samson spit out his sickly, infectious blood. He was not alone for long before he could hear a dozen pairs of footsteps rushing his way. Samson found himself fighting against six officers that had been alerted of the situation by the one that had fled. The officers were a soft, mongrelized unit unaccustomed to altercations with a resistant, virile male with a white coat. Samson was able to slay three officers, but not without sustaining nearly fatal wounds. The remaining three officers cowardly retreated.

Lowering himself to the ground in fatigue, Samson was now alone again with the incessant buzzing resonating in his ears as he laid motionlessly on the ground for what seemed like a lifetime. His eyelids were nearly shut before he was awakened by intensified buzzing and blinded by glaring lights. Giant hands groped beside him, picking up the deceased. He was closer to the gods right now than any mortal had lived to tell. A cold hand then gripped his wearied body and began to lift him into the light. *I am not ready to go; my work here is unfinished.*

Electrified, he felt power surge through him once more. Sinking his teeth into the hand that grasped him, he felt its grip loosen and a thundering roar erupted above him. Against his conscience, he followed the source of the sound. Scaling the white robe of the arm that had clutched him, he saw the face of the god.

Before he could strike the face of the god, a powerful swipe by the other hand of the god cast him off his path. He fell for what seemed like miles before he hit a polished stone floor. A once minor nick to his artery from his previous battle tore on impact, and blood flooded the sterile, otherworldly ground. He felt his consciousness float upwards towards the light above, swimming through a sea of undulating vibrations until he drifted off into an endless fog.

*   *   *

Dabbing an antiseptic on his wound, the doctor cursed under his breath as the solution began to fizz. After dressing the wound, he slipped on a new nitrile rubber glove and sighed.

"Well, the little bugger is worse off than I am," he mused as he glanced down at the lifeless albino lab mouse on the linoleum. Picking it up by the tail, he placed the limp body on a small tray at his workstation and began making incisions on it.

"Is everything okay, Doctor?" Asked an intern with concern as he opened the door to the laboratory. "I thought I heard you shout a moment ago."

Deaf to the intern's inquiry, the doctor fastidiously collected tissue samples and recorded his work. Once satisfied with his specimen, he handed the samples to his bewildered intern.

"Please prepare these samples for genetic preservation and cloning."

"Yes, Doctor," the intern replied, turning to leave the laboratory with the samples. But as he approached the door, he noticed a small pool of blood on the floor and paused. "What happened here?"

Scribbling down notes, the doctor responded, "A differentiated specimen from our twenty-fifth experiment. I would like to analyze this stock again in the next cycle of this behavioral sink study."

With a nod of understanding, the intern left the room.

Now alone in the laboratory, the doctor looked up from his notebook and gazed pensively at one of his lab mice running on its exercise wheel, the bearings faintly squeaking with each counterclockwise cycle. However, his meditative state was broken by the relentless hum of deteriorating fluorescent ceiling light ballasts above. Taking leave from his workstation, he resolved to fix it.

Doom Foresayer

Theodore Xavier

A great falcon shot down from the firmament like a bolt of lightning —so rapid it was—the auburn mass seemed like a flicker in the distance. But then it came closer; or rather, the one viewing it had inconceivably changed position, as if standing under the beast. The cry of that creature could be heard alongside the scream of a maiden, undoubtedly dressed in the manner of a princess, who could now be seen dangling from its man-sized claws as it lifted itself into the sky. The viewer was consumed with the desire to . . . to do something . . . but felt stuck, as if . . . he had to help her. . . . he had to . . .

Anacletus awoke suddenly, shook. Opening his eyes, he reached out with a sturdy arm and felt his grayed-out beard. As he arose and said his morning prayers in his cell, he could not help the growing conviction within him that what he had seen in his sleep was no nightmare—it was a vision of the future. By the afternoon, he was assured that it was a future that he *had* to prevent from coming to pass.

While he was tending to his garden behind his rustic shack, he turned over the images in his mind, for they remained more vivid in his memory than any dream or nightmare he had experienced before. Amid the details he had missed in his initial viewing of that chaotic scene, he could recall a road and a carriage bearing the insignia of the House of Clermonte: a white cross encased by a shield of red. Pondering this further, he realized that a king of that house ruled not far from him, the seat of his power being the city New Teryn.

Perhaps I may have an audience with him, he thought. *But how would I travel hence? New Teryn is many miles away, and I have only foot and simple shoe—*

A shout interrupted his flow of mind; looking up, he saw the form of a man beside his wooden fence—evidently some traveler—and responded, bidding him answer with a beckoning gesture.

"Good sir monk," the young man appealed, "aid of my carriage, I beg of you. I must bring many goods to New Teryn and have lost the way, for I am a stranger in these parts—help me, else my family who wait on me at distant home will be ruined."

Two marvelous words came to the monk's mind—*Deus providebit*.

"Worry not, troubled son," Anacletus responded, feeling a calm smile form on his face. "I know the way there, for I was brought up in a village in her vicinity. Allow me to accompany you."

"God bless you sir!" the jubilant man exhaled with apparent relief. "Come with me, then."

With careful step the monk met the merchant on the path of earth a short walk from the abode, and both boarded the carriage. They tarried not long, and departed for New Teryn.

*　　　*　　　*

The sun was setting in the horizon by the time the men had come to the high stone walls of the city and its open portcullis, flanked by towers—appearing like the facade of a cathedral. Anacletus observed the merchant's astounded look, which clearly revealed he had never seen the like; therefore, the monk explained to the young man that these structures were, in fact, quite common in the old cities of the Empire's Eastern regions. Nodding, the young man looked to him and joked with levity that in the Western country (the place of his birth) they would soon be catching up to speed. The monk smiled and gruffed.

"Men build walls and gates for protection," he said. "Are the wars not over? Have they not been since I was a boy? Perhaps there are new ones. Do tell me if there are. Otherwise, what will piling stones do you out there?"

"Ah Brother Anacletus," the young man answered (for the two had learned their names by this time), "you are quite right. There are no wars, even though there are occasional raiders that come into our lands from the other side of the Law. But you must admit that there is a certain visual appeal in a work such as this," and after a brief gesture to the arch-like shape they were now entering, concluded, "for not all of us have sworn to an ascetic way of life."

The monk was pensive for a moment. "Richard," he observed, "you are correct on your main point. But," he continued, "do not think that the ascetic excludes the aesthetic. That was one of the faults of the Plymouthers, but it was never ours."

"Ah, it was a mere generalization, sir monk," Richard replied meekly.

"That it was indeed," Anacletus remarked. He was thinking over what to say next, but then a flash came to his mind—

From a distance, as if on a mountain, he could see colossal towers piled down with massive holes within them, like voids of darkness. Many smaller buildings surrounded the zone, mostly dull square- like structures that had much of their shape effaced by the growth of foliage. He was not in New Teryn anymore, but in a place he recognized from descriptions from elders who had spoken to him of it when he was a boy . . . indeed, it had to be, for it bore the evident marks of a city from the Dark Age despite the vivid green of trees effacing much of the grid-like overlay. But then his position changed; he was now inside one of the fallen towers, and could see the pale white walls within, though discolored significantly by age. Then his focus was centered: he saw the great falcon again! It had built a nest here, and was tending to its young. Suddenly it raised its head and gazed into him with piercing yellow eyes—it stepped forward awkwardly and squawked, until . . .

"Sir monk!" the young man cried out, returning him to reality. "Are you possessed?" he stammered, asking. Anacletus was startled.

"No," he answered dimly, "I bear a message to the king—a portent of the future." The young man, taken aback, started the horses again and knew not what to say.

After they had passed the vast market square, they ended at the carpenter's guild. There Richard bid Brother Anacletus well, and the good monk blessed the traveling merchant.

Now the mission had really begun. He asked one of the carpenter's apprentices the whereabouts of the king and his residence, and thus discovered that he did indeed allow layfolk and religious to come to him during some of the morning hours. From that same man he found out the place of an order that would provide him sanctuary for the night, and bid that helpful soul a blessing. Taking those directions upon the way, he found a friendly brother at the door of the Savonarolites, was promptly given room with their community for supper, and after Vespers, was provided with lodging.

*   *   *

A happy sleep and a fruitful morning met Brother Anacletus; after Mass he was sorry to depart as were the other brothers to see him leave. But he tarried not, going upon the way to the palace of the king, his heart aflame with the message he was to bring.

The grandness of the palace's facade amazed him; the marble arch that encased the door was imposing, carved with reliefs that detailed stern knights and ancestors—rightly so, for he was to meet the lord of the realm, the highest civil servant of the emperor in this region. He gave reason to the doorkeepers, two guards in armor, obliquely informing them he had an important message to relay to the king. They respected him, and gave him admission, though made him wait on the account of a widow who had just been let in prior to the monk. When she came out, he saw a relieved face of a meek young woman under a shawl, modestly looking down as her steps joined the way.

Anacletus mentally said an Ave for her, and went inside the open doors. A great hall was before him; the walls were illumined by the fire of torch and the light that was let in by stained glass windows. Mosaics drawn from the lives of saints and the deeds of heroes who fought in the Wars of Unrest decorated the walls, animating the place with a sense of the sublime. He stepped near the throne, beyond the sight of armed guards before him, he saw there the king sitting upon the golden seat; a man younger than himself, though his features revealed him to be no youth. Beside him sat the queen, a woman who looked younger and gentler than the man of authority. Both wore the imperial purple, and beside them stood noblemen dressed in fine garments. Of greater import, however, was the presence of the princess herself—Anacletus recognized her easily as the maiden in his dream. He was further confirmed in his mission, and overcame the weight it imposed upon him, a weight of one almost overcome by the awe of authority.

The old monk cleared his throat, and after a bow and a brief introduction, began recounting his dream and the ill fate it bore for the daughter of the royals. All seemed captivated by his message—especially the princess herself. The king, with a pensive look and scepter in hand, stood to address this visitor.

"Brother Anacletus," he spoke with an air of respect. "I have no doubt you are sincere, but I do doubt your message. A creature as you describe has not been seen since the days that the iron wings sailed the skies. We do not heed the wishes of a doom foresayer; begone."

And with a return to his seat, he motioned to the guards, who promptly ushered the monk out, though with honor befitting of his state.

Seemingly defeated, the now downcast Brother Anacletus found himself on the way once more. The thought occurred to him that this was a trial. Though he had faced others before, this was unlike any he had undergone. But that did not discourage him; for he understood his mission to be a divine thing. Had not the prophets been the subject of greater scorn than him? One did not, he thought, have to travel that far into the past—had not the luminous Savonarola undergone even a false excommunication and yet kept faith? Was that not the same of those two great prelates of the twentieth century? Thus, after pondering his condition, he decided to return to the Savonarolites.

He soon found himself within the oratory's church and kneeling upon the cold ground before the altar and crucifix. Light poured in from the world through stained glass windows; beside him, the red garment of a Christ bent the colorless substance into hues of red. Brother

Anacletus found his mind shifting as he felt the silence penetrate him. Neither father nor brother joined him, for the recluse knew that these men were now laboring; for they ran a school for the children of the neighborhood.

He therefore attempted to pray alone—something he had grown accustomed to in his rustic him—but here a haunting question oppressed him: *are my visions true?*

And when he refused to answer himself, a volley of other questions shot at him:

Am I being uplifted by pride on the basis of some connections between these visions and reality? I have fled the world to embrace the calling of God; why then have I been called back to it? To be a holy fool —no, a fool! For in undertaking this mission, am I not forsaking my vocation?

Ah, so much noise! he thought. *But if I cannot fly the questions, I might as well attempt to put them to flight. Miserere mei!*

Let me see, he trailed on in his head. *I was a young man once; and indeed when I was first called to this life, many temptations assailed me, did they not? But they were different—the pang of marital desire struck me then, no vision. Yet I have not been given a vision of Jesus, Mary, or any of the saints; only something from this world, and what seems to be an ill possibility for the realm. Possibility, perhaps . . . and it is precisely this possibility that torments me.*

Then looking up to the pained face of the Christ, he felt his eyes bore into that mystery of love and death. He paused, and reopened his interior:

Not only, Lord, the possibility of death for one of your dear innocent ones; but also the possibility that I am being led astray by false lights. Let then thy light enlighten me in this Gethsemane!

He silenced himself. Though arrows of discouragement came to him still, he kept watch over his soul and pushed them out.

*   *   *

Remaining in the church at length, the sun told him that hours had passed. Hunger wearied him, but only slightly: for though he had gone without breakfast, his body was well attuned to fasting. But he was eventually roused from the quiet of his soul; a young brother touched his shoulder and beckoned him to follow, and they passed into the common house.

The matter was quite significant: A youthful messenger had come to the door, and almost interrupted Terce to deliver news that the oratory that the king wished to see this "doom foresayer" and now even offered to house the monk at his expense. Brother Anacletus therefore bade the black-cloaked fathers and brothers a "God be with you" the second time, and joined the bearer of this word. On the way to that place, the monk could not help but notice the fascinated eyes of the people watching him, whatsoever class they were—whether on the way or from the windows of their houses of wood or stone. Evidently, they had heard the rumors; whatever they even were to begin with. Anacletus felt almost without his robe, so embarrassed he was by this attention, and prayed he would speedily be in the company of the king.

Without much haste, he was once again in front of the royal court. He bowed, and the king rose from his throne and spoke for all.

"Brother Anacletus," he began, "it seems that your word has been vindicated by very recent events. Have you heard of them, good monk?"

"No, your majesty," the monk meekly responded.

"This afternoon I received a report from a village in this province that a creature like that of your 'great falcon' was sighted carrying a calf away," he said grimly. "We even were granted a feather that had been collected by one of its inhabitants as further proof of the affair."

The brother gave a look of concern. He clung to every word—for he knew that he had to save this princess, even if her father was against it . . .

"Though my daughter was due for an important diplomatic visit," the king continued with an air of stately gravity. "I will therefore retain her to prevent what you described from coming to pass. We invite you to stay the night with us, and as many more after that until this beast is destroyed; for perhaps the Lord may have some other message of import to give to you, and we despise not prophecy." Concluding, he added, "You may speak now, good monk."

Brother Anacletus now felt relief pass over him; but then he noticed the girl's expression of dismay.

"Your daughter is dismayed, your majesty," he sadly remarked. "Allow her to speak, and I will attempt to ascertain the matter."

The king gave an affirmative nod, and then looked over to the princess. "Speak then, daughter," he commanded.

"Very well, father," she said, her eyes now downcast. Softly, she continued, "I think postponing the visit is unwise. Could I not take some guards with me and travel there this night?" Her voice became more nervous. "For I fear the prince of Ottica may not believe us, and complain to his father, and then will his father complain to the emperor about us. I hate to be the subject of our realm's possible trouble, father." And looking up to meet her troubled blue eyes to those of the monk, added, "And that is what troubles me too, sir monk."

"Dear sister," Brother Anacletus said in a fatherly tone, "you must deny yourself this fear. A political trouble with that other realm will be meager in comparison to what will happen if your father perishes without an heir. You must—" He paused, his mind struck.

A considerable pain came upon him, not from that hall but from somewhere else . . . and his vision faded and then floated to another place. . . . *A great falcon shot down from the firmament like a bolt of lightning—so rapid it was—the auburn mass seemed like a flicker in the distance. But then it came closer; or rather, the one viewing it had inconceivably changed position, as if standing under the beast. The cry of that creature could be heard alongside the scream of a maiden, undoubtedly dressed in the manner of a princess, who could now be seen dangling from its man-sized claws as it lifted itself into the sky. The viewer was consumed with the desire to . . . to do something . . . but felt stuck, as if . . . He had to help her . . . he had to . . . open his mouth, and shout!*

"You must not go! You must not!" he cried, finding the words.

And suddenly he was returned to the court—a now shocked court, as was apparent to him. The princess began to shed tears.

Mending and Making

Zach Yatso

The snow fell soft and steady, like ash from a quiet fire, blanketing the cobblestone streets in the advancing twilight. It was the kind of snow that made the world feel hushed, as if the earth itself were holding its breath. A small boy picked his way down the lane, moving deftly in the ebbing light, coming to a stop at a humble shop door, beneath a weathered and peeling sign that read simply: "Mending and Making. By Hand, By Heart." The boy adjusted his grip on the hefty parcel tucked under his arm and raised his free hand to knock.

Ivan the tailor sat at his workbench, his hands moving with the calm certainty of a man who knew his craft. A knock sounded at the door. Ivan's fingers hesitated over the fabric spread before him, then he raised himself and moved to answer. Opening the door brought a gentle swirl of snowflakes and a rush of cold air into the shop, followed closely by the boy.

"Pan Petrov, a delivery for you!" gasped the boy, and he thrust the parcel toward Ivan. "Sasha, what are you doing running errands at this hour . . . so near blackout? Very well,

come in and have a cup of tea." The large paper-wrapped package crinkled as Ivan accepted it. He pushed aside the unfinished garment on his workbench, set the package down, then went to fetch tea while Sasha settled into the reading chair by the fire and began warming his hands.

Inside the shop, the air smelled of wool and thread, of beeswax and the faint tang of iron from the sewing needles. The space was cluttered, alive with the hum of creation—bolts of fabric leaned against the walls like old friends, spools of thread perched in every open space and shone in the dim light, and half-finished garments hung like ghosts waiting to be born.

Ivan brought a small steaming cup of tea to the boy, double-checked that the thick curtains covering the windows were fully drawn, and lit a second lamp from the fireplace. He sat at his workbench and lifted the package into his lap, examining its careful wrapping.

"What is this then, from whom?" He glanced at Sasha, his curiosity mirroring the boy's.

"A lady by the mill gave me three whole kurisa cents to bring it to you tonight." Sasha beamed between sips of tea. "So I came straight away, bog the curfew."

Ivan raised his eyebrows. "Did she mention her name?"

"I . . . didn't think to ask." The boy lowered his gaze, but recovered quickly. "She spoke kindly and smiled and seemed sort of sad and offered coin and I wanted to help and . . ."

"That's all right, Sasha. You did well. Shall we see what's inside?" Ivan loosed the knot of twine binding the brown paper parcel and stripped it open to reveal a bolt of brilliant modro-dyed wool, topped with a crisply folded note. He inhaled sharply. The fabric held the deepest indigo, a robust intricate weave more magnificent than anything he'd ever worked with! Sasha leaned forward in his chair as Ivan carefully opened the note and read aloud the faltering, scrawled handwriting.

For Pyotr Vasiliev. An overcoat. The finest you can make.

Silence stretched for tens of seconds, like the quiet snow falling outside. Ivan had heard the name, of course. Everyone had. Sasha sipped his tea and brusquely offered, "He's that old recluse plays the piano, lives near the bridge by Lesser Town with his daughter. I heard he's been whistertouched."

Pyotr Vasiliev, a musician and composer, a man who spoke more through his music than his words. They said he was dying, that his composition—the one he'd been working on for years—would never be finished now. A certainty if exposed to whist. Ivan didn't know much about music, but he knew what it was to leave something unfinished, to feel the weight of what might have been. And now this most unusual commission. He felt a strange stirring in his chest.

"I must speak with him. Do you know the place?"

"Aye," said the boy, drowning the rest of the tea and springing to his feet. "Meet me around fourth bell on the bridge, late morn . . . for a cent?"

Ivan laughed, "Yes, of course. Lead the way." He ran his fingers across the luxurious weave of fabric in his lap. Sasha grinned and slipped out the door into the gentle snow, vanishing into the muffling blanket of white.

*   *   *

The next morning was blindingly bright with reflected sunlight as Ivan exited his shop, and though light snow continued to fall, it was largely the wind stirring and swirling delicate flakes through the air. His feet crunched down the lane as he made toward his rendezvous with Sasha, inhaling the crisp winter air.

Scanning the ordinary, familiar vista of streets and shops for something, anything more profound and grandiose, Ivan was uninspired. He desired a goad for his creativity, like last night's unexpected package. A feeling that he hadn't felt in some time. The overcoat commission was great; it was a challenge, a chance to prove himself against some dismal stalemate.

Nearing the bridge, Ivan was reminded of the nightly threat, those gaudy posters desperately clinging to walls and windows, warning of whistfall: "Don't Become a Target! Lights Out after Curfew." and "If the Snow is Black, Turn Back!" He scoffed, and distracted, barely dodged the snowball that sailed past his head. Ivan spun, glaring at a smirking Sasha.

"A rude greeting, and worse aim, you lout!" he shouted, but his eyes betrayed kindness.

Ivan drew a cent from his coat, held it toward the boy, then feinted

282

returning it to his pocket. "You promised . . ." whined Sasha. Distant church bells began to toll the hour.

*　　　*　　　*

Sasha led Ivan down winding lanes, humming fragments of a lullaby as they moved. "Where'd you learn that?" Ivan asked. The boy shrugged. "Heard it somewhere. Tune's

older than whist." They paused in a quaint row of homes and Sasha gestured toward a door. Ivan stepped up and knocked. After a moment, the door opened, revealing a woman with storm-gray eyes and a quiet strength that seemed to radiate from her. She was tall and slender, her dark hair pulled back into a loose braid, and she wore a simple dress that spoke of practicality rather than vanity. Her gaze met Ivan's, lingered, flitted for a moment to the audacious boy standing behind him, then back to Ivan.

"You're the tailor," she said, her voice soft but firm. It wasn't a question. "But you've brought the runner, too?"

Ivan nodded. "I am Ivan Grigoryevich Petrov, proprietor, I received a commission. This is Alexander Volkov . . ."

"I'm Sasha," the boy interrupted, stepping forward, "You're the Pani, from the mill." It also wasn't a question.

She regarded the pair, then bowed slightly. "Anya Petrovna Vasilieva. I am Pyotr's daughter, his caretaker, and the commission is from his hand. He will be pleased by your visit." She stepped aside to let them in.

They entered into a small and tidy kitchen rich with the scent of tea and herbs. Anya ushered them down a short passage, leading them to a cluttered room. Sheet music, books, and knick-knacks were piled on every surface. A fire crackled in the hearth, somber and warm. The room with its objects surrounded a worn piano, the centerpiece, a testament to a space devoted to art.

Seated at the piano was an old man who seemed carved from the same ancient wood as the instrument he leaned upon. His gaunt and

283

angular form turned slowly to regard the visitors.

Whist had whittled him down to his barest essence. His face was a map of time and torment, lined with the deep grooves of a life spent wrestling with beauty and despair in equal measure. His cheekbones jutted sharply beneath skin that was pale, almost translucent, streaked with the telltale scars of whistburn. Yet, for all his frailty, there was a fire in him—a spark that burned in the depths of his sunken eyes, the color of storm-tossed seas, gray and restless like his daughter's, searching for something just beyond reach.

"Father, here is the tailor and the messenger . . ." Anya breathed.

Pyotr nodded feebly. Brief and awkward introductions were made. Pyotr's voice, when he spoke, was a low rasp, like the creak of an old door, but it carried with it a gravity that demanded attention, a resonance. He sat at the piano, his body seemed to merge with the instrument, his spine curving gently as he leaned into the keys, his fingers hovering above them like a bird poised to take flight. And then he played, there was a sadness in it, a melancholy that clung to his edges like frost on a windowpane, but also there was hope.

Pyotr's hands, though trembling with age and illness, were still the hands of a musician—long-fingered and delicate; joints swollen but their movements precise. He continued to play with his left, and lifted his right to indicate the sheet in front of him. "Each neume marks a sound, a pitch. They move with the tempo. Listen and see." He played with his left hand while his right traced the intricate symbols in time.

Ivan moved closer, observing the lines and patterns and absorbing the corresponding sounds. He was always taking in details others missed: the way a seam could be strengthened, the way a hem could be hidden, the way a garment could be made to fit not just the body but the soul. "It's like fine embroidery on a cuff . . ."

"Ah," A smile crinkled Pyotr's tired face and he turned and fixed Ivan with his eyes, like a needle pinned to fabric. "You understand what it means to make something . . . beautiful. You understand what it means to create from raw nothing, to pour your heart into your work. I've endeavored to shape these patterns, large sections, but I've failed to join them. You could stitch them together?”

“I’m just a simple tailor.” Ivan protested. The old composer’s fingers trembled over the piano keys, and Ivan saw the unspoken truth: this coat wasn’t just wool and thread—it was Pyotr’s last testament. The weight of it pressed against his ribs. Could his stitches carry a man’s soul?

“When I’m gone,” Pyotr said gently, “someone will have to continue it. The commission is yours.” Ivan felt a stubborn spark flare in him. He found himself nodding, not trusting his voice.

Anya entered with tea and ginger biscuits, serving her father first, then Ivan and Sasha.

Her hand brushed Ivan’s as she handed him his cup, and she whispered desperately, “He’s fading, Pan Petrov. Every day, a little further away . . . for him. I want it to be . . . he chose you.” She retreated, flushing.

They spent several hours in conversation. Pyotr exhibited his compositions, demonstrated musical notation, and offered the chaos of his thoughts. Ivan was attentive, overwhelmed, and bursting with creativity, exposed to this new imaginative dimension. Anya’s affect was domestic, respectful and determined, undermined by a palpable, impendent sadness. Sasha remained unusually silent, following it all, content to sip his tea and nibble confections.

Sasha suddenly stood and bowed deeply. “Pan Vasiliev, Pani Vasilieva, we have to go, the weather is turning.” The city’s bells began to ring in warning.

Ivan placed a hand on the old man’s shoulder, “Thank you, Pyotr. For your trust and encouragement. I’ll visit again as soon as I’m able.” He turned to Anya. “I hope we can speak again soon, too.”

She smiled, and her voice caught, “It’s cold out there. Be safe!”

Sasha gestured to Ivan and moved quickly toward the entrance, stashing several uneaten biscuits into his pockets. They burst onto the street, snow falling harder now, clouds thick with the mawkish ugly color of impending whistfall.

Ivan cast a concerned glance at the boy, but Sasha just grinned. “I’ll be alright, though you'd best make haste." They traveled with increasing urgency as the storm gathered.

*   *   *

Safely returned to his shop, the blackout curtains drawn and secured, Ivan settled into the familiar reading chair and reflected on all that had come to pass. He was a man of modest ambitions and quieter dreams, his life measured not in grand gestures but in the steady rhythm of needle and thread. He spread the fingers of his hands in front of him, facing the fire. Fingers calloused and strong, yet capable of the most delicate work. Stained with the faint marks of his trade: the blue of indigo dye, the dark of charcoal patterns, the occasional pinprick of blood from a needle's slip.

Pyotr's patterns burned in his imagination as surely as falling whist could burn his flesh. Sound and stitch would tell a story—an agency beyond the ability of words. He yearned to create something beautiful, something lasting and tangible. Joy, sorrow, love, endurance—emotions united celebrating an imperfect goal. Ivan moved to his bench and began to work.

He traced and cut fabrics, his blade whispering through the patterns like a secret, motivated by a desire he couldn't name. Ivan worked with focus, indifferent to the dangerous storm growing outside. Whist began to pelt the worn roof and windows of the shop, vainly seeking any exposed light.

Modro wool was quilted over a fine linen, interlined with canvas. Sewed with a half- placket front and a high collar, Ivan turned his attention to the embroidery. Deep into the night, in red and gold thread, he stitched all of the melodies he could recollect. Slow and sweeping ballads sung during the solstice, comforting like an old friend. Bars of the boisterous tunes belted drunkenly during the Springtide's festival. Meandering snips of melody, haunting and ancient, that the boy would quietly hum when he felt content and safe.

He slept when tired, or ate a meager meal of haricot beans and lean

286

gammon when he was hungry (all kept such safety stores). There was always tea.

On the second night, Ivan's needle snapped. The fabric puckered like a scar, the embroidery threads snarled. One misplaced movement, a bad stitch, would disrupt the entire piece. A small something that could change everything. He cursed, carefully backing out the threads. Starting over. Outside, whist hissed against the windows, mocking him. Pyotr was dying, and he was wasting time like a fumbling apprentice! He unspooled fresh thread and sipped his tea. It was alright; sometimes there was silence between notes. He would work this new defect into the pattern.

For three days the storm persisted, and Ivan stitched. Sometimes he would lose track of the time, only realizing it was a new day by the faint acrid smell of the whist boiling off into the morning's sunlight. It would fall again in the night. On the fourth day, as Ivan drew water for tea from the cistern and began to worry that he should have put up more, the city's bells began the slow toll signaling 'all clear'.

Emerging into the daylight, Ivan wrinkled his nose at the residual whist. Inert now in the sun, an ash-gray dust marring the formerly pristine snow. After such storms, the familiar cinder gangs moved carefully down each street, wearing their distinct protective leathers. Sweeping and prodding, overturning this and that, ensuring none of the noxious stuff remained hidden. Ivan watched the nearest group, when a small figure detached himself and hailed with a familiar voice: "Oy! Pan Petrov!"

*   *   *

Sasha marveled at the completed overcoat: covered in intricate embroidery, stitches curved along the hems and seams, across the breast and collar. To Ivan it was imperfect, every small mistake felt like a failure. He was prepared to confess defeat, that he hadn't done his best, that the stitches were wrong. Music wasn't cloth, it couldn't be forced into seams.

When he looked up, Sasha was already two steps out the door, coat folded against his chest, heading for Pyotr's house. Ivan rushed after him with a shout.

The bridge to Pyotr's house loomed, its stones slick with whist-tainted snow. Sasha darted ahead, kicking up gray slush. Ivan forced his legs onward, and when he turned the corner, the boy was already presenting the coat to Anya. Her eyes were red with weeping, but they still held that quiet strength.

"Pani . . ." Ivan panted.

"Hush. Come, there isn't much time." She led them to her father.

Pyotr sat very still at his piano. His hair fell across his forehead in uneven strands, and his breath was shallow. Anya gently opened the overcoat and spread it on the piano above the keys. Pyotr reached out a trembling hand and touched the fabric. "Beautiful," he said, his voice a rasp, like wind through dry leaves. He began to play.

Slowly at first, delicately, then gaining energy, he shifted from one stitch to another, the melodies mixing and moving together. Unique but complementary. His fingers were as light as snow falling on the keys, bright with reflected sunlight. Pyotr improvised when he came to an imperfection, moving through them as if they were an intentional part of the composition. And then he came to the collar, a familiar lullaby.

Sasha quietly hummed along with the melody, his eyes closed. Then he began to sing, in a bright, crystal countertenor:

Oh, the night is not yet done,
Oh, the stars are cold and thin,
Who will sing the morning in?
Who will sing the morning . . .

Oh, the wind is at the door,
Oh, the fire sinks so low,
Who will keep the ember's glow?
Who will keep the ember . . .

Pyotr halted his playing, unable to continue, though there was a happy smile on his face and in his eyes. Anya supported his feeble frame, with tears now streaming down her face. Ivan was speechless.

Pyotr looked at them each in turn. "You've done well. We've done well . . . to create." And outside, the snow continued to fall, enveloping the town in its quiet stillness.

Honorable Mention in Short Story

A Letter to Julia

By Hecataeus

A.D. 2749, April 15th. Aboard the legion carrier Aeneas, orbiting [REDACTED: Sensitive strategic information].

To my beautiful Julia Taylor, soon to be Julia Clarke; from your beloved Titus Clarke.

I write this letter through the archaic mode of pen and paper, intending that you will never see it, that you will only hear from my own voice. This is simply an audit of my own heart, a confession of things which I want to tell you, yet also never want you to know. Even then, I cannot shake the feeling that it should be written, even if only for my eyes.

I should briefly recount my time in this war—from the day I left you to now. The invasion of the Milky Way, as we all know, struck without warning, but at the opposite side of the galaxy from Earth and her colonies. We believed—rather, we hoped—that our distant, non-human neighbors would clean it up quickly. And yet eight years later, that Andromedaean horde—the Atrocity—is at our doorstep, thousands of scorched worlds and trillions of corpses in their wake. It had long been clear to us; nothing less than the extermination of all other races, mankind included, is their goal.

Thus, just over a year ago, I volunteered for service in the Terran Union's Coalition military, through the established defense apparatus of our home system, the glorious Europa Nova, and our home-world Britannia Secunda in particular. I had proposed to you just before then, and still now I remember the scene better than any simulation could produce; the rolling hills of our shire, the cloudless day, the balance of sunlight and breeze on my skin as I laid back on a blanket, which was covered with treats you had spent the whole day prior baking. I remember your braided hair, your marble skin glistening in the daylight, your blue eyes—like gemstones in the sand—your floral dress, and your aroma, a mix of that Terran perfume I gave you with your natural cleanliness. My heart aches as I write this; how badly I want to hold you right now! But forgive my purple prose.

June 22nd last year, I departed our planet with my legion, having seen you one last time at the farewell parade. I do not regret the dressing down I received from my superiors for breaking formation and running to you, to embrace you one last time. Of course, I ~~knew~~ believed then that it was not really the last time; I would go, lay waste to the enemy, and return home to you, drenched in glory and medals. The concepts of "duty" and "sacrifice" lived comfortably in my head, and I really believed in them—at least, I "believed" in them. In retrospect, my mind dressed up those abstractions as direct knowledge of the thing itself. "Duty" felt great, as long as the job was easy. "Sacrifice" was exciting, as long as I kept all my limbs. And the Atrocity? A threat, sure, but a good part of a galaxy away, and so in my mind little more than a dummy I could daydream a thousand ways to kill, and, amazingly, I would always come out victorious.

Beyond all that, I knew I would be home in short order, a hero of mankind, and bringing with me all of the benefits and prestige of war, nothing more, nothing less. Such was my psyche when I reached the legion carrier at the edge of the system. I then joined my *contubernium* —a twelve-man unit—and settled into our shared quarters.

After a day of getting established in the carrier, we commenced the journey to the battlefront, which was beyond the systems controlled by human states, but fast approaching them. My comrades and I had plenty of time bonding time, beyond drills and training. Our stories differed wildly, as did our personalities. I came from a farm, another from a megacity. I was a Christian; another, an adherent of the Restored Pantheon. By the time of our first engagement we were practically childhood friends, knowing each other's darkest secrets, the kind that even parents and siblings are oblivious to.

Though our differences were countless, we all shared two traits without exception; we all of us loved mankind, and we were each a glory hound. All of us bought the illusion of an easy duty, and many a dinner in the hall was choked with our daydreams on how we will slaughter the enemy and bets on who can kill the most, our meals sometimes going cold before the second or even first bite. They were special, my Julia, these friendships I made. Our brotherhood was forged before even a lick of the refining fire. Not even a week since meeting them and I was being kicked on the ground by another unit for gut-punching one of their own. I assure you that I did not start it, but it is a long story for another time.

Three months into the journey is when we made first contact with the enemy, some scouting parties darting between systems, harassing allied fleets. The first to approach us was chased and destroyed by a fighter wing; my cousin was one of the pilots, incidentally. The second time, the enemy dropped a few squads on the legion carrier, intending to set explosives along critical points of the hull. Our cohort was deployed in response, and my team specifically was the vanguard against one of those squads. From the little we saw of their attempts they had next to no idea where to plant their charges or look out for attacks. We thus maintained surprise and wiped them out in barely a minute, letting their bodies float into the void. An easy victory, and a strong affirmation of our boasting.

On October 5th, our first direct engagement took place. Months of training and daydreaming hero moments were now to be fulfilled, and our lust for glory satisfied with leftovers. I have spent at least ten minutes at this point on my bunk in silence, just mentally sifting through words to describe the feeling. Just writing the prior sentence now gave me the one appropriate word; indescribable. But now too an utterly inadequate analogy comes to mind, yet which is the best I can conceive; that stretching of the arms for a final swing that fells a tree.

I stepped into the designated landing craft, then the rest of my contubernium—my brothers—after me. We secured ourselves, gave our pilot the thumbs up, and our craft departed the carrier, alongside hundreds of others. The journey from orbit to surface would take only a few minutes, yet felt like hours, but not at all from fear. We stood at the ready, silent and bubbling with adrenaline, waiting only to feel the bump of a landing and for the doors to slide open, then sprinting out and slaughtering every non-human thing that fell in our line of sight. Those few minutes later our pilot instructed us to loosen our straps, and so we did. Then we felt the bump of landing; a mere moment later, the doors slid open, revealing a vast beach, and behind it an immense forest. We sprinted out the doors that very second.

A wall of bullets and energy beams fell upon us that same instant. Then, a brother dropped dead. A few more steps, and another fell flat with a hole in his chest. I saw two brothers die in seconds, yet the adrenaline numbed me to the sight, so I kept running and dove behind a boulder to shield myself. I could not leave the cover, lest I be shredded immediately. I watched, unable to act, as other comrades took three, five, a dozen rounds to the body and dropped dead in the sand. I watched as hundreds of others leapt from their transports only to meet the same fate. Limbs were blown off; heads were turned into mist. It was not long before the blood of my fallen brothers pooled together in a ditch just behind me. Precious few of us could return fire—and even then, only in the vague direction of the forest, by which our enemy was perfectly obscured. I let off a few rounds from my cover, only for a second at a time. Despite this, a hostile round mangled the barrel of my rifle; I was now stuck. Worse, the enemy saw us writhing in ditches and charged from the forest. Now I could see that their grotesque appearance was clearly toned down in training; blackened, seemingly decayed skin, hairless, and monstrous roaring. They jumped atop the injured and those pinned behind cover, not killing them efficiently, but ravaging them like bears, even employing "creative" methods which I dare not describe here. They enjoyed the taking of life, the tearing of flesh from bone and organs from within. A couple of them jumped me but I took them down with my sidearm after a brief and terrifying struggle. I showed them greater mercy than they did my brothers.

How any of us managed to reach the return transports I cannot explain. Still, seven of my brothers died on the field, and another in the carrier's infirmary. Nearly three quarters of my contubernium, three quarters of my only family a fraction of a galaxy away from all I have ever known. I survived, not unscathed, but intact—physically, that is. We who remained said nothing on the return transport; not a word as we took apart and packed our combat gear; not a whisper on the walk back to our quarters. As written earlier, I joined only knowing of duty and sacrifice as abstractions; that day, on the beach, I met them in the flesh, and I hated what I saw.

When I mentally came to in my quarters, after an hour or so of laying numb on my bunk and staring at the ceiling, the whole experience replayed itself from the beginning, but with my full attention. I again saw my brothers die, but without the numbing of adrenaline. I saw the hundreds of other comrades drop into the sand, dead and mangled. The vanity of glory had evaporated immediately in the battle, but seemed to reassemble itself and dissolve again in my quarters, though now with full granularity, like witnessing a live dissection with a fixed head and translucent eyelids. Worse yet, news from the front offered little but rare victories, a few stalemates, and a long string of defeats. I wanted no more of this war. I had to get home.

I discreetly flipped through the legion manual for ways to be discharged. The clearest option, I presumed, was just requesting a dismissal from the hierarchy. Such would bring the shame and mockery of the entire cohort upon me, but what would that matter? Everyone in the know who does not also transfer out will be dead within months in this interstellar meat grinder. But a real problem would preclude this avenue anyway: this is a war of annihilation, so the ordinary procedures of discharging are almost all annulled (per the modified manuals we were given), because the army cannot spare relieving men for the mere fear of death. The other option was to injure myself, but anything less than fatal could be patched up by the carrier's own facilities, and I would back in fighting condition in short order. Severe psychological injury could work, but why live at that point?

I was stuck. Command admitted an intelligence cock up in our debriefings and assured us this would not happen again, but how could they guarantee such? For five days I dreaded the announcement of our next engagement, and when it finally came, I saw the timer on my life begin to count down. I and my surviving comrades were introduced to the reserves sent to replenish our ranks. Completely fresh, no bond like that with our fallen brothers, and infuriating in their nativity and arrogance—though, in retrospect, no different to us barely a week earlier. I took the initiative to disabuse them of their vainglory; they signed up to their own doom, and they must swallow that pill if they are do go out with dignity. As you may have guessed, I was not popular at breakfast, lunch, or dinner.

Another week later, we were at another world occupied by the Atrocity. We stepped into our drop- ship and secured ourselves to the ceiling connectors. When we were all ready, the doors shut, and at that moment my stomach dropped, knowing that I was to die within the hour. My innards churned for much of the trip, and my mind was a husk. But something then happened for which I still have no explanation. Some neuron in my brain fired and forced my conscience to interrogate me. "Why be afraid? Why cower from the inevitable? Your despair cannot save you, so why endure such pain?" This thought stewed in me for a good minute, until another followed; "Gird your loins, O man, and expend what energy you still have before the end; pour out the last of your wrath and embrace eternity." In mere moments, my insides settled, and the anchor attached to my mind was cut. For the first time in nearly two weeks, I knew peace. And not just the peace I had known before that first battle, before deployment, even before the war; a truly perfect peace, flowing in my blood and washing through my brain. Was this peace? Or had I just become high? To my shame I have experienced the latter, yet I could not distinguish it from what I was feeling now. Is this, I thought, a final mercy from God before my flesh is shredded? Or, in retrospect, was it a divine reassurance that I had a greater purpose?

Our transport made the final approach for landing. My brothers and I stood at the ready, and I spontaneously gave them a few words of motivation; the blood was pumping in all of us. We felt the bump of the landing, the doors slid open, and we jumped onto the field and ran to our designated covers as the wall of gunfire enveloped us—the same kind that tore us apart in our first engagement. Somehow, we all survived disembarkation. Was it our planning? Was it our will to live? Or was it the hand of divine providence? Given all I have experienced, it could not be anything but all three. "The fool says in his heart, 'There is no God.'" So sang the blessed David.

Though not without losses on our part, this battle was truly glorious. We knew where the enemy was this time and struck accordingly. We [REDACTED: Sensitive combat information].

When the last of them lay dead at my feet inside one of their own compounds, I knew we had won, and not as an abstract fact of history, but of personal, nay, spiritual experience. Defeat was not inevitable; the horde could indeed be stopped. We merely acquired the will to take victory without being moved by the size of the enemy.

Upon our return to the carrier, my contubernium was lauded by the hierarchy for our effective fighting. Some, my own men included, praised my performance above all; one of the lads even said I looked "possessed." I guess I was, in a certain sense. And this would only increase in the battles following, instilling the legion with real hope. After this victory I came to an epiphany, that I had a divinely-ordained purpose in this war. I signed up in chase of glory and medals, but through the baptism of blood had shed off these vanities and, after much suffering, discerned the real significance of this struggle and my place in it. I now knew what duty and sacrifice really were, and though initially rejecting them, I came to embrace them, for without such my race will surely die.

Over the months following we fought the enemy everywhere; on planets, orbital stations, ship-to- ship. Some were tougher than others, and I would lose men with time, including the rest of my first brothers. Yet the legion had struck a rhythm, and we took victory after victory. Then, my dream was granted. The string of victories by the legions across the front and the arrival of extra legions prompted the hierarchy to offer a select few exemplary men an honorable discharge home, in part to incentivize better performance across the legion. I was one of those selected.

I'm sure, my Julia, that you are tempted to tear up and throw away the letter at this point, knowing what comes next. I was naturally ecstatic at the offer, ready in a heartbeat to pack my quarters and jump on the transport home. But my conscience—once my greatest comfort —pulled me back by the neck and forced me to appreciate consequence. I have become the glue of my contubernium, arguably of the entire cohort. My initiative on the field has saved countless men, slaughtered whole divisions of the enemy; could I afford to be replaced? Command assured me that the incoming reinforcements were more than competent. A reassuring claim, until I remembered that the same leadership still made one colossal mistake before. So, *maybe* the leadership has good information; *maybe* our replacements can pick up the slack. Or, they may be wrong again, and the legion will pay the price.

They gave us three days to make a decision. From what I gathered, everybody else to whom the offer was made accepted it on the same day, perhaps one of us took two days. Five days later and I was still gnawing at the matter, having requested more time to consider. As a final kick in the guts, my turn for the occasional tachyon call home was scheduled the following day. So, I was forced by conscience to make the necessary choice.

Having made my decision the day prior, the wait for your call tortured me. Upon being notified that you were online I ambled to the VR comms room. Each step was a new agony, bearing the weight of the pain I was to inflict upon you. I felt as though I were an army messenger, preparing to deliver news of my own death. And upon entering the room and seeing your projection, I could barely feign a grin. It hurt beyond imagining, seeing your beaming smile at the sight of my entry. I kept my words to a minimum, just so I could hear the music of your voice, and all the little details of life at home that you wanted to share. It was, per the ancient saying, a spoonful of sugar to make the medicine go down.

But what happened next will haunt me without end, until I see you again. You asked how deployment was treating me, that you were always worried for my safety and would even weep in bed on occasion over the mere thought that I may not come home. This prompted me to inform you of the offer, and that I rejected it. The way your face sunk and voice shattered, how you collapsed to your knees and screamed at me through streams of tears. The sounds of your pain haunt me worse than the butchery of the battlefield and the blood-choked shrieking of my brothers. These horrors shook me, but your cries broke me. That call replays in my head without end; at breakfast, at briefings, at deployment, in bloody combat. Please, my Julia, do not leave me for this. I cannot lose you, I cannot lose you, I can— [TRANSCRIPTION ERROR: Sentence illegible due to water damage]

*   *   *

It is the 16th now, took the rest of yesterday to reset. There are few things the carrier's stocks of whisky cannot drown.

About that same call: it was the only time we did not end with a mutual "I love you." That fact, more than all else, terrifies me. The real possibility that this could have been our last goodbye made me want to vomit the instant I grasped it, a day after the fact. I did not eat for two days since. Shortly thereafter Command surprised the legion with a "holiday" to the carrier's resort facility, one cohort at a time for three days each, a rare treat most legions will never have. Me? I stayed in my quarters, haunted day and night by your despair—by the fear you might abandon me for another.

It has been two weeks since that call. I am certain you agonize over the question of why: Why am I still here? Why am I voluntarily risking death? Why will I not come home and start our dream life together? My beloved Julia, oh my sweet Julia; I want to be with you for the rest of my years, tending to our modest farm and raising beautiful children until I pass away in my sleep, my last thought being of family. But my dream cannot answer this one question:

If not I, then who?

If I come back, some kid will take my place, almost certainly to die within a month. Outlasting my original contubernium made me the cream of the crop, a real asset in the war, however modest my contribution is on the galactic scale. Take me out, and my replacement will make mistakes, failing to cover a corner and letting the unit be picked off, then the cohort, then rippling into millions more dead; at worst, the defeat of mankind. There is a salient poem I learned in a lecture on Ancient Terran History:

For want of a nail the shoe was lost.
For want of a shoe the horse was lost.
For want of a horse the rider was lost.
For want of a rider the message was lost.
For want of a message the battle was lost.
For want of a battle the kingdom was lost.
And all for the want of a horseshoe nail.

So, if I gave in and left for home now; if my brothers were to do the same, to what would we return? For the moment, the warm embrace of our loved ones—and a little later, the rape, mutilation, and eradication of the same. It is from this calculus that my final lesson came, that to which the war in my mind resolved itself: Duty to my race comes first, for it is the life of my race that secures the existence of my family, and that of all other families. The fruits of labor that I enjoy— that *we* enjoy, are not the product of an individual, nor even a family, but of the toil and sacrifices of a whole people under the grace of God. Thus, as my people gave me life and comfort, I owe the loss of the same to them when their collective survival is threatened.

I therefore resigned myself to this possibility, that I may never enjoy these particular fruits, that I may have at first unwittingly—but now, willingly—foregone the comfortable life, the life where I come home to children screaming "Daddy!" as they run to me from the house, and to a wife waiting at the door, another child in hand; a life where I hold my woman in my arms as we watch the sun retreat behind the horizon; a life where I can see my sons and daughters grow, marry, and have their own children; a life where we kneel before God as a family and each thank Him for His bountiful gifts. I want this, oh does Christ know how badly I want this! But I would sacrifice it all that my race may endure, and that by denying myself this beautiful life, innumerable others may yet experience it.

All these things I say without reservation; I have laid my heart on the table bare. But as written at the start, I intend for you, my darling Julia, never to see this letter. By the grace of God, I will survive this war, and the day I land back on Britannia Secunda, I will scrunch it up and throw it in a river, before running to you, taking you in my arms, and announcing from my own lips how much I love you. I long to see you again, to cup your face in my hands, feel your heartbeat against my chest, and above all, for you to be mine, and I, yours. How long I will still be out here I am not sure, but I will remain as long as I am needed, painful as it is knowing that I am but one call to my superiors away from a return home.

I love you with my whole heart and soul, my dearest Julia.

I will see you soon,
Titus

*   *   *

ITEM IN THE CUSTODY OF THE TERRAN UNION OFFICE OF MORTUARY AFFAIRS DO NOT REMOVE

Item no.: #13-02-05-01-01
Date of reception: 14/05/2749
Type: Personal letter; handwritten (automated transcription)
Status: Next of kin informed—ready for collection.

The Weight

By Michael Calloway

The heater coughed again, spitting rust-colored air through the vents. He pulled the blanket tighter around his shoulders, watching the job board refresh like something was going to change. Same listings. Same scams. Same "competitive opportunities" that required ten years of experience to stock shelves or "deliver secure packages to exclusive clientele." He clicked *apply* anyway.

It didn't matter anymore. There used to be pride in this place. Factories, mills, union halls where guys slapped you on the back if you showed up early and didn't mouth off too much. Now they're vape shops, strip churches, and busted-out windows with *for lease* signs no one takes down.

He'd joined the Army at nineteen. Not because he believed in anything. Just because it was a way out. They said he tested high—real high. Could've gone officer. But the paperwork got lost. Or maybe someone needed the slot more. Either way, he ended up in logistics, babysitting pallets and watching contractors skim fuel from convoys. No medals. No trauma badge. Just four years of bureaucratic rot in a desert full of sand and broken people.

His old man had served, too. Back when uniforms still meant something—Desert Storm, maybe Kosovo. The details changed every time he told it, depending on the bottle and the audience. But there was always that look in his eyes when the anthem played, like he still believed it all. Still believed that the brass gave a damn about the boots.

They didn't. Not then. Not now.

What the Army gave him was moldy barracks, broken generators, and PowerPoint lectures on extremism delivered by majors who couldn't spell "morale." They taught him how to fill out forms in triplicate, how to spot IEDs from a safe distance, and how to nod during briefings that lasted longer than the missions. He'd once spent six weeks prepping a shipment of replacement boots that never arrived. They vanished somewhere between Kuwait and Kandahar— like everything else.

The best soldier in his unit got discharged for making a joke in a group chat. The worst one got promoted for ticking the right boxes.

He'd stopped caring by year two. Just kept his head down, hit the gym, avoided eye contact. Nobody looked out for you—not the sergeants, not the COs, not the flag. You looked out for yourself, or you got swallowed.

He came back stateside with a limp that didn't show up on x-rays and a resume that made employers smile and then throw his name in the trash.

The heater groaned again, like it was giving up. He rubbed his hands together and blew warm breath into the cracked gloves. The fingers were stiff and thinning. He'd meant to buy a new pair last winter, but Mom needed a new prescription and Medicaid hadn't kicked in yet. So he'd waited. Then spring came. Then summer. And now here they were again—cold creeping in under the doorframe and a disconnection notice on the kitchen counter.

He glanced toward the back room. The light was off, but he could hear her soft breathing. Shallow. Wet. COPD from a lifetime of factory air and bargain-bin menthols. She used to be tough—worked the floor at the plastics plant until her legs gave out. Now the walk from the bed to the bathroom left her winded for half an hour.

He was behind on her meds again. She didn't say anything—just smiled and turned the TV up when the bill collectors called. He was all she had left. And the VA disability check didn't stretch like it used to. Not with rent. Not with gas. Not with eggs at five bucks a dozen.

He'd applied for every warehouse, grocery store, call center job in a hundred-mile radius. Resume: Caleb Rusk. Twenty-three. Army logistics, four years. Not a hero, not a case study. Just another name in a system that ran out of space a long time ago.

He still had some GI Bill left, technically. Online courses he didn't have the energy for, not with Mom wheezing in the other room and the fridge nearly empty. What was the point of a degree when half the damn country was in a hiring freeze and the other half paid in exposure and meal credits?

The headlines called it a "market correction." The landlord called it a seventy-five-dollar rent hike. The phone buzzed.

Unknown number. Local area code.

He let it ring once. Twice. Thought about ignoring it. Then swiped. "Yeah?"

The voice on the other end was calm, professional, the kind you'd expect to hear at a car dealership or a bank. The kind that was used to not being told no.

"Mr. Rusk?"

He hesitated. "Who's asking?"

"You filled out an interest form last month. Delivery services. We have a client in need of immediate assistance. Cash on hand."

Caleb's throat tightened. He didn't remember filling out any form like that, but hell, he'd applied to so many things in so many windows he barely knew what was real anymore.

"I don't do drugs," he said, more out of instinct than conviction.

"You won't be asked to. You deliver a package. You get paid. That's all."

What's the catch?"

A pause. The hum of a diesel engine in the background.

"Meet us behind the old pharmacy on twelfth. Nine p.m. No phone." The line clicked dead.

Caleb stared at the screen until it dimmed, then slowly lowered it.

He looked back toward the hallway. The sound of his mom coughing echoed weakly through the cracked door. A wet, rattling sound that scraped at his nerves.

He opened the fridge—half a carton of expired milk, mustard packets, and a few eggs. Closed it again. Rubbed his temples.

This wasn't what he wanted. But wanting didn't matter.

Pride didn't cover heat. Hope didn't refill prescriptions.

He thought of her lying in that back room, eyes sunken, lungs crumpling like paper bags. All she had was him.

And if he didn't do *something*—anything—then what the hell had all of it been for?

The Army. The busted knees. The years spent babysitting gear for generals who forgot his name the second he saluted. The job apps, the rent notices, the promises he'd whispered to her on better days: "Don't worry, Mom. I got this."

He grabbed his coat.

The zipper was still broken, same as always. Nine o'clock. Pharmacy. No phone.

He was halfway to the door when her voice croaked from the bedroom. "Caleb?"

He froze, hand on the knob.

A pause. Then the soft rustle of her sheets, the wheeze of lungs trying to catch up with her words.

"Where you going, baby? It's cold out."

His jaw tightened. "Just out," he said.

"Out where?"

He hated how small her voice sounded. Like it knew it didn't carry weight anymore. "Nowhere. Just . . . job stuff."

Another pause. Then the sound of a pill bottle clattering to the floor. She didn't ask him to pick it up. She never asked for anything.

"You eating tonight?"

He felt that one like a nail in the ribs.

"Yeah," he lied. "Grabbin' something while I'm out."

"You sure you're, okay?" she said, barely audible now. "You've been . . . quiet."

"I said I'm fine," he snapped, too fast, too loud.

The silence that followed was thick and sharp. He exhaled, long and bitter. Ran a hand down his face. "Look . . . I just gotta check something out, alright? I'll be back in a bit."

She didn't answer. Just turned the volume up on the TV. Some old black-and-white movie playing reruns on public access. The kind with men in hats and women in pearls, back when the world still pretended to make sense.

He opened the door and stepped into the cold. Didn't look back. Couldn't.

The wind hit his face like sandpaper as he shoved his hands into his pockets. The snow had started again, light flakes falling like dust over the dead town. Streetlights flickered yellow. A stray dog darted across the intersection. Somewhere down the block, a siren started up, then cut off just as quick.

He picked up the pace, head down, boots crunching on salt and ice. The pharmacy wasn't far.

It used to be one of those big branches, back before the chain closed half its stores and turned the rest into ghost shells. The sign was still up, faded to pale blue and sun-bleached red, with half the letters missing. The automatic doors were boarded, and weeds pushed through the cracks in the parking lot like they'd declared independence.

Caleb walked around the side, past the loading dock. Snow crunched under his boots. There were no cameras—he checked without thinking, muscle memory from the desert. The alley behind was narrow, boxed in by dumpsters and stained cinderblock walls.

One wall caught his eye. Spray paint—faded red, half-washed by snowmelt.

A rough stencil: a man holding a rifle in one hand, a crutch in the other.

Above it, in block letters, chipped and weathered:

IF NOT US, THEN WHO?

The kind of slogan someone once believed in.

Recruiter bullshit, maybe. Or a vet trying to remember what it was all for—trying to carve meaning into brick and paint before the whole town forgot it.

Maybe they'd sprayed it after a funeral. Or after a second eviction notice. Maybe it was the last thing they had left to say.

He stared at it for a long moment.

The paint was old, crusted by years of freeze and thaw, but the message hadn't peeled.

IF NOT US, THEN WHO?

Then the wind cut through his coat again, sharp and familiar, and he moved on—pretending he hadn't read it twice, as the cold slipped through his coat and settled in his bones. For a second, he thought about walking away. Just turning around, going home, pretending this was all a misunderstanding.

Then headlights swung into the alley—slow, confident.

A black SUV. Not new, but well-maintained. It rolled to a stop a few yards in front of him. Tinted windows. Engine idling like it owned the place.

The driver's door opened.

And Caleb froze.

The man who stepped out—same sharp features, same smug professionalism—was the one who signed him up. Sergeant First Class William Trager. Recruiting office, strip mall south side. Ten years ago, same winter wind.

Back then, Trager had a buzzcut, a flag pin, and a gleaming smile full of "opportunity."

Now? Long coat. Leather gloves. No uniform, but the same "I'm doing you a favor" tone behind the eyes.

"Rusk," he said, as if nothing was strange about this at all. "Didn't think you'd be late." Caleb's lips parted, but nothing came out. Late. Funny.

"You brought gloves?" Trager asked. Caleb held them up automatically.

Trager walked to the back of the SUV and popped the hatch. Inside was a duffel bag. Plain. Heavy. Familiar in its military neatness.

"You take this to the address on the slip. Knock twice, leave it, walk away. Don't look inside."

Caleb just stared at him. "You're a recruiter," he finally muttered.

Trager shrugged. "Was. Everyone's gotta adapt, Rusk. You should understand that better than most." Caleb clenched his jaw. "You told me the Army would set me up for life."

"I told you the Army would give you a future. It did. Four years, room and board. You got out clean. That's more than a lot of guys get."

Something in Caleb's chest twisted.

"You're running . . . this?" he asked. "This is what you do now?"

"I move things," Trager said calmly. "Just like you used to. Only difference now is I don't lie to myself about where it ends up."

He handed over the bag. The weight of it hit Caleb's arms like a dare. "You want the money or not?"

Caleb stared at him, then slowly took it. The weight settled deep, like an anchor. Trager handed him a slip of paper.

"Address. Back door. Knock twice. Don't stick around."

Then, with no goodbye, Trager climbed back into the SUV and pulled off into the dark, leaving Caleb alone in the alley behind a dead pharmacy.

Caleb stood there a moment longer, holding the duffel bag like it might start bleeding.

He stared down at it—just canvas and zippers, military-grade, same as the ones he'd loaded by the dozens during deployment. But this one felt heavier. Not in weight, but in meaning. Like it knew something he didn't.

He glanced at the slip of paper. No name, just an address up in the hills. Not the kind of neighborhood he ever got invited to. Big houses with gated drives and lawn maintenance crews. Where people didn't work at all, or worked in ways that never made sense.

He stuffed the slip into his coat and started walking.

The town looked worse than it did six months ago. Somehow. Cracks spidered across every sidewalk. Empty storefronts had their windows tagged or blacked out with garbage bags. Even the gas station looked like it was holding its breath, waiting to be condemned.

He passed a church where a man in a neon vest was sleeping in the vestibule. The banner out front still read "fall food drive," even though it was January. A little farther down, a sign blinked through half-lit letters.

He'd been hearing it for years: things were getting bad. The recession, the inflation, the fentanyl, the layoffs. But now that he was walking through it with a bag full of god-knows-what under his arm, he realized it wasn't "getting" anything anymore.

It was done.

This was it. This was *normal now*.

And Trager—Trager, the man who'd told him the Army would "open doors"—was part of it. Running jobs behind a pharmacy like it was just another mission brief. No uniform. No flag. Just a new chain of command.

Caleb tried to picture what the man had looked like back then. Tight haircut. Recruiter's smile. The goddamn brochures with the paratrooper silhouettes and the bold, block-letter promises: *DISCIPLINE. BROTHERHOOD. PURPOSE.*

Now he was moving silent bags in alleys for people with no names. Like it was nothing. Like **this** was the natural progression.

Caleb's breath fogged in the air. His fingers were numb again.

You want the money or not?

That line kept echoing in his head. Not a threat. Not even pressure. Just inevitability.

Everyone had adapted. Everyone was surviving. The ones with real money didn't get their hands dirty—they hired guys like Trager. And Trager hired guys like Caleb.

He reached the edge of downtown. From here, the hills began to rise—the houses got cleaner, the driveways longer, the streetlights less flickery. The rich part of town wasn't big, but it still felt like another country.

The houses got bigger as Caleb moved uphill. Porches with string lights still on from Christmas. SUVs in every driveway. Some of them probably hadn't been driven in a week—just showpieces. Caleb kept his head down and walked the sidewalk like he belonged there, even though he didn't. Not in these neighborhoods. Not anymore.

He was two blocks from the address when he saw the headlights. A cruiser, rolling slow.

Caleb didn't look up, didn't speed up, didn't freeze. Just kept walking, one foot after another, duffel bag slung low at his side.

The cruiser pulled up beside him. Window rolled down. "Caleb?"

He stopped.

The voice was older. Familiar.

Officer Jim Hale. Sheriff's deputy for as long as Caleb could remember. Used to come over for dinner when Dad still worked maintenance. Had a dog named Buck and always smelled like motor oil and mints.

Caleb turned. "Evening, Deputy."

Hale leaned out the window. He hadn't changed much—maybe a little greyer, bags under the eyes deeper, but still looked like the kind of man who believed in the town, even if the town had long since stopped believing in itself.

"Didn't expect to see you up here," Hale said. "Just out walking," Caleb said. "Needed some air."

Hale's eyes flicked to the duffel bag. Didn't ask about it. Not at first. "You still living over on Linwood? With your mom?"

"Yeah."

"She doin' okay?"

"She's hanging in."

A beat passed. The cruiser's engine idled like a slow, tired heartbeat. Snowflakes drifted between them.

"You hear what happened to the McKays?" Hale said suddenly. "B&E last week. Right down this road. Real mess. House torn apart. Took the safe, TV, even the silverware."

"Damn," Caleb muttered.

"Yeah," Hale said. "People don't ask questions anymore. Just . . . take." Another silence. This one heavier.

Hale tapped the steering wheel.

"You, uh . . . heading somewhere in particular?"

"Just walking," Caleb said again, firmer.

The deputy nodded slowly, eyes going back to the duffel.

Caleb could feel the moment coming like a freight train. Hale didn't want to ask. Didn't want to press. But he had to.

"You mind if I take a quick look in the bag?"

A pause.

"I can't let you do that, Jim."

Hale looked at him for a long time. Not angry. Not shocked. Just . . . tired.

"You know I knew your dad. He used to say you were the smartest kid on the block. Said the Army'd make a man out of you."

Caleb's jaw tightened.

"Yeah, well," he said. "Turns out it just made me good at carrying shit."

Hale didn't smile. He just stared, like he was trying to see through the coat, the bag, the bullshit—like maybe there was still some of that kid left, the one who used to race bikes down Miller Hill and talk about going to state.

"Caleb . . ." Hale sighed, like the wind had gone out of him. "You know what's happening around here. You know where that road leads."

"I know where staying put leads too," Caleb said. "I've seen it."

"You think I haven't?" Hale's voice cracked just a little, his hand tightening on the wheel. "You think I don't wake up every morning wondering if it's the day I find some kid with his jaw shot off in an alley? Or worse—one I know?"

Caleb looked down at the bag. Couldn't meet his eyes anymore. "You want to stop me?" he asked quietly.

Hale didn't answer right away. He opened his mouth, then closed it again. "No," he said finally. "No, I don't."

The snow fell between them, soft and unhurried, like nothing mattered. "I just wish . . ." Hale trailed off. Shook his head. "Never mind."

He rolled the window up, one slow mechanical groan. Put the cruiser in drive. Caleb didn't move. Couldn't.

Hale looked at him one last time through the glass. "You make it home safe tonight, son," he said.

Then he drove off, slow and steady, tail lights glowing in the snow like dying embers. Rusk didn't move. Not for a long moment.

Because he'd seen that look before—the one Hale wore as he pulled away. Tired. Hollowed out. Like the job still meant something, but not in any way he could name anymore.

His dad had it too, toward the end. Long after the jokes stopped and the pride turned into something brittle. When the uniform started hanging on him like a costume. When he couldn't quite look Caleb in the eye anymore.

That same distant stare. That *quiet guilt.* Like he knew the ship was going down but couldn't say when or how—just that it would, and he'd helped build it.

Back then, Caleb hadn't understood. He thought his dad was just worn out. Old. Bitter. Now?

Now he got it.

You serve something long enough, it stains you. You keep your head down, follow orders, adapt. Then one day you wake up and realize the good guys aren't clean either. That the people you protected got eaten anyway. That maybe the worst things weren't done by strangers at all—but by the ones who told you to stand still and salute.

He adjusted the duffel bag on his shoulder.

The wind cut through his coat again, sharp and personal. The houses ahead were getting bigger. He was close now.

Too close to turn back.

He passed the old elementary school on the way up the ridge. The chain-link fence out front was rusting through, bent inward where someone's car had tapped it and nobody ever came to fix it. The marquee still read Winter Festival—Dec 16th, even though it was January. The flag out front hung limp, caught halfway up the pole, frayed out.

He stopped for a second. Looked at it.

If not us, then who?

The thought came out of nowhere—uninvited, sharp. It made his stomach twist.

He pulled his coat tighter and kept walking. He looked down at the bag.

Still sealed. Still heavy.

He kept walking. But something itched inside him now. The wind. The line. The silence. The way Trager had said "don't look" without saying it. Like he *expected* Caleb to be too far gone to even try.

He cut through the snow behind a row of houses, lights glowing warm behind tall hedges. When he found a quiet spot—no windows, no cameras—he set the bag down on a stone bench and crouched beside it.

His fingers hovered over the zipper.

One pull.

That's all it would take.

He told himself it was stupid. That it didn't matter. That he didn't want to know. Then he pulled it anyway. The zipper opened with a quiet rasp.

Inside was paperwork. Not cash. Not pills. Just files. Neatly stacked, tabbed, and bound with thick rubber bands.

He pulled one out and cracked it open with numb fingers.

Medical records. Names, dates of birth, insurance information. All from his county. Half from clinics he recognized—Urgent, Memorial, even the pharmacy next door before it shutdown.

The first few pages were controlled substance logs. Prescriptions for oxycodone, hydromorphone, fentanyl patches. Dosage escalations marked in columns . . .

He flipped to the back.

"Prescriber Behavior Monitoring—Internal Use Only." Each doctor had a number. Each number had a rate.

Most were flagged "Compliant—High Output."

A few were marked "Pending Review."

One was stamped "Terminated."

No names. Just codes. Like it was all normal. He shoved it back—then pulled another.

This one wasn't medical—it was logistics. Distribution flowcharts, client lists, and "alternative courier chains." His eyes traced the hierarchy. Trager's name wasn't on it—but a regional code matched the SUV's license plate.

It wasn't just backdoor pill running. It was bigger. Cleaner.

The documents tracked private contracts between "pain management consulting groups" and pharmacies across three states. Boxes marked "Compliant Markets," with rural counties like his highlighted in green.

There were margin forecasts. A spreadsheet of deaths cross-referenced against refill dates.

Loss ratio: within acceptable range.

That line stopped him cold.

He closed the folder. Sat there with the snow starting to soak through his jeans, breath coming out in short, wet bursts.

He was a logistics guy. Not combat. Not Intel. But logistics guys see everything. And what he saw now was simple: they were moving *evidence*. Physical records. Something no lawyer could FOIA, no watchdog could leak. Something that couldn't be hacked or traced—just handed off in duffels by nobodies in gloves.

He stared down at the bag, the cold forgotten. Then he stood.

He didn't go toward the house.

He turned back toward town.

Downhill. Toward the last payphone he knew still worked—outside a shuttered diner near the edge of the strip mall, the same one where he'd seen Trager's recruiting posters years back. The one his mom used to call from during graveyard shifts.

He trudged through the dark, bag still slung over one shoulder. A man in the wrong place with the wrong cargo, heart hammering behind his ribs.

The booth's plexiglass was cracked, the receiver grimy with age. A smear of someone's spit or blood— or both—streaked one corner of the casing.

He dropped a quarter in, dialed the burner number Trager had called from. It rang. Once. Twice.

Click.

"Yeah?" Trager's voice, cool and unsurprised.

"You knew I'd look," Caleb said.

Trager didn't bother denying it. "Doesn't matter what's in there, Rusk. The delivery's still due."

"Due?" Caleb barked. "Like it's a damn invoice? You think I'm some broken forklift that needs to stay useful?"

A pause.

"That's exactly what I think."

Something inside Caleb cracked. Not like a snap—more like a *tear*. Slow. Ugly.

"All that shit you used to say," Caleb spat into the receiver. "Service. Honor. Integrity. Brotherhood. What was that? Just ad copy?"

Trager's voice was steady. "It was true. Then."

"Then when?" Caleb hissed. "Before you were running kill counts for pharma execs? Before you started treating towns like mine like testing grounds?"

"You don't have the luxury of righteous anger," Trager said, a little colder now. "None of us do. You want to survive, you adapt. Just like we were trained."

Caleb laughed bitterly. "You call this surviving?" Trager didn't answer.

Caleb went on, voice rising. "You sent me to Iraq to count pallets while contractors skimmed fuel and our COs covered it up. Then you dumped me back here, told me to get a degree, get a job. What job, Trager? You seen the town lately?"

"I picked you," Trager snapped. "You think I call everyone? No. I called you because you're not a junkie. You're not a loudmouth. You're trained. Efficient. Quiet."

"I'm not quiet anymore."

Another pause.

"No one cares what you think, Rusk. Not really. You think I believe in this? I don't. But I've got a mortgage. I've got a wife who still thinks I wear the uniform. We all got our compromises."

"Don't lump me in with you," Caleb said. "You're not a recruiter anymore. You're a fucking middleman for poison."

"You're a delivery boy," Trager shot back. "That's the part you're missing. You don't *matter*. You're a cog. You do the job, you get the check, and no one ever asks your name."

There was a long, humming silence. The payphone buzzing in Caleb's ear like a static curse. Then quietly, through clenched teeth:

"I should burn this bag."

Trager didn't flinch.

"Go ahead," he said. "Burn it. Just know this—there's no second call."

Silence buzzed on the line.

"You think anyone's hiring guys like you, Rusk? Limp, broke, angry? This *was* the job. You burn that bag, you burn your last chance."

Click.

Caleb stared at the receiver, heart pounding.

Snow gathered in the phone's metal cradle. Somewhere, a dog barked. The world didn't care.

He looked down at the duffel. Then at the town around him—quiet, crumbling, waiting for someone else to fix it.

His breath curled white into the air.

Trager's voice still echoed: *There's no second call.*

He bent down. Picked up the bag. Slung it over his shoulder.

Stood there for a long moment, eyes on the horizon, the street, the silence.

The snow was falling heavier now, soft and soundless. It blanketed the sidewalk, the shuttered diner, the streetlight with its dying flicker. The world didn't notice. The world didn't wait.

He looked toward town. Then toward the hills. Two directions. Same story.

One offered heat. Maybe. A few bills to keep the lights on, to push the hunger back another week. The other offered nothing.

No flag. No anthem. No clear right answer. Just the question.

If not us, then who?

He didn't have an answer. He didn't want to hand it off.

Didn't want to be *that guy*—the one who said nothing, did nothing, and convinced himself he didn't have a choice.

But the rent wasn't going to vanish. And his mom wasn't going to get better. And nobody—was going to swoop in and make any of it right.

So what was he supposed to do?

He let out a sharp breath, bitter and shallow. He wanted to walk away.

God, he *wanted* to.

But he couldn't take another step until he figured out what it would mean—to walk away, or to go through with it.

Either way, he was going to have to carry it. One path just meant it stayed on his back.

The other? It followed him forever.

He stared at the snow as it collected on the corners of the bench, the edges of the phone booth, the seams of his coat.

Then, slowly, he sat back down. Bag in his lap. Not running. Not delivering.

Just—sitting. Thinking. Weighing. Maybe for the first time in his life.

The snow fell heavier now, clinging to his sleeves, his boots, the seams of the bag. His fingers were numb. His jaw ached from the cold.

He thought of his old man. Of Hale.

Of all the years they wore uniforms and saluted flags and talked about pride—*and still* let the town rot around them.

Let it fill with pills and silence and shuttered windows.

Let it die a little more each year while they told themselves it wasn't their fault.

Maybe they were tired. Maybe they meant well. But they hadn't stopped it.

They hadn't done a damn thing.

And now it was his turn.

His choice.

And God, he hated it.

Hated that it fell on him. Hated that doing the right thing felt like stepping off a ledge with no one waiting to catch him.

Hated that there *wasn't* a better option.

That there were no clean hands left—just his, frozen and cracked, clutching a bag full of someone else's mess.

All he wanted was a goddamn heater that worked. A fridge that stayed full. His mom to breathe easier.

He closed his eyes and exhaled through his teeth. He thought of an apology—but decided against that. Something more resolute came over him.

This time, it wasn't going to be passed along. It was going to end— right here, with him.

The Coming Africa

By Christopher Jolliffe

Lieutenant Colonel Harry Stevenson tapped his pen against the desk rhythmically. It was a Friday, and usually he enjoyed Friday afternoons; a weekend spent with his wife and children in leisure awaited. But not today. A bomb had crossed his desk. He reread the report in irritation.

Attn. Lt. Col Stevenson,

Reporting the arrest and detention of Private Richard Hartley on April 29th, 1962 and awaiting further orders re: legal proceedings.

Hartley was arrested in Bulawayo on charges of disorderly conduct on April 26th.

Special Branch advised his arrest and referred the matter to Division.

Hartley deserted from RLI on September 9th, 1961. He claims to have joined a mercenary organization active in Katanga and was actively engaged in operations there.

Please find transcript and notes included from his recorded interview. We have organized legal counsel for him pending court martial at his request.

Awaiting your sign off and instruction.

Ordinarily Stevenson would not worry. Desertion was uncommon but not unknown and military justice swift and to the point. But the mood in Southern Rhodesia was bad. He knew there would be political considerations that went beyond the operational purview of the Rhodesian Light Infantry. He worried as well that this new regiment, minted only twelve months ago and his first substantial command, would suffer reputationally. This would hurt him and his prospects as much as the standing of the unit, a thought that he inwardly checked. Thinking that way—well, that way led to scoundrelry.

He pushed back his thinning fringe and looked out the window. Inwards drifted the clear sunshine of the African autumn. It was a *lekker* place to live, so different from the England he had briefly known as a young man. He had visited after wartime internment to be greeted by bombed-out cities, economic ruin, the grotesquery of the postwar rebuild and listless demobilization. The Britain his father had known seemed no longer to know itself. Southern Rhodesia promised much for men looking for opportunity, to escape what had happened in the thirties and forties and yet take a piece of the homeland with them. The last holdout of empire, where men wore wide-brimmed hats in summer and gazed over expansive estates and still remained part of modern life. It seemed *large*, when really it was very small. There were only 270,000 whites in Southern Rhodesia. And many millions of blacks.

There came a knock at the door. Tentatively his adjutant, Captain Johannes De Wit, entered the room. He was a South African who fit the bill for the Cape Dutch: tall, blonde, built to play rugby. A candidate for the Waffen SS, had he been born in another time and place, as Stevenson sometimes joked. He moved to Southern Rhodesia when he was young, as some Afrikaners had; Stevenson, who maintained that prejudice was not proper for an Englishman, spurned the disdain many of his countrymen felt toward Afrikaners in the South Rhodesian military.

"You've seen this report, Johannes?" Stevenson tapped the pages with his pen.

"Yes, sir. Very troubling."

"We will need to convene a court martial for next week at the latest. The bugger will be looking at a few years in the jug."

"You've read the transcript, sir?" said Johannes.

"Yes. Very troubling indeed. The press will be all over this if they get a sniff. We have to move quickly to settle matters before it ends up public."

Joahnnes, who was still standing, took the seat that Stevenson offered with a wave of his hand. He liked the Lieutenant Colonel, and his commanding officer returned the sentiment. The regiment was young but hoped for great things, and the optimism matched the spartan quarters Stevenson kept. The office was so new it had barely been decorated: only a rug of reedbuck skin and the voluminous *History of the English-Speaking Peoples* perched atop the mantlepiece. Stevenson considered himself well-read; he enjoyed literary references and historical anecdotes. Johannes had read History at Cape Town University and graduated with a first, so he made for good intellectual company, which was part of the reason they got along so well—even if, as is the case for men of different ranks, he was deferent. Johannes had quietly noted during drinks at the officer's mess that while he spoke English very well, it was not his first language. Might those who read Churchill consider him a peer? He had said as much in his best impersonation of well-bred English inflection. Stevenson had clapped him on the back.

"Of course, old boy."

The Lieutenant Colonel had been in African nearly a decade and a half. Johannes had been born there, as had his parents, and his parents' parents. His line preceded the arrival of the Bantu peoples in the south. The continent had primordial bones, depths not easily plumbed, forces that worked beyond the ken of the men who'd conquered it, who seemed to think they could transcend it, who believed tea and good manners and English liberties were sufficient tonic for all the world's woes. Johannes at times wondered at Stevenson's naivety, but concluded this was a symptom of his good character. He depended on Stevenson for his own advancement, as an Afrikaner in a dominion suspicious of the Cape Dutch. Thus he liked him.

"I'm afraid the press have already got wind of it, sir," said Johannes. "There were inquiries not even an hour ago from both the *Rhodesia Herald* and the *Bulawayo Chronicle*."

"Damn," said Stevenson. This complicated matters. A military trial was a closed-door affair, but public interest would be piqued. All remembered with trembling the refugee convoys heading south as the Belgian Congo disintegrated in 1960. They were the subject of every nervous dinner conversation. *Could it happen here?* Land Cruisers with every belonging strapped to the roof, dirt roads halfway to mud, driven by men formerly members of the Belgian administration, hoping against hope they did not blow a tyre or a head gasket, which meant capture and mutilation and death. Women and children bearing haunted eyes. The stories like something out of the American West in the Indian Wars, only worse, because there was no US cavalry coming.

Instead had come the mercenaries, and then the UN. "This place leaks like a bloody sieve," said Stevenson. "How could they have got hold of this so quickly? Was it leaked by us?"

"Perhaps the police. It is hard to know, sir."

"If it was leaked by regimental staff, there will be a second court martial, I can promise you that."

There was a polite silence. Stevenson sighed. "Very well, Johannes, I suppose we better meet with this boy today. It is only proper. Organize a driver, will you?"

There was still the promise of light refreshments in the mess and then a weekend of leisure. It was not so bad.

*   *   *

Stevenson and Johannes met with Private Hartley in the duty officer's quarters at the military prison. The young man was lean and tanned, twenty-three years old and Salisbury-born. His eyes glittered. If he was afraid in the presence of rank, he did not show it.

"At attention, private. You are, for now, still a member of my regiment—if one in disgrace," said Stevenson, and when satisfied, allowed the young man to sit. "Quite a mess we have here, boy."

"Yes, sir."

"Have you anything to say?"

There was a pause while Hartley considered his words. "I suppose only that, while there was a shooting war just north of us, it seemed wrong to sit around. Sir."

"You made an oath and signed your name," said Stevenson, "and that means that what you did was wrong by any measure."

"I suppose so, sir."

"But I did not come here to give you a lecture," said Stevenson. "Your transcript, assuming it is true, is explosive. I need to hear it from the horse's mouth."

"Of course, sir. What would you like to know? Begging your pardon, sir, but I did ask for a lawyer."

"Quite so. But you will see that I am taking no notes, and nor is Captain De Wit. We are interested in the facts of what happened, and nothing said here will enter into legal matters. You've already given a statement and a recording has been made. That is sufficient."

Hartley seemed satisfied. He reached his hands behind his head—insolently, thought Stevenson. "I joined Mike Hoare's 4 Commando in Katanga, at Shinkolobwe, sir. I got there through an ex-army bloke here who was his recruitment contact in Bulawayo. I've already given his name—but everybody knows who he is, and what he does is legal. We fought the Baluba tribesmen to protect the Europeans evacuating south. Most of it was around the Lubumbashi River. That was in September last year. We disbanded in December and I came back to Bulawayo. Sir."

"The stories of cannibalism," said Stevenson, "did you witness this?"

"Yes, sir. The Blacks would cut the arse off any man they killed and eat it—excuse my language. They had a special knife, a *makraka*, to do it. We found many bodies this way. They would use poison arrows and were always high on drugs. They used rotten crocodile brains as poison. They raped hundreds of Belgian girls before we arrived."

"And you were strafed by aircraft?"

"Yes. Ethiopian, I think. A Saab, sir."

"And there were other Rhodesians with you?"

"Many in the unit, sir, many who did a stint in the army. Many others who were not in the unit, but told Mike Hoare what was what."

"And they were freelance, like yourself?"

"Not all of them, sir."

"For whom did they work?"

"For the government, sir."

"For our government?"

"Yes, sir."

"Do you remember their names?"

Hartley paused and thought. He did not remember their names. He knew this was his only card and he had to play it carefully. "Some of them, sir."

"And what did they do?"

"They helped plan the operations with Mike Hoare. They organized resupply when we were low toward the end of September. It's all in my statement, sir." He smiled an innocent smile.

Hartley looked at this self-important officer and his mind raced. He had seen him before on parade, giving speeches; Duke of Wellington, the men called him, because he seemed to think he was a great military leader. But Hartley had fought under the mercenary leader Mike Hoare, had fired his FAL until the barrel was too hot to touch, had gone hungry and thirsty and contracted dysentery and bilharzia, had been paid close to a thousand pounds for his work. He had shot many Baluba, but fewer than he'd have liked. He'd shot at the Malayan UN contingent, too, though only to suppress their movement and from a great distance. About that he'd at first had mixed feelings, but concluded they'd thrown their lot in with the devil and received their due. Eventually 4 Commando abandoned their positions and made a fighting retreat south, running out of everything that mattered, before Mike Hoare had declared the action concluded.

Mike Hoare was the real thing, an Irishman who led his men how he pleased, who did not sit in a barracks completing paperwork when Europeans were being killed one country over. *You can't win a war with choirboys,* he'd said. Well, I am no choirboy, not anymore. And the men were like brothers, in a way that his barracks mates never were; around them he felt joined to something dangerous, vital, exclusive, that was past the point of propriety, and thus not bound by its imperatives. They did what others refused, those who laundered their cravenness with extravagant words like duty and service.

But I am not too keen on going to prison. What did I do wrong, exactly? Desertion, but for good reason! Isn't that the white man in Africa, an individual sovereign-born, who makes his own fate?

But the pencil-pushing Duke of Wellington would not understand that. And they think it won't come here. They think the workers in the townships and the witchdoctors and men like Mobutu will be happy to drive their cars and wash their laundry forever. No, it is coming. It was coming in Kenya and then it was coming in Congo and then it came to Katanga. It will come here. It is better to know what to expect. And now I really am a man among men. The Rhodesian Light Infantry thinks itself an elite formation, but they parade, while Europeans are killed practically on the border. What else does a future for White Europeans in Africa require? No, my conscience is unbothered. I did what was right.

"Thank you, Private. I have organized the court martial for next Tuesday, to give you time to meet with your lawyer. It's a sorry business. You're dismissed."

"Thank you, sir." And Hartley saluted and left.

*　　*　　*

The two officers made their way back to their car. Across the road was Centenary Park, planted with European trees amidst Rhodesian Teaks, which shimmered in the heat. It was unusually warm for autumn. Then a voice called out from down the street.

"Harry Stevenson?"

Stevenson turned and saw a wry man in a suit waving him down. "Good Lord," he said, "Dave Walker!"

"Well met, Harry," said Walker and clasped his hand. "Fancy seeing you here. Haven't seen you at the club lately."

"It's been busy over at Brady Barracks," said Stevenson.

"I heard they gave you a regiment. Long overdue," said Walker.

At once Stevenson was mentally catapulted back to his time with the Eight Army, the Rhodesian platoons in the thick of the dust and the

327

beating sun and the smell of engines and oil and cordite, the march west from Mersa Matruh, the harrying of Rommel's men, skirmishes with panzers and gabbling Italians who surrendered happily with bottles of wine they'd swiped on their way over. The best time of his life. He and Walker served together in North Africa before Stevenson was made prisoner at Gazala in June 1942. He'd spent a month interned before Walker joined him, captured when Tobruk fell. Encirclement and surrender to the Germans, who were hard and cold like ice and very different from the Italians: years then in camps, in Italy and Germany, with never enough to eat, until in a second surrender he became accustomed to camp life. He ceased dreaming of escape and resigned himself to parading in the cold and counting the men and counting the rations. The worst time of his life. But Walker had scavenged parts enough to make a radio, at grievous risk to his own life, and they had kept track of the Soviets in the East and the Allies in the West. They held a small celebration when the Allies crossed the Rhine. The Germans noticed, and detained Walker, and Stevenson was white and tense with worry. Discovery of the radio signified certain death. But death did not come. The war had ended and they had gone home; Stevenson into the Southern Rhodesian army, Walker to vagaries in the Southern Rhodesian government.

"My adjutant, Captain Johannes De Wit," said Stevenson by way of introduction, and the two men shook hands.

"I wonder very much if I might borrow your commanding officer for a stroll through the park, Captain," said Walker. "We haven't seen one another in a long while."

"By all means," said Johannes, and sat in the car. It was hot. He had a feeling he knew what this was about, and expected they would be a while.

"Come, old chap," said Walker. "It's too nice a day to waste."

*   *   *

328

"The truth is, I didn't come upon you by accident," said Walker, "the government has an interest in the Hartley case, and I'm here to put forward the official position."

"I guessed as much," said Stevenson, and he tried to laugh, but found he couldn't. "Intelligence men up to no good in Katanga, eh? Not you, Walker?"

"I'm too old for that sort of thing, if that's what you think, Harry. No, nothing like that. Obviously, there are things I can't say, even here in the park. But there are two reasons the government would like things handled discretely."

"Go on," said Stevenson.

"First, this will embarrass the Federation. It is bad enough that Rhodesians were involved, but when it comes to men who've passed their term of service, it can't be helped. But men deserting a new elite regiment to join ragtag mercenary outfits is worse, and we know that someone's tipped the press. It's worse again if allegations that we sanctioned operations underway comes to light—which of course is all conjecture. The Federation is committed to multiracial stability and black advancement and eventual suffrage. Becoming involved in a breakaway state like Katanga? Certainly not."

"Mmm," grunted Stevenson. "And the second?"

"The second is purely political, old boy. And don't pretend an officer who's been around as long as you doesn't have an appreciation for this sort of thing. The government's worried that this will be a propaganda victory for the Rhodesian Front, who will make a martyr out of Hartley and demonstrate that the Federation sides with African Nationalists over our own. It risks becoming a coup d'état for those who want a Rhodesia independent from Britain. Clearly the narrative's nonsense, but with elections coming up and things so precarious, you understand the concern."

The Rhodesian Front, thought Stevenson. A newly-minted party, a rabble of reactionaries and racialists, formed from the wreckage of the Dominion Party that preceded it, not even a month old, led by a rogue's gallery who wanted independence from Britain at any cost. Surely the Federation had nothing to fear from such a medley.

"I see. A real pickle. You can't admit you were there, which would solve the second problem. I appreciate the difficulty," said Stevenson.

"Thank you, Harry. We had in mind a charge for being absent without official leave. A suitable fine for Hartley, of course. He should know in no uncertain terms that charges will be reviewed if he speaks to the press or divulges any information we consider sensitive."

Stevenson swallowed. This was a bitter pill. "There are considerations when it comes to the health of the regiment," he said. "I am reluctant to let Hartley walk so easily."

"Of course," said Walker, "but I know you appreciate that the health of the regiment and the health of the government are not so different. I know you're an honorable man, who will do the right thing once the picture is made clear to you."

Stevenson looked away. In the distance were the crowns of the Matopo Hills. Great kopjes and bush on all sides. Civilization tiny islands amongst it. "Is it true you bribed the Commandant to avoid being shot for the radio?"

Walker was taken off-guard by the sudden change in conversation. "The war was nearly over and a good word from a British officer was more valuable than an execution. Fascinating, isn't it? Those Teutons were sticklers most of the time, and they went berserk in other camps. We got lucky."

"The Commandant was a tyrant," said Stevenson.

"Indeed he was," said Walker, "but you must bend sometimes. You, Harry, have always stood tall. Admirable. You would have stood tall as they marched you out and lined up to shoot you. You would have saluted the King. But in this world, you have to bend."

"Bend? Or just bloody compromise?"

"Don't be getting upset with me, old boy. They're just words," said Walker, who gave a sympathetic smile. "I hope you see the sense in bending on this occasion."

"Very well. But I would like you to lodge my strongest objections," Stevenson said. "It's supposed to be my damn regiment."

Walker spread his hands. "It's a difficult situation. The situation is only going to become more difficult. The country has been unsettled since the Monckton report, since the crown started threatening majority rule. Britain is leaving Africa, Harry. We will need to be wise as serpents, but perhaps not gentle as doves."

"We're Englishmen," said Harry. "Englishmen don't abandon their own."

"I better get you back to your Captain," said Walker. "Come by the club sometime?"

"He's not my bloody wife," said Harry in irritation. They walked back to the car.

*   *   *

Later Stevenson allowed himself to be convinced by Johannes to have afternoon tea at the officer's mess. He had a gin and tonic and a few hors d'oeuvres he moved around the plate absentmindedly with his fork. He had no appetite. It was a day of being outflanked: outflanked by Hartley, who didn't seem to see any problem with what he'd done—who was *proud* of it—and by Walker, who had made Stevenson privy to things he should have already guessed but about which he was only dimly aware. He had been made brutally aware of his shortcomings and impotence, and was afraid that he did not have as good a read on things as he thought. Too much time on parade and weekend reading, not enough time taking in the *mise en scène*. Yes, that was it. I will have to read more of the damned newspapers.

"Another gin, sir?" asked Johannes.

"Please," said Stevenson. Concentrate on the regiment. It's new and they gave it to you because of your combat record. That Hartley thinks he knows what it's about, but the Germans were real adversaries. Not bushmen with arrows. Does he think he's the first man to ever fire his rifle in anger?

"I know it's not very English of me, sir," said Johannes, "and hardly very Afrikaner. But you are the commander of the regiment and I am your adjutant, and therefore your state of mind is important."

"Quite improper, Johannes," said Stevenson. "A man should be left alone with his thoughts."

A junior officer on the other side of the room was playing billiards. He said something that drifted across the breezy mess. Outside the perfect autumn day continued.

"You know, they call me the Duke," said Stevenson, "the men."

"The Duke of Wellington, sir."

"Quite so," said Stevenson. "Rather nice of them."

Johannes did not share that it was not complimentary. Instead, he brought the gin bottle to the table. "The decision on Hartley will be relayed to division. You should receive word back on Monday."

"No shop talk in the mess, Johannes," said Stevenson. "You know the rules."

They were quiet for a while. The gin worked in his blood. Stevenson felt better. "My friend Walker seems to think that the independence movement is a credible threat. I can't quite believe it."

Johannes refilled his glass. "The Rhodesian Front is popular. Independence is inevitable if Britain is set upon a course of majority rule for Southern Rhodesia."

Remarkable, thought Stevenson. "You don't seriously believe that, do you? An independent Southern Rhodesia?"

Johannes was happy that the Lieutenant Colonel had drank enough gin for frank conversation. "I'm afraid so, sir. There is no way that the voting White population will accept universal suffrage. They will be outvoted in an instant and ruled over by the Black majority. It would be the end of everything here. It would be another Congo."

Stevenson leaned back in his chair. He thought about Hartley's statement before dismissing it. "I've always maintained that a stable black middle class is the answer. Education is a civilizational force. That's always been the British mission here in Africa. We can share power with men of good heart who are united by bonds of class and nationality before race."

"May I be frank, sir?" said Johannes, and Stevenson nodded genially. "The African Nationalist leaders are all members of that Black middle class. They went to Oxford and Cambridge and learned about Marx and nationalism. Fifteen seats reserved for them in a parliament where the other fifty seats are held by White men is unacceptable. They are the reason there is a movement for African rule to begin with."

"That's because we've excluded them from proper avenues for advancement here," said Stevenson. "In thirty or forty years, they will be doctors and engineers and live alongside us as equals. They will have a stake without taking it by force."

"We do not have thirty or forty years," said Johannes, testing the boundaries of rank. "Britain wants to offload its colonial possessions like bad investments. Five years at the most."

"I'm afraid I must disagree," said Stevenson, "Perhaps Northern Rhodesia, which isn't full of settlers, and Nyasaland, for the same reason. But Southern Rhodesia is a little slice of England far away. Many of us served in the war, fought for the mother country. We won't be cast off like that." He clicked his fingers.

Caution pricked Johannes. He wondered how much he should fly his colors. "Think of English history. The Scots and the Irish, and all the trouble with them, and they more like the English than not. There is no precedent for managing a multiracial society like the one here. This is a problem the British will never have at home and thus do not understand abroad. They think that abstract English principles will bridge divides they do not properly understand." He thought about the Monckton Report, which talked rosily about 'awakened Africa.' Then he too thought about Hartley's testimony.

Stevenson wondered for a minute about the Afrikaner. The Boer War, the deep bitterness that followed, the Afrikaners who had refused to serve in the war, who took the jobs vacated by British men of conscience, who established Apartheid in South Africa. He remembered how his comrades called them Hitlerites during the war. "Dammit, man," he said. "A man is a man is a man. A creature of incentives. A thing that can be molded by good example."

Stevenson couldn't stand to be thought a racist. His sister taught Black children to read and write in the local township. He employed seven Blacks in his home, and trusted them completely. They lived among his children. But do I *know* them? They were everywhere but nowhere. Intimately woven into the fabric of white life, but completely sundered from it in the same moment.

"In the camp were Indians and Nepalese. We shared our rations and worked together. A man is a man."

"But four million men is a different matter," said Johannes. "The numbers are against us." He poured the Lieutenant Colonel another drink.

"You talk like a reactionary," said Stevenson. "They are part of us."

"Perhaps you should ask them if that is how they feel." Johannes thought, the only thing we have in common with Britain is that we are an island. They are an island in a sea that protects them. We are a White island in a Black sea, where there is no protection.

Stevenson bristled. He believed in the invincibility of the English mission to the world. They had fought racialism and won. English liberties had formed the foundation of the United States. It was the dream of Rhodes. Rhodesia was part of that dream, the heart of that dream.

As if reading his thoughts, Johannes said, "Think about the United States. All the trouble they are having with race—and there the white man is an overwhelming majority."

Stevenson sighed. "The White Man's Burden, Johannes. It's in Kipling. No choice but to shoulder it and carry on."

"Half devil and half child?" quoted Johannes. "Reap his old reward?"

Stevenson refilled his gin. He was quite drunk now, his face red, his brow sweaty. His earlier bad mood had returned. "Next you'll tell me you've joined the Rhodesian Front."

Johannes gave no reply. He looked out the window.

"Dammit, man, you have, haven't you?" said Stevenson. "Did you leak the Hartley report?"

"Certainly not, sir." But Johannes had leaked the report, and did belong to the Front.

Stevenson stood up unsteadily. The bottle toppled off the table and smashed. The junior officers playing billiards paused and looked over, horrified.

"You're an honorable man, sir," said Johannes, "We all know the regiment is in good hands."

"You're the second man to say that to me today," said Stevenson. He thought: you mean I am a *stupid* man. But I am not a stupid man. We will see. On the wall was a portrait of the Queen. He looked at it, in that strange and sentimental state of mind that drunkenness can bring. He didn't want to go home too sloshed to his wife. "Let's walk outside, shall we?"

In the corner of the room the Shona servant, Phineas, waited until the two men had left. He took his broom and judiciously swept the shattered glass. The officers had quarrelled. He would report this upwards. Carefully he picked up the larger pieces, jagged and slick with remnant gin. Yes, they were worried about the coming Africa. They should be.

*　　*　　*

Hartley stepped into the Bulawayo streets and felt the autumn sun hot on his brow. He couldn't believe his luck; a hundred pound fine and dishonorable discharge. Perhaps there is a moral economy in the universe. He felt young and vital and above all free: free of the constraints of rank, of obligation, of mawkish propriety. He hailed a taxi. In the wind were rumors Mike Hoare was setting up 5 Commando. They would go back to the Congo. There he could strike a blow for a European Africa, in the mud and heat and sweat, and earn a packet in the process. The coming Africa was a land of opportunity that rewarded the brave. He longed for a drink with his brothers, most of whom were still in Bulawayo, and the touch of women easily impressed. Stevenson and his ilk were yesterday's men. The world was changing, and only fools were left behind.

ENJOYED THIS BOOK?

TO READ MORE, VISIT US AT

ANTELOPEHILLPUBLISHING.COM